The Urban Crucible

The Northern Seaports and the Origins of the American Revolution

D0111580

The Urban Crucible

The Northern Seaports and the Origins of the American Revolution

GARY B. NASH

Harvard University Press
Cambridge, Massachusetts
and London, England

This volume is an abridged edition of *The Urban Crucible: Social Change, Political Consciousness, and the Origins of the American Revolution,* published in 1979 by Harvard University Press.

This book is printed on acid-free paper, and its binding materials have been chosen for strength and durability.

Library of Congress Cataloging-in-Publication Data
Nash, Gary B.
    The urban crucible.
    Abridged version of the 1979 ed.
    Bibliography: p.
    Includes index.
    1. United States—History—Revolution, 1775–1783—
Causes. 2. United States—Politics and government—
Colonial period, ca. 1600–1775. 3. United States—
Social conditions—To 1865. 4. United States—
Economic conditions—To 1865. 5. Boston (Mass.)—
History—Revolution, 1775–1783—Causes. 6. New York
(N.Y.)—History—Revolution, 1775–1783—Causes.
7. Philadelphia (Pa.)—History—Revolution, 1775–1783—
Causes. I. Title.
E188.N382   1986   973.2   85-13980
ISBN 0-674-93058-4 (alk. paper)
ISBN 0-674-93059-2 (pbk. : alk. paper)

70916

Contents

Illustrations

Preface to the Abridged Edition

ALTHOUGH eighteenth-century America was predominantly a rural, agricultural society, its seaboard commercial cities were the cutting edge of economic, social, and political change. Almost all the alterations that are associated with the advent of capitalist society happened first in the cities and radiated outward to the smaller towns, villages, and farms of the hinterland. In America, it was in the colonial cities that the transition first occurred from a barter economy to a commercial one; that a competitive social order replaced an ascriptive one; that a hierarchical and deferential polity yielded to participatory and contentious civic life; that factory production began to replace small-scale artisanal production; that the first steps were taken to organize work by clock time rather than by sidereal cycles. The cities predicted the future, even though fewer than one in twenty colonists lived in them in the period 1700–1775 and even though they were but overgrown villages in comparison with the great urban centers of Europe, the Middle East, and China.

Given the importance of the cities as dynamic loci of change, it is surprising that historians have written far more about the early American inland villages, whose households numbered only in the hundreds, than about the colonial urban centers. Nothing published in the past generation has gone much beyond Carl Bridenbaugh's *Cities in the Wilderness: Urban Life in America, 1625–1742* (New York, 1938) and *Cities in Revolt: Urban Life in America, 1743–1776* (New York, 1955). Moreover, these pioneering works, though richly textured and elegantly written, are descriptive rather than analytic, deal primarily with institutional history, and are based primarily on town records, newspapers, and personal accounts.

This book proceeds from a different conception of how urban societies changed in the eighteenth century and is based largely on different sources. On a general level it is concerned with the social morphology of America's colonial cities and how it was that urban people, at a certain point in the preindustrial era, upset the equilibrium of an older system of social relations and turned the seaport towns into crucibles of revolutionary agitation. More particularly, it is concerned with how people worked, lived, and perceived the changes going on about them; how class relationships shifted; and how political consciousness grew, especially among the laboring classes.

Historians of early America have avoided the issues of class formation and the development of lower-class political consciousness not only because of an aversion to Marxist conceptualizations of history but also because of the persistent myth that class relations did not matter in early America because there were no classes. Land, it is widely held, was abundant and wages were high because labor was always in great demand; therefore, opportunity was widespread and material well-being attainable by nearly everybody. If low or middling social and economic status was only a temporary condition, a way station on a heavily traveled road to the top, then the composition of the various ranks and orders must have been constantly shifting, and class consciousness could be only an evanescent and unimportant phenomenon. Thus our understanding of the social history of the colonial cities has been mired in the general idea that progress was almost automatic in the commercial centers of a thriving New World society.

Only recently has the notion of extraordinary elasticity within classes and mobility between them begun to yield to a more complex analysis of how demographic trends, economic development, the spread of a market economy, and a series of costly wars produced a social, political, and ideological transformation. Historians have begun to create a far more intricate picture of social change by studying the extent of vertical and horizontal mobility, the degree of stratification, the accumulation and distribution of wealth, the social origins of the elite, the changing nature of economic and political power, and the shaping of class, ethnic, and religious consciousness. Historians are also beginning to discuss not how *the* community was affected but instead how different *groups* within the community were affected. Armies were supplied by some urban dwellers and manned by others, and those who gained or lost were not randomly selected. Price inflation and monetary devaluation caused problems for the whole society, but the burdens were not distributed evenly. A sharp rise in overseas demand for American grain might increase the profits of inland farmers and seaboard merchants but also undercut the household budget of urban laborers and artisans.

Much of this book is about the people occupying the lower levels of urban society, who frequently suffered the unequal effects of eighteenth-century change. This focus reflects my conviction that the best way of measuring the success of any society is not to examine the attainments and accumulation of those at the top but to assay the quality of life for those at the bottom. If this appears to be the approach of a utopian socialist, it was also the notion of an eighteenth-century English aristocrat whose essay circulated in Boston. "Every Nation," wrote Sir Richard Cox, "has the Reputation of being rich or poor from the Condition of the lowest Class of its Inhabitants."[1]

In examining the lives of the lower classes in the eighteenth-century American cities I have repeatedly encountered evidence of social situations for which the standard scholarship provides no account. Boston, I have found, was not only the commercial and intellectual center of New England Puritanism, as we have been taught, but also, by the 1740s, the New England center of mass indebtedness, widowhood, and poverty. By the end of the Seven Years' War, in 1763, poverty also existed in New York and Philadelphia on a scale that urban leaders found appalling. The narrowing of opportunities and the rise of poverty are two subthemes of this book. True, compared with most places from which the colonists came—at least those who were white and free— the New World offered far more favorable material circumstances. Comparisons between life in the colonial cities and life in Europe, however, like comparisons today of the plight of the urban poor in Chicago and Calcutta, miss the mark. An indebted shoemaker in Boston in 1760 took little satisfaction from the fact that for many of those who worked with hammer and awl in Dublin or London, life was worse and the future even bleaker. People's sense of deprivation is not assuaged by references to remote places or times. Like their social or economic betters, they measure the quality of their lives by conditions in their own locales and make comparisons primarily with the world of their parents.

To study those at the bottom of the seaport societies it is also necessary to study those in the middle and at the top. Neither the reaction of the poor to the new formulas for dealing with urban poverty nor the role of the crowd in the Stamp Act demonstrations of 1765, for example, is explicable apart from the ideology and conduct of men at the higher levels. It was, after all, with those who possessed economic, political, and social power that the lower orders ultimately had to negotiate about property, employment, and credit.

The concept of class is, then, central to this book. But the term has a different meaning for the preindustrial period than for a later epoch. In the following chapters it serves as both a heuristic and a historical category. The concept of class helps us to understand how urban people gradually came to think of themselves as belonging to economic groups that did not share common goals, began to behave in particular ways in response to events that impinged upon their well-being, and manifested ideological points of view and cultural characteristics peculiar to their rank. This is not to say that all carpenters or all shopkeepers occupied the same position along the spectrum of wealth or that all ship captains or all caulkers thought alike or that merchants and shoemakers consistently opposed each other because they occupied different social strata. Nor can class be determined simply by notations on a tax assessor's list or by occupations given in inventories of estate. Moreover, evidence is abundant that vertical consciousness was always present in a society in which movement up and down the social ladder never stopped and in which the natural tendency of economic networks was to create a common interest among, for example, the merchant, shipbuilder, and mariner.

Eighteenth-century society, to be sure, had not yet reached the historical stage of a mature class formation. To ignore class relations, however, creates a greater problem. The movement between ranks and the vertical linkages that were part of a system of economic clientage did not preclude the possibility that horizontal bonds would grow stronger. Many urban Americans, living amid historical forces that were transforming the social landscape, came to perceive antagonistic divisions based on economic and social position; they began to struggle in relation to these conflicting interests; and through these struggles they developed a consciousness of class. This evolution is quite different, as E. P. Thompson points out, from the argument "that classes exist, independent of historical relationship and struggle, and that they struggle *because* they exist, rather than coming into existence out of that struggle."[2]

In their evolving relationships different groups of urban people were subject to historically rooted changes that may have been as perplexingly intricate to them as they have been to historians since. We can gain greater insight into the urban social process between 1690 and 1776 and can understand more fully the origins and meaning of the American Revolution by analyzing the changing relations among people of different ranks and examining the emergence of new modes of thought based on horizontal rather than vertical divisions in society.

This shift in social alignments continued after the Revolution, not moving with telic force toward some rendezvous with destiny in the industrial period but shaped by historical forces that were largely unpredictable in 1776.

This book also employs a comparative approach. By examining concurrently the process of change in Boston, New York, and Philadelphia, it shows how specific factors intertwined in each city to hasten or retard the formation of class consciousness and to give a particular texture to social discourse and political behavior. These three cities provide useful evidence not only because they were the largest northern maritime centers and the seats of government, but also because their populations differed significantly in racial, ethnic, and religious composition and in the legacies of their founders. Class consciousness developed according to no even-paced or linear formula. It emerged and receded depending on conditions such as cultural traditions, the presence or absence of leadership at the top and the bottom, and economic factors. The comparative approach also shows that the Marxist maxim that the mode of production dictates the nature of class relations has only limited analytic potential for explaining changes during some eras. It is not different modes of production that account for the striking differences among the three port towns in the historical development of class consciousness, but the different experiences of people living in three urban societies that shared a common mode of production. Thus it is necessary to go beyond determining objective class structures and objective productive relations and instead to examine "the specific activities of men [and women] in real social and economic relationships, containing fundamental contradictions and variations and therefore always in a state of dynamic process."[3] Bostonians, New Yorkers, and Philadelphians experienced their situations differently between 1690 and 1776 because different factors impinged upon them, ranging from their proximity to Anglo-French theaters of war, to the development of their hinterlands, to their cultural heritage.

In the following chapters the term "laboring classes" denotes the common people of the northern port towns. The term takes account of the fact that before the American Revolution—and indeed for more than half a century afterward—there was no industrial working *class* composed of a mass of wage laborers who toiled in factories, with a capitalist class wholly owning and controlling the productive machinery. Several broad groupings of people worked with their hands but were differentiated by skills and status. Thus the laboring *classes* included slaves, whose bondage was perpetual; indentured servants, whose unfree status was temporary; and free persons, whose independence could be altered only in unusual circumstances. The laboring ranks also ascended from apprentice to journeyman to master craftsman. Likewise, there were gradations among ill-paid merchant seamen, laborers, and porters, at the bottom; struggling shoemakers, tailors, coopers, and weavers, who were a step higher; more prosperous cabinetmakers, silversmiths, instrumentmakers, and housewrights; and entrepreneurial bakers, distillers, ropewalk operators, and tallow chandlers. There was, in short, no unified laboring class at any point in the period under study. That fact, however, does not mean that class formation and the shaping of class consciousness were not occurring.

Despite the importance of economic and social factors, ideology in many instances was a powerful motive force among urban people of all ranks and was not always a mere reflection of economic interests. Ideology, however, was not simply established by educated individuals and powerful existing groups and then obligingly adopted by those below them. Slaves, indentured servants, the laboring poor, women, and the illiterate also had an ideology, although few of them expressed ideas systematically in forms that are easily recoverable today. Their ideology consisted in their awareness of the surrounding world, their penetration of it through thought, and their reasoned reactions to the forces impinging on their lives. People living in communities as small as the prerevolutionary port towns, linked together as they were by church, tavern, workplace, and family, exchanged views, compared insights, and through their face-to-face associations arrived at certain common understandings of their social situations. They may have comprehended their world imperfectly, but they acted upon reality as they understood it, whether they were university trained and rich or could barely keep their shop books by crooked hand in a rented room.

It is impossible to fathom the social changes that transformed the urban centers of colonial America or to get a glimpse of the lives of the mass of obscure urban dwellers by consulting only the most accessible sources—newspapers, municipal records, business accounts, diaries and correspondence, and published sermons, political tracts, and legislative proceedings. Vital though these sources are, most of them come from upper-class merchants, lawyers, clergymen, and politicians. Such documents are silent on the lives of those low in the urban hierarchy and only occasionally reveal subsurface social processes. On the one hand the gentry were not interested in illuminating the lives of laboring-class city dwellers, and on the other hand they were often unaware of, mystified by, or eager to obscure the changing social, economic, and political relationships in their cities. Therefore, to provide at least a general picture of ordinary people's lives and of how conditions changed in the colonial cities, this book draws extensively not only on the traditional sources but also on less familiar documents, virtually all of them unpublished and many of them fragmentary: tax lists, poor-relief records, wills, inventories of estate, deed books, mortgages, court documents, and portledge bills and wage records. It also infers lower-class thought from lower-class action, an approach that is justifiable when action is adequately recorded and is repetitive.

This volume is an abridged version of *The Urban Crucible: Social Change, Political Consciousness, and the Origins of the American Revolution,* published in 1979 by Harvard University Press. I am indebted to Aida Donald at Harvard University Press for her suggestion of a shortened version and for her continuing interest and encouragement. To reduce the length of the book and thus make it more accessible to undergraduate and general readers, I have omitted the appendixes and many details and historiographic observations found in the original edition and have compressed the notes. The main points of analysis and interpretation presented in the original work, however, have been preserved.

In preparing this edition I have received indispensable editorial assistance from Norma Farquhar and, at Harvard University Press, from Ann Hawthorne. Ruth McGuire provided excellent stenographic service. I thank them warmly.

The Urban Crucible

The Northern Seaports and the Origins of the American Revolution

The Web of Seaport Life

Chapter 1

WATER DOMINATED the life of America's northern seaport towns in the seventeenth century, dictating their physical arrangement, providing them with their links to the outer world, yielding up much of their sustenance, and subtly affecting the relationships among the different groups who made up these budding commercial capitals. Boston was built on a tadpole-shaped peninsula jutting into island-dotted Massachusetts Bay and was connected to the mainland only by the mile-long causeway called the Neck. New York was literally an island, set in perhaps the finest natural harbor on the continent and separated from its hinterland by the East and Hudson rivers. Philadelphia, almost one hundred miles from the sea, was planted on a broad strip of land between the Schuylkill and Delaware rivers—the latter providing its access to the ocean. These colonial seaports gathered in timber, fish, and agricultural produce from the rural settlers who made up the vast majority of the colonial population, sent it to West Indian and European markets, and distributed finished European goods throughout the regions they served.

At the end of the seventeenth century the seaport towns were really only overgrown villages. Boston was the largest. Founded by English Puritans in 1630, it reached a population of about 6,000 by 1690. New York, founded as New Amsterdam by the Dutch West India Company in 1625, numbered about 4,500 in 1690. Philadelphia, planted in 1681 by William Penn, had only about 2,200 inhabitants by the turn of the century. None of the American port towns could compare with even the secondary commercial centers of western Europe such as Lyons, which had reached 45,000 in the 1530s, or Norwich, which had grown to 19,000 by the 1570s. Nor could they vie with the cities of the Spanish and Portuguese colonies to the south, where Bahia, Cartagena, Potosí, and Mexico City numbered 50,000 or more by the end of the seventeenth century.

The American port towns were small because they served sparse regional populations. In 1690 the population of Massachusetts was less than 50,000, while the agricultural populations served by New York and Philadelphia numbered about 14,000 and 12,000 respectively.[1]

Social Relations

The reduced scale of life in these late seventeenth-century ports, whose buildings huddled along the waterfront, made face-to-face relationships important. Craftsmen did not produce for anonymous customers or distant markets but labored almost entirely at turning out "bespoke goods"—articles made to order for individual customers. Even in the middle of the eighteenth century one prominent Philadelphian could remark that in his city of about 13,000 he "knew every person white & black, men, women & children by name."[2]

Even in the relatively large seaport towns, society was strongly familial in organization and still reliant upon oral discourse rather than the written or printed word for communications. Seventeenth-century American families were generally nuclear in structure, and slaves, indentured servants, and apprentices, as well as children, were integral parts of this family network, working, eating, and learning together in close quarters and subject to the authority of the patriarchal father-employer.

No less familial in form was the wider network that bound together several households. In churches and in the organization of poor relief, the kinship orientation was pervasive. The family, according to the Puritan leaders of Boston, was a "little commonwealth."[3] The town, a collection of families, was a larger commonwealth, recognizing the common good as the highest goal. And all the towns in the Bay colony made up the Commonwealth of Massachusetts. The corporate whole, not the individual, was the basic conceptual unit.

Few features of the late seventeenth-century towns would be recognizable to the twentieth-century urbanite. Cows were commonly tethered behind the crudely built wooden houses, for milk was a commodity that most householders could not afford. Hogs roamed the streets, feeding on household wastes that were emptied into ditches running down the middle. Indian shell beads, called wampum, were still in use as a medium of exchange in New York, and paper money was unknown except in Boston, where it made its first appearance in

1690. No newspapers were printed in the colonies before 1704, when the *Boston News-Letter* was first published. Philadelphians had no newspaper until 1719, New Yorkers none until 1725. Lawyers were everywhere regarded with suspicion, and the few who practiced were largely untrained, unorganized, and little respected.

The seaport towns were not traumatized by the witchcraft hysteria that swept Salem, Boston's neighbor, in 1690, but most town dwellers believed in the existence of witches. As late as 1727 an earthquake that shook most of New England was interpreted by the lettered and unlettered alike as evidence of God's displeasure with the inhabitants.

Among other casts of thought inherited from the Old World was an unquestioning faith in the indispensability of social hierarchy. Virtually everyone of wealth or position in the port towns adhered to the axiom that rank and status must be carefully preserved and social roles clearly differentiated if society was to retain its equilibrium. As John Winthrop, the leader of the Puritan Massachusetts Bay Colony, put it, "In all times some must be rich, some poore, some highe and eminent in power and dignitie; others meane and in subjeccion."[4] Puritan clergymen perpetuated this conception in Boston for many decades. There was every reason for the officials and the mercantile elite of the port towns to echo such ideas, which justified the position of those at the top and encouraged those at the bottom to believe that their lowly positions were divinely willed.

In New York and Philadelphia it was much the same. The religious impulse was weakest in New York, the least utopian of the northern capitals, but there, too, those at the apex of the social pyramid subscribed to the notion that all men, by God's design, were created unequal. Likewise, William Penn believed that the success of the "holy experiment" depended on orderly patterns of taking up land, on economic regulation, and on firm lines of authority. Quakers were not levelers, even though they opposed social deference when it fed arrogance and abuse of power by those who held it. Their quarrel was not with the need for a structured society but with its social conventions.

This perpetuation of social hierarchy was apparent in many of the conventions of urban life at the end of the seventeenth century. Puritans were assigned seats in church according to their rank in the community. In New York, whipping, the most common punishment meted out by the courts for minor offenses, was not permitted for men of rank, although the stripping away of the right to use "Mister" before one's name, or "Gentleman" after it, may have been more painful than the lash. By their dress, speech, manners, and even the food on their tables, urban dwellers proclaimed their place in the social order.

Social Mobility

Although this replication of traditional European attitudes regarding the structuring of society was widespread, it was not universally accepted; nor was it unaffected by the New World environment. Those in positions of authority or economic advantage were the principal proponents of a paternalistic, hierarchical system, for they were the chief beneficiaries of such an arrangement. Those lower in the social order were often less eager merely to recreate the past in the new land. As early as 1651 in Massachusetts the magistrates of the General Court expressed their "utter detestation and dislike that men and women of meane Condition should take upon themselves the garb of Gentlemen by wearing gold or silver, lace or buttons, or points at their knees or to walk in bootes or women of the same rancke to weare silke or tiffany horlles or scarfes, which though allowable of persons of greater estates, or more liberal education, yet we cannot but judge it intollerable in persons of like condition."[5] Here was a signal that many early Bostonians had improved their condition and had used their newfound prosperity to enhance their wardrobes, thereby upgrading their class identification, of which clothes were a primary badge.

Although almost every urban dweller knew instinctively his or her relation to those below and above, there was much crossing of social lines and, even as early as the 1690s, a long history of undeferential behavior among plebeian sorts. To us, "deference" describes the unquestioning acceptance of the superior wisdom of an elite by the broad mass of people. In the seventeenth century, to be sure, many urban people deferred because their economic security was bound up with a landlord, employer, or creditor. Yet the obliging comment and passive demeanor of a journeyman carpenter or merchant seaman could melt away in moments of passion or collective action and often did not extend at all to other powerful figures whose control was less direct. Many vertical links bound urban society together and inhibited the formation of horizontal solidarities. But time and circumstances altered social consciousness, wore away at deferential behavior, and gave rise to feelings of unity that were based on occupation, economic position, and class standing.

Closely tied to attitudes about society's structure was the urban dweller's sense of whether his or her community functioned equitably, expressed in the gap between aspiration and achievement. Contemporary expectations of success have little relevance to those of preindustrial people. In the late seventeenth century few Scots-Irish or German immigrants in Philadelphia, Dutch residents of New York, or English inhabitants of Boston dreamed of becoming wealthy merchants or country gentlemen. In the society they had left, intergenerational movement was almost imperceptible, sons unquestioningly followed their fathers' trades, the Protestant work ethic did not beat resoundingly in every breast, and security from want, rather than the acquisition of riches, was the primary goal. Modest opportunity (access to sufficient capital, land, and labor to produce material well-being) rather than rapid mobility (social ascendancy at the expense of others) was most important in their calculations of equity.

Much of the urban laborer's sense of what was possible was shaped by the distinctly premodern nature of economic life in the port towns. Routinized, repetitive labor and the standardized work day, regulated by the clock, were unknown. Work patterns were dictated by weather, hours of daylight, and the erratic delivery of raw materials. When winter descended, business often ground to a halt. Even in the southernmost of the northern ports, ice frequently blocked maritime traffic. The result was slack time for mariners and dockworkers, just as laborers engaged in digging wells, building roads, and excavating cellars for houses were idled by frozen ground. The hurricane season in the West Indies forced another slowdown; few shipowners were willing to expose their ships and cargoes to the killer winds that prevailed in the Caribbean from August to October. Food and housing cost money every day of the year, but in calculating his income the urban dweller had to count on many "broken days," slack spells, and dull seasons.

Although resettlement in America could not change the ragged work patterns of preindustrial European life, it did bring an adjustment in thinking about what was achievable. Many contemporary observers noted these rising expectations in North America—a psychological transformation heavy with implications for notions about the structuring of society. Land-hungry Europeans, arriving on the western shore of the Atlantic, found river valleys spread before them beyond their wildest dreams. Their aspirations and their behavior consequently changed, and not always for the better from the viewpoint of their leaders.

In the seaport towns aspirations were somewhat different. Open stretches of land meant nothing to the artisan or shopkeeper, but the availability of work, the relationship of wages to prices, and the price of a lot and house meant much. In all of these matters the seaport dwellers could anticipate more favorable conditions than prevailed in the lands that they or their parents had left. Unemployment was virtually unknown in the late seventeenth century, labor commanded a better price relative to the cost of household necessities, and urban land was purchased reasonably. Even so, it still usually took years of hard work and frugal living before the immigrant could purchase even a small house. Modest ambitions were the rule.

Social Structure

In their social structure the late seventeenth-century colonial port towns differed in several important ways from European commercial centers.

At the bottom were black slaves. Slavery took root early in the northern port towns and persisted there throughout the colonial period. By 1690 slaves represented as large a proportion of the northern urban centers as they did of tobacco-growing Maryland and Virginia. From 1638 on, when Bostonians exchanged captured Pequots for West Indian slaves, there was a small but steady flow of slaves into the Puritan capital. The number might have been greater if more slaves had been available, but Boston was farther from the source of slave labor than were the West Indian or Chesapeake colonies. Even so, slaves made up about 3 to 4 percent of the population in 1690, and about one of every nine families owned at least one slave. Most of the slaves were held by well-to-do merchants and officials of the community, who employed them as house servants, or by the best-established artisans, who taught them skills and turned them into mastmakers, bakers, blacksmiths, seamen, shipwrights, and the like.[6]

New York's connection with slavery stemmed from the extensive early Dutch participation in the international slave trade in West Africa. When the English captured New Amsterdam in 1664, its population was 20 percent black, about four times the proportion of blacks in Virginia and Maryland at the time. The English imported fewer Africans than the Dutch, but they made no attempt to phase out slave labor. By 1698, when the first English census was conducted in the city, Negroes formed more than 14 percent of the population, and almost 35 percent of heads of household owned slaves. Five years later the percentage had increased to 41.[7]

In Philadelphia the earliest settlers eagerly received their first shipload of African slaves only three years after the town had been established. By the last decade of the seventeenth century one of every fifteen families owned slaves.[8]

Above slaves in the urban structure were indentured servants. Trading four to seven years of their labor for passage across the Atlantic and sold at dockside to the highest bidder, they were circumscribed so thoroughly by the law that until their terms of service were up they lacked most rights regarded as basic to English citizens. They formed an important part of the labor force in New York and Philadelphia but not in Boston. Indentured servitude in the cities was never so exploitative as in the early Chesapeake tobacco colonies, where most servants did not survive their term of bondage and only a few of those who did achieved freedom from want along with legal freedom. Yet it is evident from the considerable number of suicides and the great number of runaways that the life of the servant-immigrant, who was typically between thirteen and twenty years old, was frequently miserable.[9]

Above slaves and indentured servants—bound laborers who occupied a kind of subcellar of society from which ascent into the main house was difficult or impossible—stood apprentices and hired servants. Apprentices were servants too, but they differed from indentured servants in serving in the locale where they were born, usually in a family known to their parents, and contracting out to another familial setting by consent of their parents or guardians. Unlike indentured servants, they were rarely bought and sold. Especially in Boston the apprentice system bolstered familial forms by training up the young in the families of friends and acquaintances who were usually coreligionists. In all the port towns the principal purpose of apprenticing was the same as it had been for generations in England—to educate the youth in the "arts and mysteries" of the various crafts, thus providing an adequate pool of skilled labor.

Free unskilled laborers formed the next rank of society. They provided the essential raw labor associated with construction and shipping, loading and unloading and manning the vessels that provided the lifelines between the seaports of North America and the world beyond. Each of the northern port towns had hundreds of such laborers. They are perhaps the most elusive social group in early American history because they moved from port to port with far greater frequency than other urban dwellers, shifted occupations, died young, and, as the poorest members of the free white community, least often left traces of their lives in the tax lists or in land and probate records. Of comparable social status were common laborers who stayed on land. In the port towns, they were the diggers of basements and wells, the pavers of streets, the cutters and haulers of wood, and the carters of everything that needed moving. Of the 304 estates of decedents inventoried in Boston from 1685 to 1699, less than one-fifth belonged to this group. Yet together with apprentices, indentured servants, and slaves, these free laborers probably formed as much as half the labor force at the end of the seventeenth century.

Artisans—a large and diverse group—filled the wide social gap between laborers and the upper class. Most of them were proudly self-employed, and they included everyone from silversmiths and hatters to shoemakers, tailors, and mast- and sailmakers. Within the artisanry a wide range of wealth and status existed. In part this diversity reflected the age-old hierarchy of apprentices, journeymen, and master craftsmen within each craft. With each step upward the artisan could normally expect economic security and material to increase; thus the range of wealth observable in the tax lists for, say, carpenters in Boston or clockmakers in New York reflects to some degree the age of the particular artisans and the acquisition of skills associated with their work. Other factors affecting an artisan's prosperity included craft skill, business acumen, health, luck, and choice of marriage partner.

Status also varied among occupational groups. A hierarchy of trades existed in all the towns—after the Revolution this was sometimes symbolized by the marching order of the various crafts at public celebrations—and to some degree the success of individual mechanics can be predicted by the trade they followed. Everyone knew that artisans working with precious metals got ahead faster than those who worked at the cobbler's bench and that house carpenters were far more likely to become property owners than were tailors and stocking weavers. Nonetheless, young men tended to base their choice of a career far more on those of their fathers—or of their uncles, older brothers, or cousins—than on a rational calculation of future material rewards. Nathaniel Adams, a Boston boatbuilder from the 1650s until his death in 1690, was followed in his craft by his son, grandson, and great-grandson. Along the Philadelphia waterfront the name Penrose meant shipbuilding for four generations before the Revolution. Such intergenerational continuity was one more proof that most urban artisans held to traditional modes; a decent subsistence or a slow inching forward was more the norm than the rapid aggrandizement of wealth.

At the top of the urban pyramid were two groups, one distinguished by high social status and the other by wealth. The first of these was composed of the professionals—government officials, doctors, clergymen, schoolteachers, and, eventually, lawyers. Often they were rewarded more by the community's respect than by material benefits. Public school teachers in Boston, for example, earned only about £25 sterling per year in the 1690s and only £30 sterling in New York forty years later. The congregation of Old South Church allowed its pastors, Benjamin Colman and Thomas Prince, only £73 sterling annually in 1725.[10] Professional men tended to do better only when they used their social prestige to arrange a propitious marriage. The fact that these educated professional men were so modestly rewarded serves as a reminder that parallel hierarchies of wealth, power, and prestige did not precisely overlap.

Held in lower regard but dominating economic life were the seaport merchants and, to a lesser degree, the shopkeepers, who often aspired to merchant status. These were the importers and exporters, wholesalers and retailers, builders of ships, wharves, and warehouses, without whom there could have been no commercial centers. They quickly gained a disproportionate share of economic leverage and political power. How this power was used would become one of the most enduring issues of the eighteenth century.

Wealth and Poverty

The differing levels of economic success achieved by the port dwellers were eventually reflected in the community tax lists and in the inventories of decedents' estates. Despite certain distortions inherent in these records, tax lists and inventories are a generally reliable index to wealth distribution in the seaport towns and can be used to measure long-term secular change.[11] These records reveal that the division of wealth in the three cities, despite marked differences in their age and religious and ethnic composition, differed only slightly at the end of the seventeenth century. Boston in 1687 and New York in 1695 were more than half a century old and had populations of nearly 6,000 and 4,700 respectively. Philadelphia had existed for only a decade and had about

2,100 inhabitants. But wealth in the three communities was similarly distributed.

In each of the towns the bottom 30 percent of wealthholders possessed only about 3 percent of the community's assets. Among these were men at the beginning of their careers, who had accumulated only meager taxable assets; and older residents, including seamen and laborers, many widows, a scattering of carpenters, shoemakers, coopers, tailors, and joiners, and an occasional shopkeeper or merchant whose luck or business acumen had failed him. Some of them lived in stark penury, such as Boston mariners Robert Oliver and Henry Johnson, who died in the 1690s with the clothes on their backs, a sea chest, a Bible, and a few nautical instruments. But most maintained a rudimentary existence, renting a small, sparsely furnished house and owning the tools of their trade and a few household items. About one in twenty had scraped together enough money to purchase real estate, usually a small lot with a rude wooden structure on it.

The second tier of society, composing the next 30 percent, included artisans, smaller numbers of mariners who had prospered modestly, merchant-shopkeepers who had not, and the inevitable widows. This group commanded 11 percent of Boston's collective inventoried wealth and 16.5 percent of Philadelphia's. In Boston about half of them owned real estate, usually a small lot and house valued at not more than £150. Caleb Rawlings of Boston, a house carpenter who died in 1693, stood near the median of this group. He owned a house and lot worth £117 sterling, which he left to his wife. The house was plainly furnished with tables, chairs, chests, three bedsteads, and two spinning wheels, pewter and brassware worth about £5, a looking glass, and a few rugs. The additional mention of musket, bandeliers, and sword indicates that Rawlings may have been a militia officer.

In the upper-middle tier of urban society stood the prospering merchants and shopkeepers, a sprinkling of master craftsmen, and securely situated widows. In Boston almost three-quarters of these persons passed on to their heirs substantial amounts of real estate, including wharves, shops, and warehouses, as well as land and houses. They lived comfortably, with mahogany furniture in the parlor instead of oak, canopied beds, fine linens, silver dishes rather than wood or pewter, imported clocks, books, and other symbols of moderate affluence. In this period 20 percent of decedents in the sixty-first to ninetieth percentile owned slaves, compared with 4.4 percent in the bottom 60 percent of society. In all the port towns this upper-middle group held about 40 percent of the collective assets in their communities.

The top 10 percent—the economic elite—were almost all office-holders, merchants, and others closely associated with mercantile pursuits, or their widows. Among the thirty-one Bostonians of this rank who died in 1685–1699, for example, there were nineteen merchants, four sea captains (who also usually acted as importers on their own), two officeholders (including Governor William Phips), and a distiller, house carpenter, brazier, butcher, miller, and minister. This wealthiest tenth controlled about 40 percent of the total taxable assets or inventoried wealth of their communities.

Such a distribution of wealth—with the top tenth of society controlling 40 percent of the community's assets and the bottom half possessing only about 10 percent—was entirely normal, especially in urban centers, where the division of material goods and property was almost always less even than in the countryside. In fact the wealth of European towns in this period was probably far less evenly distributed.

Laborers in the colonial port towns were far better off than their counterparts in English towns, where unemployment and acute poverty were major problems and political economists were busily planning workhouses to absorb the jobless poor and set them to hard labor that would cut the taxes of property owners. The incidence of poverty in the New World was in fact extremely low and was confined for the most part to the widowed, disabled, and orphaned. Townspeople regarded the small number of indigents as wards of the community. Little stigma was attached to poverty, for it was generally due to circumstances beyond the individual's control. Legislation passed in New York in 1683 directed local officials to "make provision for the maintenance and support of their poor."[12] In Philadelphia the law until 1700 required justices of the peace to see to the needs of the indigent. In this social system, fundamentally based on family and kinship, remedies for dealing with the community's unfortunate were familial in form. Most often, persons in need remained in their homes or in the homes of others and were given "out-relief"—clothes, firewood, bread, and often small weekly cash payments.

In none of the towns did poor relief burden the taxpayers. On average, Boston needed less than £100 per year for poor relief in the 1690s, and Philadelphia probably less than half that. In 1688 New York required only £20 for the care of the needy.[13] Only twice in the late seventeenth century was there widespread deprivation in the seaports, and in both cases it was caused by war. The first crisis came in 1676, when Native American tribes in Massachusetts devastated dozens of inland communities, sending refugees streaming into Boston in search of safety and aid. Boston's leaders, ignoring the rule of corporate responsibility to the larger community of Massachusetts Bay, tried to convince the General Court to allow the eviction of these "strangers." But the crisis soon passed, and Boston returned to the traditional system of caring for its small number of resident indigents.

The second crisis followed the outbreak of war with France in 1689. By excluding refugees from towns along the Canadian frontier or by "warning them out," a legal procedure that permitted them to take up residence but disqualified them from public relief, the town again acted to hold down taxes. But Boston now had a resident poverty problem of unprecedented proportions. Many Boston seamen and foot soldiers had taken part in the disastrous expedition against Quebec in 1690, an abortive offensive against French Catholic power in North America. The deaths of scores of these volunteers put their widows and children on the town's relief roll. Bostonians alone among late seventeenth-century urban dwellers knew at first hand the debilitating effects of war, but they continued to regard poor relief as a communal responsibility.

Whereas laboring people at the bottom of northern seaport society enjoyed more benefits than their European counterparts, the colonial economic elite of Boston, New York, and Philadelphia cut far poorer figures than the overseas traders of Bristol, Hull, Cork, Dublin, and Edinburgh. In the New World the gap between rich and poor was one of those measures by which ordinary town dwellers and even upper-class leaders judged equity and virtue in their society. Nobody questioned the right of the rich to their worldly goods. But too much wealth was suspect, especially in Boston and Philadelphia, where the Puritan notion that profits should be put to public uses and the Quaker emphasis on "plain living" subtly curbed the accumulation of large fortunes.

The opportunities for amassing great wealth were in fact few in the late seventeenth-century port towns. Even the wealthiest men were primarily rich on paper, since their main assets were large tracts of land outside the towns, which would wait another generation for buyers. Likewise, urban real estate was appreciating in value but would not deliver substantial rewards until the next generation, when it would double and redouble. The inventories make clear how small was the apex of the pyramid of wealth. From 1685 to 1699 only eleven individuals in the three port towns left personal estates worth more than £2,000 sterling. Shipbuilding was Boston's chief industry, but neither this nor fishing and lumbering had the potential to generate great wealth.

Still, a small number of Bostonians accumulated minor fortunes, and some had adopted lifestyles that shocked the town's moral guardians. Samuel Shrimpton, for example, the son of an immigrant brazier who had speculated in Boston real estate, consolidated the family fortune by investing in the fish and logwood trade and likewise speculating in real estate. Shrimpton owned one of Boston's few coaches in the 1690s, and he scandalized Puritans with his sinful extravagances and public displays. Samuel Sewall, a devout merchant of modest estate, described one drunken coach ride made by Shrimpton and his friends from Roxbury to Boston, where "they stop and drink Healths, curse, swear, talk profanely and baudily to the great disturbance of the Town and grief of good people."[14] Other prospering merchants, such as Andrew Belcher, arrived at balls in carriages attended by liveried slave footmen. And merchants were beginning to build Boston's first three-story brick houses in the North End. But for all these pale imitations of European aristocratic life, this was still an elite very much in the formative stage.

The leading merchants of New York and Philadelphia were even less affluent than those of Boston. New York's merchants, a mixture of Dutch, English, and French, gleaned their profits from a far less developed hinterland than New England's, and in the late seventeenth century they were caught in a transition period, with mercantile activities shifting from connections with Amsterdam and the Dutch empire to London, the West Indies, and other parts of the English-controlled colonial world. In Philadelphia, an elite had not yet crystallized by the end of the century. Only one inventoried estate there exceeded £2,000 sterling. This telescoped social structure was accentuated by the Quakers' emphasis on simplicity and avoidance of ostentation. In its early years Philadelphia disguised the growing gap between top and bottom as did no other town.

By European standards, which, after all, provided the American urban dwellers with their frame of reference, the relationships among the constituent parts of society in all three ports functioned in a generally equitable fashion. Lower-class artisans and laborers might regard upper-class leaders as too inflexibly committed to the concept of an ordered and immobile society; and upper-class merchants and professionals might see dangerous leveling tendencies in lower-class pretensions to a more genteel manner of living. But most people took satisfaction in the fact that William Phips, a sheep farmer and ship's carpenter from Maine, could rise to the governorship of Massachusetts in 1692 and that Griffith Jones, a glover from Surrey in England, could become mayor of Philadelphia in 1704. If the expectations of every inhabitant of the port towns were not fully met, there was at least a general sense that life was fulfilling and the future bright.

The Concept of Government

"Were it not for Government, the World would soon run into all manner of disorders and confusions," wrote a Puritan clergyman early in the eighteenth century. "Mens Lives and Estates and Liberties would soon be prey to the Covetous and the Cruel" and every man would be "as a wolf" to others.[15] Few contemporaries, Puritan or otherwise, would have disagreed with this claim, for the concept that government existed to protect life, liberty, and property was well established in every part of the English-speaking world. Equally uncontroversial was the notion that behind all good government stood good law: the lines between acceptable behavior and unsanctioned acts had to be precisely drawn so that offenders could be quickly apprehended and punished. A third widely acknowledged tenet of government was that political authority existed not only to keep order and promote harmony but also to protect members of the community in the free exercise of their just rights—rights that had been defined over the centuries in England and had become embodied in the common law carried to the New World. In theory, all of these precepts of government found general acceptance among the urban societies of the 1690s, just as they did within rural communities.

Between theory and practice in political life, however, lay difficult terrain. The social harmony so widely desired was rarely achieved by Englishmen either at home or overseas. Agreement was rare concerning exactly what constituted "good law." How far individual rights extended was a subject of never-ending debate. Especially thorny were the questions how far protest against established authority could go and what forms it might take. What were the limits of the ruler's power? When was his encroachment on the people's rightful liberties serious enough to warrant his exclusion from office? Who was to determine this and how was an unjust ruler to be ousted? What kinds of dissent should be allowed?

Such questions were especially pertinent in the colonial seaports, where provincial government in the northern colonies was centered. Legislative assemblies convened in Boston, New York, and Philadelphia; the will of the mother country was promulgated in them; and royal officials charged with its implementation resided there. In fact political life in general operated more vibrantly in the towns than in the country because the urban communities required a greater degree of government, given their size and commercial character. Social structure and economic conditions also changed more rapidly in the northern colonial commercial centers than in the smaller towns and hinterland; thus political life, which necessarily responded to these alterations, was most dynamic there. Many of the changes that would transform the political system as a whole appeared first in the prerevolutionary maritime centers. It was also in the seaports that rapidly changing economic and social conditions engendered new kinds of political behavior, demanded new political institutions, and led to the articulation of new political ideas.

The Political System

These changes occurred within a political context that was itself shifting at the end of the seventeenth century. English political theory, from which American thought was derived, was evolving from faith in the God-given authority of the monarch to a "civic humanism" that achieved stability by balancing the interests of monarchy, aristocracy, and democracy—represented by the king, Lords, and Commons. The governments of most of the colonies were so modeled, distributing power among governor, council, and assembly. The governor was appointed by the king and acted as his agent overseas; the council was appointed by the governor and sat as a pale equivalent of the House of Lords; and the assembly was elected by the freeholders, who regarded it as a replica of the House of Commons.

The freeholders of Boston, New York, and Philadelphia experienced this "republican" form of English government in slightly different forms. The governors of Massachusetts and New York were royally appointed. Pennsylvania governor was appointed by William Penn, who had received a vast proprietary grant from Charles II in 1681. More important to seaport dwellers were differences in selecting the council and assembly, the lawmaking bodies in each colony. In Massachusetts the councilors were selected annually by the elected assembly, voting with the councilors of the previous year, the selection being subject to the veto

of the governor. In New York and Pennsylvania, councilors were selected by the governor. Thus a popular element was present only in
the election of the Massachusetts council.

The election of an assembly was widely regarded as the most important feature of the legislative power of the people. In Boston and
Philadelphia, elections for the assembly were held annually. In New
York they were held only when the governor pleased, although eventually a law was passed requiring elections at least every seventh year.
Voters had to own real property capable of producing an annual income
of 40 shillings, in addition to satisfying fundamental requirements
related to age, sex, and sometimes religion. This requirement excluded
the poor and propertyless from politics and favored landed wealth over
liquid wealth, such as bonds, bills, book credit, mortgages, and stock
in trade. The result was an antiurban bias, for in the dynamic, commercial maritime towns liquid capital was unusually important if not
dominant.

In Massachusetts the definition of political competence underwent
many changes before 1690. Certainly by 1690 the franchise was not
as open as in 1655, when, according to a committee of the General
Court, "Scotch servants, Irish, negers and persons under one and twenty
years" were voting.[16] The charter of 1691 abolished the church mem-
bership requirement and extended the vote to those who held real
property worth 40 shillings per year in rent or property of any kind
worth £40 sterling. Despite low voter turnout before 1698, the franchise, undoubtedly broad by English standards, probably included a
majority of adult males.

In New York the basic suffrage requirement was also a £40 freehold,
and as in Boston it seems to have embraced a majority of the free male
members of the community. In 1699, 632 voters in a population that
included only 800 eligible taxpayers went to the polls. Even with some
absenteeism allowed for, this turnout strongly suggests that the £40
property requirement was generally ignored.[17]

Pennsylvania also had a liberal franchise, extending to anyone owning 100 acres of land, which could be purchased for £2 in the early
1680s, or who paid a householder's small municipal tax. Thus a large
majority of free adult males was eligible to vote. In 1696, when the
Quaker-dominated assembly was concerned about the heavy influx of
non-Quakers into Philadelphia, it narrowed the franchise to exclude
anyone without a £50 estate free of debts. Nevertheless the new legislation still permitted a majority of free males to vote.

Voting for the assembly was a treasured privilege of the urban electorate at the end of the century; but of equal, if not greater, importance were their municipal governments. Tax assessors, tax collectors, overseers of the poor, selectmen, sheriffs, and constables were the officials most closely tied to the concerns of daily life. In some towns, notably Boston, the economic qualifications for voting in local elections differed from those for provincial elections. More important, the range of elected urban officials and the dynamics of the municipal political systems varied markedly in the three seaports. In Boston, political life centered on the town meeting, which annually elected six selectmen to serve as a municipal governing board. The meeting also selected many minor officeholders such as assessors, constables, overseers of the poor, hog-reeves, town criers, measurers of salt, scavengers, firewards, and auditors, who carried the authority of the town to every inhabitant. Many of those elected to serve did not themselves have sufficient property to vote. With one-tenth of the adult males holding office every year, nobody could gain a reputation for sobriety and industry without quickly finding himself elected to some municipal post.

This widely participatory system of local government did not mean that Boston's politics were democratic in the modern sense. Hierarchy characterized town affairs. The most important offices—representative, selectman, clerk, treasurer, and town meeting moderator—were regularly filled from a small pool of acknowledged leaders to whom the lesser people ordinarily deferred. A second level of offices, including the sheriff, overseers of the poor, and tax assessors, was almost always occupied by men of high social standing and economic position. Left to ordinary town dwellers were the supervisory and regulatory minor offices, which were more burdensome than honorific; artisans and shopkeepers often preferred to pay a fine rather than serve in these positions. Nonetheless, substantial numbers of Boston's inhabitants regularly became public servants involved in making decisions and discharging responsibilities. In this they were unique among residents of the northern capitals.

Boston was also unique in that decisions were made by majority vote in town meetings, the deliberations of which were open to all inhabitants, whether propertied or propertyless, free or bound, male or female. Boston thus had a built-in mechanism for resisting concentrated political power.

New York and Philadelphia had less participatory town governments. New York's first elections for aldermen, assistants of the newly chartered municipal corporation, and constables were held in 1686. The governor, with the approval of the council, appointed all other offices, including the mayor, recorder, town clerk, sheriff, tax assessors and collectors, and clerk of the market. In Philadelphia, where at first the suffrage was the broadest of any of the seaport towns, the structure of municipal government was the most conservative. Under a city charter granted in 1691, sheriffs, commissioners, tax assessors, and coroners were elected annually, but the municipal corporation, the chief agency of city government, was a self-perpetuating body of aldermen and councilmen who were initially appointed by William Penn with tenure for life and who thereafter selected their own successors. This kind of city government, largely immune from public opinion, was patterned after the closed corporations in England, which exercised extensive powers, including almost exclusive jurisdiction in civil and criminal courts and the right to pass municipal laws, erect public buildings, and appoint municipal officers.

Consistent with this corporate pattern, Philadelphia and New York operated carefully regulated public markets where foodstuffs and many nonperishable items were sold by schedule several times a week. "Among the corporation-owned stalls," writes one historian of Philadelphia, "strolled corporation officials employing corporation standards of weights and measures to gauge the produce sold by corporation-licensed butchers and corporation-admitted freemen."[18]

Boston exercised no corporate control over public marketing, but even there economic life was managed according to the traditional ethic, in which unrestrained competition was an alien notion. The selectmen strictly regulated the price at which bakers could sell a loaf of bread, fixing the price according to the price of flour. Tanners could not market hides that did not meet standards established by law. Mariners received wages in accordance with schedules set by the General Court. Town officials carefully regulated weights and measures. But unlike New York and Philadelphia, Boston did not restrict vocational opportunity by limiting the number of men who could enter specific trades, and in general it allowed a freer movement of labor and goods.

The structure of town government and the size of the electorate cannot alone describe the political world of the seaport towns. Also of great importance were the values and social customs that informed political discourse and legitimated political decisions. In the late seventeenth century, social and political ideas, like political theory, were in flux. Certain assumptions, however, had wide currency among town dwellers: first, that those of substantial wealth and high social status were best qualified to hold positions of power; second, that the people en masse, however lowly in education, occupation, or material achievement, were entitled in special circumstances to make judgments regarding the actions of those entrusted with power and to act accordingly; third, that those who held civil power ought to promote no special interests but be zealous for the commonweal; and last, that partisan politics, with "factions" and "parties" competing for power, were to be avoided. These precepts, which were part of a collective consciousness rather than a written doctrine, informed people's actions and views of events.

The limited geographic areas and small populations of Boston, New York, and Philadelphia permitted intimate contact between the rulers and the ruled. The structure of town government, particularly in Boston, ensured that matters of concern were quickly known and often quickly acted upon by the commonalty. Even in Philadelphia, where there was no popular election of officers of municipal government, the fluidity of early immigrant society brought to office men of modest wealth and only faint aristocratic pretensions. Annual assembly elections kept those with legislative authority responsive to collective interests. This was not democracy, to be sure; all of these facets of urban politics operated within a framework, which ensured that those of inferior rank would normally bow to their superiors, accepting the legitimacy of a structured society, even regarding it as divinely ordained. But it was a system in which the contractual relationship between rulers and ruled could be breached if the rulers acted irresponsibly. At these times, which occurred far more often than is generally believed, deference quickly crumbled. These elements combined in each seaport in different ways in response to particular circumstances shaping moments of political crisis.

The Glorious Revolution

Political turmoil broke out in Boston in the spring of 1689. Three years before, the English government had launched a bold administrative experiment to unify the northern colonies under a political authority more responsive to London. This move was thought to be particularly necessary in the case of New England, where for two generations an autonomous spirit had reigned, not the least of which was widespread evasion of English commercial regulations. The in-

1. Plan of Boston in 1722 by John Bonner

strument of English determination to rationalize and discipline its growing empire was Sir Edmund Andros, who arrived in Boston in December 1686. Escorted by a company of English grenadiers, Andros assumed the governor-generalship of the Dominion of New England, the new political entity invented to encompass Massachusetts, New Hampshire, Connecticut, Plymouth, Rhode Island, New York, New Jersey, and part of Maine.

Andros was a determined crown administrator with a military background that had taught him how to bring the recalcitrant into line. Bostonians soon hated him heartily. He abolished the General Court and lodged all civil power in the hands of appointed officials; thus the people had no opportunity even to debate, let alone consent to, his subsequent imposition of taxes. Boston's cherished town meeting was muzzled by an order that it meet no more than once a year for the purpose of electing town officers. Congregationalist Puritans in Boston were also appalled at the establishment in their midst of the Church of England, against which their forefathers had rebelled. Their rage was further heightened by Andros's land policy, which required quit-rents on new grants of land and called into question all old land titles. Employing the methods of the army officer rather than those of the diplomat, Andros tried to impose discipline and a proper sense of mercantilist subordination on a people who for many years had blandly ignored English regulations.

When news reached Boston in April 1689 that William of Orange had landed in England to end the hated Catholic regime of James II, Bostonians lost no time in overthrowing their tyrant in residence. To the beat of drums the inhabitants streamed into the streets, formed units with the militia, and surrounded the Town House, the center of government. A committee of safety, composed mostly of merchants and ministers, assumed control and quickly seized and imprisoned Andros. No blood was shed, for the governor-general, aware that his tiny garrison could not overpower the town, offered no resistance. Within hours the Bostonians had set up provisional authorities, arrested most of Andros's supporters, and issued a declaration justifying their seizure of power.

How had the highest authority in the land been so quickly overturned? Edward Randolph, royal customs collector and crown investigator, believed that "a violent & bloudy zeal" had been "stir'd up in the Rabble, acted & managed by the preachers."[19] To the imperious Randolph, however, everyone beneath the upper class was "the Rabble." Preachers, merchants, and former magistrates led the rebellion, but city folk of all classes, about a thousand strong, united to overthrow the governor. In doing so they were reflecting a colonywide animus against Andros. They were also trying to preserve their power against the threats of a thoroughly aroused rural populace, which was ready to unseat Andros if the city people would not. Tyranny in Boston had been stopped because the mass of people had collectively taken the law into their own hands. They had done so, however, under the leadership of the town's foremost men, who never lost control of the situation.

Community consensus did not last long after the overthrow of Andros. Many upper-class Bostonians who had detested Andros and participated in his overthrow had no wish to give up control of political affairs. On the other hand many townsmen drawn from lower in the social structure now desired greater participation in public affairs. Many who had not enjoyed freemanship under the old charter of 1629, including nonchurch members of all ranks, had been in the crowd surrounding the Town House in April 1689, and they subsequently showed an unwillingness to withdraw quietly from the political arena. To the Puritan elite such perversity was alarming.

As the interim government sought to establish its authority while awaiting instruction from England on how the post-Andros government should be constituted, these former outsiders pressed for a new role. They petitioned for a change in the colony's suffrage law that would extend the vote to qualified property owners who were not church members. The council of state acceded, granting the franchise to most property owners. Less peaceful demands followed in July 1689, when the interim government allowed Joseph Dudley, one of Andros's chief officers who was roundly detested in Boston, to return home on bail from the Boston jail. To allow this henchman of Andros to go free was more than Boston's populace could abide. A crowd appeared in the streets, composed of "women boyes and negros," according to one unsympathetic observer, broke all the windows in Dudley's house, and demanded his reincarceration.[20] Several magistrates reported that "the tumult in the town is so great and sudden that no reason will be heard or regarded."[21] Bowing to public pressure, the president of the interim government, who was Dudley's brother-in-law, convinced him that he must return to jail, lest the crowd take further action. There is not sufficient evidence to determine the social composition of the July mob, but it is unlikely that the governing council would have yielded to a street gang composed only of "women boyes and negros." It seems clear that a more broadly based populace had abandoned its deferential stance and taken matters into its own hands, increasing the pressure on the provisional magistrates "to justify their policies before the people."[22] "Anarchy" was the word chosen by Samuel Willard, minister at Boston's Third Church, to tar the popular spirit he saw unloosed in Boston in the aftermath of Andros's ouster.[23]

This feeling of political importance, together with the dawning notion that the public good was better served if the common people exercised a watchdog role rather than electing eminent men to positions of power and trusting them to exercise it for the commonweal, marked a turning point in politics. After 1689 the political consciousness of ordinary people began to grow. There were those in New England who believed that the overthrow of Andros had uncovered a "levelling, independent, democratical principle and spirit, with a tang of fifth-monarchy." It was said that some deluded New Englanders now wished to form "an Oliverian republic."[24]

Phrases of this kind carried enormous emotional freight. "A tang of fifth-monarchy" and "an Oliverian republic" called to mind the bloody English civil war of the previous generation, the rise to power of the radical dictator Oliver Cromwell, and the emergence of millenarianists, radical utopians, and social reformers in the 1650s and 1660s. These were events within the living memory of many Bostonians and well known, through story and book, to the younger generation. England in the mid-seventeenth century had in fact witnessed "the greatest upheaval that has yet occurred" in that country.[25] At the center of the turmoil were the efforts of common people, enlisting in popular movements such as the Ranters, Levellers, Muggletonians, Quakers, Diggers, and Fifth Monarchists, "to impose their own solutions to the problems of their time, in opposition to the wishes of their betters who had called them into political action."[26] Whereas the gentry revolted against an absolutist king, arbitrary taxes, prerogative courts, and feudal tenures, the radical sects warred for a far-reaching democratization of political and legal institutions, establishment of communal property, disestablishment of the church, and leveling of class distinctions and wealth. The Fifth Monarchy Men, who believed that the Lord Jesus would return to earth to help usher in the new era, were composed primarily of the urban lower classes and were often prepared to resort to violence to attain their goals. Pathetically unsuccessful, they were driven underground; but, like other lower-class groups that rose violently in quest of radical reform, they sent shock waves through the propertied, politically dominant upper class.

Boston in 1690 was not London or Bristol in 1660, of course.

Outweighing several parallels was a fundamental difference: in England lower-class reformist zeal had blossomed into a revolution within a revolution as the call went forth, accompanied by violent uprisings, for fundamental change; in Boston the lesser people were far more moderate in their proposals and far less violent. Almost nothing in the actions of the Boston commonalty suggests that they wished to level distinctions among the inhabitants or to do away with a system of private property in favor of return to a primitive communitarianism. But enough of the spirit of Fifth Monarchy had crossed the Atlantic, albeit in watered-down form, to frighten many in the upper echelon. They were witnessing an assault on the older emphasis on the primacy of social hierarchy and civil order. The belief that those at the top of society were the appropriate guardians of the public interest, the only truly disinterested members of the community, was in direct contention with the belief that it was those of modest means but common sense who could best be trusted with power. These rumblings from below had neither taken organizational form nor emerged as a clear-cut ideology but nonetheless bespoke feelings of disdain for the gentry, a predilection for egalitarianism, perhaps even the faint echo of millenarianism.

In New York, where the hard-bitten military careerist Francis Nicholson had been deputized as Andros's lieutenant governor of the Dominion of New England, word of the Boston uprising arrived on April 26, 1689. Nicholson had inflicted few of the odious new policies upon New Yorkers that Andros had applied in Boston, mostly because it was unnecessary to do so. New Yorkers had no representative assembly to suspend, no town meeting to restrict, and had dutifully paid small quitrents on their land for years. Although he alienated some in the town by bestowing political favors on a circle of powerful Dutch and English merchant supporters, New Yorkers did not regard Nicholson as a despot or as an abrogator of ancient liberties. Some did, however, regard him as a crypto-Catholic. Thus he was deeply suspect by those who applauded Boston's revolt as part and parcel of the move on both sides of the Atlantic to drive out James II and all the other "bloody Devotees of Rome," as the Boston Declaration of Grievances against Andros declared.[27]

New Yorkers did not actually overthrow Nicholson's government. It simply melted away. While awaiting instructions from the newly crowned monarchs in England, Nicholson had ensconced himself in Fort James. When the local militia, led by Captain Jacob Leisler, a petty merchant of German origin, appeared to take over Fort James on May 31, 1689, Nicholson offered only token resistance. Within two weeks he had quietly sailed for England. Leisler became the head of an interim government, ruling with an elected Committee of Safety for thirteen months until a governor appointed by the new king arrived in the colony.

New York seethed with tension during this interregnum, but, unlike in Boston, internal conflict caused it. Factional infighting was so intense that when Governor Henry Sloughter arrived in 1691 and encountered resistance by the Leisler party, the anti-Leislerians put Leisler and seven compatriots on trial for treason. Joseph Dudley, the target of the crowd's wrath in Boston four years before, presided over a less than impartial court, which found Leisler and his chief adjutant, Jacob Milbourne, guilty of treason. They were summarily hanged and decapitated. These events did nothing to reduce the enmity coursing through the town, for the Leislerians believed that their leaders had not been executed for treason but had been judicially murdered for challenging the rule of an entrenched oligarchy.

The differences between New York and Boston in their ousting of constituted authority are striking. In Boston a united populace had risen against a man seen as an invader of the people's rights but as one who upheld the rule of a distant authority rather than that of an oppressive local economic elite. In New York one part of a divided population rose to seize authority from a caretaker governor who had never reduced or struck down long-enjoyed privileges but who stood at the center of a group of local, arrogant, mercantile grandees. In both cases fission within the community followed the takeover of power. Whereas in Boston the division was caused by political activity among those who had previously played a very small part in political affairs, the split in New York represented the widening of a break that predated the Glorious Revolution and was ethnic as well as economic. Neither Dutch nor English New Yorkers had much of a tradition of participatory politics to draw upon, for the town's charter, allowing the election of a common council, had not been granted until 1686 and a representative assembly had existed in the colony only from 1683 to 1685, when it was abolished. But ethnic tension interlaced with class antagonism had permeated the town since the English takeover of New Amsterdam in 1664.

Rather than overthrowing constituted authority, Leisler stepped into a local power vacuum created by the Protestant revolt against

James II in England. His enemies depicted him as a treasonous rebel who had illegally overthrown the government in New York. But the real conflict in the town was internecine and occurred after Leisler had established an interim government. Much of this strife had its origins in the smoldering resentment felt by Dutch inhabitants toward the English of the town. Many of the Dutch merchants had adjusted to the English government after the conquest of New Amsterdam in 1664, for business was business whether conducted under Dutch or English rule. Conversely, because of the initial dearth of Englishwomen many incoming Englishmen had married into Dutch families and joined the Dutch church. But beneath the upper echelon, where economic success eased tension, incidents of Anglo-Dutch hostility were legion. In the 1670s and 1680s ordinary Dutch families increasingly felt that they were being crowded out of an economic system that they had built.

When turmoil came in 1689, New York's Dutch and English did not neatly divide into Leislerian and anti-Leislerian factions. A number of wealthy Dutch merchants who had made their peace with the English opposed the renegade leader. A few Englishmen joined him. But leadership of the two sides split along ethnic lines to a considerable degree, and among the rank and file the ethnic alignment was even more striking. It was indicative that in a town whose population was 60 percent Dutch, Leisler was tried and found guilty by an all-English jury in the spring of 1691.

Leisler's brief government radicalized New York's political life. It created a precedent for popular politics and nurtured laboring people's resentment of parvenu merchants. Leisler was not interested in traditional English liberties as they were cherished in Boston, nor was he intent on transforming society along egalitarian lines. He established almost no contact with and received little support from the communities on Long Island where migrating New Englanders had previously established town meetings and agitated for a representative assembly. When he reluctantly revived the elective assembly, mainly because he desperately needed revenue that he dared not raise by executive order, he was so angered by the legislators' attempts to discuss English liberties that he prorogued the first session and rejected a measure enacted by the second one to obtain such rights. His motivation, instead, was primarily economic and religious. A fervid orthodox Calvinist who saw a popish plotter lurking in every corner, he had detested Thomas Dongan, the former Catholic governor sent to New York in 1683. He frequently denounced his opponents as "Popish Doggs & Divells," vividly reflecting the fear of Catholicism that resonated deeply among New York's Dutch.[28] In trying to legitimate the assumption of power it was judicious for the Leislerians to argue that they had cleansed the colony of Jacobitism, just as the faithful Potestants of England had driven out the tainted James II. But Leisler and his followers lived in real fear of popish subversion and were in deadly earnest when they described Governor Nicholson as a "pretended protestant" who "countenanced the Popish party" and appointed Catholics to high places.[29]

Interwoven with Leislerian antipopery was hostility toward New York's elite—a sentiment that spread so suddenly after Nicholson's departure that even Leisler was at times powerless to contain it. Soon after their assumption of power, the Leislerians freed imprisoned debtors in New York and called for the election of justices of the peace and militia officers, who previously had been appointed. These were steps of great significance in a colony in which authoritarian and oligarchical rule had prevailed for several generations. In another move, the Leislerians tried to extend the role of ordinary people in municipal government. The second request of Leisler's deputy, sent to England less than three months after the assumption of power to gain recognition for the interim government, was that the crown grant New York a city charter like that of Boston. By this move the Leislerians were clearly asking for a more participatory system with a town meeting and elective officials.

In one other respect Leisler's government in New York departed radically from past practice. It not only drew wide support from laboring people but also gave artisans and persons of humble background positions of power. Joost Stoll, a dram seller, was chosen to represent the Leislerian cause in London in 1689. Henry Cuyler, a baker and tailor, was a prominent cohort of Leisler. Johannes Johnson, a carpenter, was appointed sheriff. Leisler's marshal, who could be seen marching at the head of a file of supporters when arrests of wealthy merchant opponents were made, was William Churcher, formerly a bricklayer. Jacob Milbourne, Leisler's son-in-law and chief lieutenant, had begun his career in America as an indentured servant and was the brother of William Milbourne, a radical Fifth Monarchy man in England. Six of the ten aldermen chosen in the year of Leisler's takeover were artisans drawn from outside the merchant elite. It was moving testimony to Leisler's popularity among the "leather aprons" that his wealthy opponents, after sentencing him to death, could find no carpenter in the town who would furnish a ladder to use at the scaffold.

The class orientation of the Leislerian struggle became further evident when Leisler's merchant antagonists, reinstalled in power in 1691, attempted to legislate lower artisans' wages and to make the requirements for freemanship more restrictive.

At times the laboring people forged ahead of their supposed leaders. Late in the summer of 1689, Leislerian mobs began attacking the property of some of New York's wealthiest merchants. Although the plundering probably never reached the extent claimed by the anti-Leislerians, the assaults on property were widespread. One of the town's principal merchants claimed that the mobs "take peoples goods out of their houses and if hindered by Justices of the peace, they come with great numbers and fetch it out of the Justices house by forse."[30] In this expropriation of property, without parallel in Boston's overthrow of Andros, "their Captains can no more Rule them," it was claimed.[31]

Attacks on the property of the rich, whether English or Dutch, are important indications of the class feeling that mixed strongly with ethnic hostility in New York. Nothing is more noticeable in the charges of the anti-Leislerians than their horror that the movement had raised up what they variously described as the "rabble," the "ignorant Mobile," the "tumultuous multitude," the "most abject Comon people," and the "drunken crue."[32] Actually there was far from perfect correlation between class and political allegiance during the rebellion. But the anti-Leislerians correctly understood how widely their enemies had appealed to the working poor, who were disproportionately Dutch. In stigmatizing the revolt Leisler's enemies were at pains to show that it was people of lowly condition, in no way entitled to rebel against civil authority by themselves, who had snatched control of the government.

It was a measure of wealthy New Yorkers' fear and hatred of Leisler that after he surrendered the government to Colonel Henry Sloughter, the newly appointed royal governor who arrived in March 1691, Leisler was tried for treason in New York instead of being sent to England. As the best legal historians of early New York history have said, Leisler "was eventually sentenced under circumstances which no amount of explanation has justified."[33] He would later be canonized by the laboring people of the town, who had been amply instructed on how far the elite was prepared to go to ensure its dominance.

Philadelphia staged no miniature Glorious Revolution because there was no local autocrat, appointed from afar, to oust. But not all was tranquil in William Penn's "holy experiment." Tension had been mounting since the first settlers arrived in 1681. It was fed by the normal confusion attending migration to a new land . . . lack of specie to facilitate trade, disagreements over the proper form of government, friction between council and assembly, competition for choice land and political preferment, and the departure of the charismatic Penn in 1684. From 1684 to 1689 Penn faced the growth of a strong anti-proprietary movement centered in Philadelphia that strove to limit severely his political power in the colony and to evade the quitrents that he collected on all property.

Disillusioned with the ordinary colonists, Penn tried to cultivate the support of a local elite. When this failed he unwisely appointed a Puritan disciplinarian, Captain John Blackwell of Boston, as deputy governor of the colony. It was a monumental blunder and Penn paid dearly for it. Puritans were cordially hated by the Quakers, especially in the New World; Friends had been beaten, mutilated, and hanged in Boston only a few decades before. Despite his years of administrative and military experience, Blackwell was no match for the Philadelphia pacifists. Within eighteen months he resigned his commission, thoroughly shaken and convinced that the mosquitoes in Philadelphia were worse than armed men, though not nearly so nettlesome as the "men without Armes," who had found endless ways to obstruct his administration of government.[34]

Stymied in his efforts to bring orderly government to Pennsylvania and to implement proprietary land and revenue policies, Penn returned the reins of government to a circle of Quaker leaders in 1692. Many of them had been among the antiproprietary faction that had developed after Penn's departure, but at a distance of three thousand miles his alternatives were limited. Invested with power, this group, composed primarily of the wealthiest Quaker merchants, removed all officeholders who had supported Governor Blackwell and began to administer government with a high-handedness that rankled elements of the lower and middle classes.

Against this backdrop of growing friction a religious schism split Philadelphia's Quaker community wide open in 1692. Known as the Keithian controversy, it took its name from George Keith, an itinerant Quaker preacher who had emigrated from Scotland to East New Jersey in 1685. A deeply introspective, moody individual, Keith was disturbed by what he perceived as the failing commitment of Quakers to the founding principles of the Society of Friends. He therefore began a crusade to institute more discipline and structure in church affairs. By

Keith's reckoning, ordinary, untutored Quaker folk, cast into a dis-integrative New World setting, would be able to preserve their faith only with a set of strict tenets to guide them and sterner tests of religious convincement to weed out superficial adherents from true believers.

Keith was soon confronting most of Philadelphia's "Public Friends," the lay leaders of the Society of Friends, who hewed to a simpler faith. They supported a less structured organization of the church and be-lieved in the ability of each Quaker to draw upon the "inner light" to fashion a godly life. They utterly rejected Keith's reform demands as "downright Popery," a phrase fraught with implications, given con-temporary fears in England of Catholic plots.[35] Soon the controversy over Quaker doctrine turned into an argument about the proper lo-cation of authority within the Society of Friends, for Keith was accusing some of the Public Friends of heretical views and demanding that they be disciplined.

The Keithian controversy was deeply rooted in issues of religious doctrine and church organization. Yet it also involved more than this. The hundreds of Philadelphians who followed Keith were drawn to the passionate Scotsman not only for ideological reasons but also be-cause political and economic tensions in Philadelphia were interwoven with disputes about Quaker belief and organization. One of Penn's supporters, writing in 1692, noted the conjunction of religious and civil conflict: "Alls a fire spiritual and temporal."[36]

The social composition of the disciples of George Keith and his opponent Thomas Lloyd (a financially embarrassed Quaker merchant who was deputy governor after Blackwell) shows the close connection between secular and religious conflict. Among the several hundred Quakers who publicly avowed their opposition to Keith, not one was known as a political opponent of Lloyd. Conversely, among Governor Lloyd's officeholders the denunciation of Keith was almost unanimous. Similarly, the most prominent Keithians were those who led the po-litical opposition against Lloyd but had lost their voice in public affairs because of their support for Penn or his deputy Blackwell. Keith also found considerable support among the town's shopkeepers and master artisans.

Thus Keithianism took on a far broader meaning for elements of Philadelphia society than Keith had initially intended in his movement to reform the Society of Friends. A stratum of lesser merchants, shop-keepers, and artisans found that Keith's program provided a way of challenging those who held high positions and who were resented for their political domination and overbearing behavior. The texture of the debates, the scurrilous language used by Quakers against each other, and the abstruseness of some of the theological issues at stake all suggest that participation in the movement was not only religiously inspired but also emblematic of widely felt political and economic grievances.

The Keithian controversy reveals a number of tendencies that were woven into the fabric of urban politics. When they went to the polls each year Philadelphians elected men who had ascended to the top of society, as measured by occupation, wealth, and reputation. At the same time they did not hesitate to oppose these figures or even William Penn, who was known and respected far beyond the boundaries of his colony. Men of middling and even lower status affixed their names to petitions, joined public demonstrations, indulged in inflammatory and hyperbolic rhetoric, refused to pay quitrents and taxes, and kept invoking the communal interest, as they saw it, in order to oppose those whom they viewed as authoritarian or inequitable. While they may have denied the legitimacy of factions, they readily indulged in factional politics, though carefully designating the other side as the violators of the public good.

What occurred in Philadelphia's early years was to some extent related to the unleashing of energy and ambition that accompanied the persecuted Quakers' exodus from England. "More and not less [liberty]," Penn would later reflect, "seems the Reason . . . to Plant this Wilderness."[37] Penn's words tap the sense of anticipation felt in Philadelphia from the outset. People whose religion and humble positions in English society had made lofty aspirations unthinkable quickly acquired in the New World an enlarged sense of self-importance and of what was attainable. Agencies of authority were also less organized than at home and to a considerable degree were instruments of the people they were supposed to control.

Special characteristics of Quakerism may also have contributed to Philadelphia's early tendency to balk at constituted authority. In the exercise of their beliefs in England, Friends had continually defied established authority to an even greater extent than the Puritans. The Friends were not unrestrained individualists; there was much in their code of values that stressed self-control and a commitment to community. But the Quaker personality had two sides, one that emphasized control, hierarchy, and community and another that celebrated freedom, individualism, and nonconformity. In Philadelphia the centrifugal tendencies seem to have overpowered the centripetal ones, even though Quakers now had control of their own government. Penn despaired that his followers, set down on the banks of the Delaware, should be so "governmentish," so "brutish," so ready to indulge in "scurvy quarrels that break out to the disgrace of the Province."[38]

Religious values in Philadelphia, though of fundamental importance in the first few decades, never stifled the quest for economic and political advantage in an environment that was fluid and abundant enough to raise the level of aspiration of a large part of the community. Quakers in England, persecuted and limited in what they could achieve, looked inward. In Pennsylvania, where they controlled the government and were discovering the limits of ambition, they looked outward. Events in New York and Boston during this period show a similar tendency.

The Port Towns in an Era of War

Chapter 2

THE HALF-CENTURY from 1690 to 1740 marked the emergence of the small American port towns into commercial centers rivaling such British provincial ports as Hull, Bristol, and Glasgow. Boston and New York reached about 17,000 and 9,500 inhabitants respectively, and Philadelphia more than quadrupled in size to about 9,000 during this period. Boston, however, had reached the limits of its colonial growth by the late 1730s, whereas the population of New York and Philadelphia would continue to increase through the second and third quarters of the century, leaving Boston on the eve of the American Revolution the third largest city in British North America.

To a considerable extent the growth of the cities and the expansion of their economies during this period was dictated by the development of the hinterlands to which they were commercially linked. Boston, for example, reached out to serve the scores of towns, many of them founded in this era, that made up New England. Regional expansion caused growth at the metropolitan center. So while New England's population tripled between 1690 and 1740, from about 50,000 to 150,000, Boston's climbed correspondingly from 6,000 to nearly 17,000. Inbound and outbound shipping also grew rapidly as the level of imports and exports kept pace with rising regional population.[1]

The same relationship between seaboard commercial center and commodity-producing hinterland obtained for the ports of New York and Philadelphia. The colony of New York increased nearly fivefold from 1690 to 1740, while Pennsylvania's population swelled more than sevenfold. This growth alone guaranteed that the two mid-Atlantic ports would rapidly close the gap on their northern competitor. By early in the eighteenth century the fertile interiors of New York and Pennsylvania had begun to establish a competitive advantage over New England, with its marginal soil. As a result their primary ports, rather than Boston, would come to dominate the West Indian and southern European foodstuffs trade and thereby earn larger balances to pay for a higher volume of imported goods than New Englanders could afford.

The impact of war also contributed to divergent economic and social conditions in Boston, New York, and Philadelphia. Almost continuously for a quarter-century after 1689, the colonists were involved in military conflict originating in Europe. Wars alternately stimulated and depressed trade. They also opened up new forms of entrepreneurial activity such as smuggling, piracy, and military contracting, provided the basis for new urban fortunes as well as for new urban misery, altered the social structure, and exposed the towns to the vagaries of the market economy to a degree previously unknown.

The Impact of War on Boston

Boston, far more than any other colonial seaport, was involved in King William's War (1689–1697) and Queen Anne's War (1702–1713)— the two worldwide conflicts that involved a contest between Britain and France for control of North America. Shipping and shipbuilding were mainstays of Boston's economy, and war made the shipyards hum as orders from England rolled in and local vessels lost to the enemy had to be replaced. In the peacetime years from 1697 to 1702 Boston's shipwrights constructed an average of fifteen vessels totaling 1,024 tons per year. During Queen Anne's War the volume of construction nearly doubled.[2] After the Peace of Utrecht in 1713 the demand for Boston ships dropped, idling many artisans employed in the shipyards.

War also altered the pattern of shipowning. In a time of great risk on the high seas only those financially cushioned to withstand short-term losses could continue investing their capital. In 1698 small investors who owned shares in no more than three ships held about 70 percent of all investments. But during Queen Anne's War their investments fell to 52 percent of the total. The five leading investors in 1698 controlled 12 percent of investments; during the subsequent war years they increased their holdings to 24 percent.[3] The largest vessels were held by fewer and fewer people, and the wealthiest shipowners, those who invested in ten or more vessels, obtained control of the colony's shipping.

While war altered the circumstances of shipbuilders and shipowners, it had far more deranging effects on those at the bottom of urban life.

Wartime shipbuilding booms kept shipwrights, mastmakers, caulkers, ropewalk workers, and blacksmiths fully employed; provisioning contracts for the royal navy aided bakers, distillers, and chandlers; and so long as trade was uninterrupted Boston's large population of merchant seamen, who may have numbered about eight hundred during this period, found berths aplenty. Beneath the established artisanry, however, was another group—indentured servants, apprentices, recently arrived immigrants, migrants from hinterland towns, unskilled laborers, and younger artisans not yet established on their own. It was from these ranks that troops were recruited or pressed involuntarily into service for the assaults on the bastions of French Canada. They cannot have enlisted for the money, for the 8 to 10 shillings per week paid during Queen Anne's War was below the prevailing wage for common laborers.[4] Fervent antipopery, dreams of glory, and, most of all, hopes for plunder from the commercial centers of French Canada probably attracted most of them, but some were involuntarily pressed into service when quotas could not be met by volunteers.

At least one-fifth of the able-bodied males of Massachusetts participated in the campaigns, and of these about one-quarter perished. Recruitment in Massachusetts was particularly heavy in the coastal ports. At the end of King William's War, in 1697, the colony was, according to one official, "quite exhausted and ready to sinke under the Calamitys and fatigue of a tedious consuming War."[5] More than a decade later a knowledgeable Bostonian recalled that the war had cost Massachusetts an "abundance of young *chosen Men*" and left it so burdened with debt that it "did not recover itself for many Years after."[6]

By the beginning of Queen Anne's War, much of the romance of bearding the French lion in his den was wearing thin. Governor Dudley had great difficulty recruiting volunteers for a British expedition against the French in the West Indies in 1702. He mustered two companies, but they were wiped out by disease. Nonetheless, Massachusetts sent 550 men on a fruitless foray into Nova Scotia in 1704, and 1,300 men on two unfortunate attacks on Port Royal in 1707.

Massachusetts mustered 1,000 men in 1709 for another Port Royal expedition, which never sailed because the expected English supporting task force failed to arrive. In the following year a combined British–New England expedition did capture the Nova Scotian port, and in 1711 Massachusetts put about 2,000 men into service in the most ambitious military exploit yet conceived—an Anglo-American assault on Quebec by land and sea. This expedition, which included sixty ships and about 6,000 British soldiers, turned into another fiasco. Ships ran aground in the St. Lawrence River, heavy casualties were sustained, and the task force never reached its objective.

The emergence of a serious poverty problem in Boston by the closing years of Queen Anne's War was clearly related to this series of calamitous campaigns, which left many war widows and their children without means of support. In 1712 Cotton Mather wrote that "the distressed Families of the Poor to which I dispense, or procure needful Relief, are now so many, and of such daily Occurrence, that it is needless for me here to mention them."[7]

While war stimulated employment among artisans who could avoid military service, it also affected them adversely in two ways. First, taxes were increased. For the luckless expedition against Canada in 1690–91, which cost £50,000, the legislature levied a tax twenty times the usual rate. The expedition's leaders hoped to seize enough enemy treasure to pay for the costs of the war, but "failure, debts, unpaid soldiers, and threats of mutiny at Boston were the actual results."[8] Among taxpayers, those at the middle and lower levels of society were probably most affected, for the method of taxation was highly regressive and struck with particular force at those with the smallest estates.

The campaigns against Canada from 1707 to 1711 also required extraordinary expenditures, which again sent taxes spiraling upward. Governor Dudley estimated the war costs at £30,000 per year and put a price tag of £50,000 on the 1711 expedition. The average householder's taxes increased 42 percent between the end of the seventeenth century and the height of Queen Anne's War. For Boston artisans, who commanded wages of about 5 shillings per day and, because of the seasonality of work, could rarely earn more than £40 sterling per year, these war-related tax increases represented a significant reduction in expendable income. Weighed down by war taxes, Bostonians had less to spend on imported goods. The subsequent drop in trade meant dead time between voyages and unemployment for the town's seafaring men at times when naval expeditions against the French were not under way.

The war economy of the two decades bracketing the turn of the century affected Bostonians of the laboring class in a second way. The heavy wartime demands on the provincial treasury could be met only by the issuing of paper money, because taxes sufficient to subsidize military operations could never be extracted from property owners' pockets all at once. Thus, faced with unpaid mutinying troops in 1690, the legislature issued paper money for the first time in Massachusetts history. In 1690–91 it issued £40,000 in paper bills; between 1702 and 1710, £85,000; and in 1711 the assembly authorized another £317,000 in paper money over the next five years. Most economic thinkers of the day, at a time when monetary theory was in its infancy, believed that the bills of credit would retain their value so long as they were accompanied by tax legislation ensuring that levies on property would be used to retire the paper currency within reasonable time limits.

Faced with unprecedented military expenditures, however, the Massachusetts legislature gradually began to extend the time for redeeming the yearly issues of paper money. It extended the retirement date of new issues of paper money to one year in the early years of Queen Anne's War, to eighteen months in 1704, to two or three years in 1707–08, and to six years in 1710, all in an effort to spread out the costs of war over a number of years. But, unexpectedly, Massachusetts currency began to lose its value in 1705, marking a depreciatory trend that was to last for two generations. The price of silver in Massachusetts paper currency remained stable at 6 shillings 8 pence from 1685 to 1704, and then rose to 8 shillings in 1706, 9 shillings in 1714, and 13 shillings in 1721.[9]

To some degree the decline in sterling value of Massachusetts money represented faltering public acceptance of the bills of credit. Another factor was Massachusetts merchants' inability to balance trade. Lacking a rich hinterland, the colony's residents were always scrambling for means of paying for products imported from England. Unable to make sufficient returns to England, especially in 1711, when the colony imposed an embargo on its own shipping in order to assemble a fleet for the expedition against Nova Scotia, merchants bid higher and higher in Massachusetts paper money for sterling bills of exchange. Massachusetts money had itself entered the competitive marketplace and fared poorly in the decade following the Peace of Utrecht in 1713.

The other effect of currency depreciation was price inflation. In 1714, when the decline in value of Massachusetts money had only begun, even an affluent Bostonian complained of the "excessive price of everything among us (and even the very necessaries of life.)"[10] A bushel of wheat had risen to 8.5 shillings, an increase of 60 percent since the early years of the century. Such increases were caused in part by the heavy demand for provisions for the royal navy and the colonial military expeditions, but they were also the result of currency depreciation. The higher cost of household commodities spelled misfortune for the average family, since wages did not increase correspondingly. It is generally agreed by economists today that in an inflationary period those at the lower levels of society are most adversely affected because it is they who spend the largest proportion of their income on the necessities of life and on taxes.

Confirmation of this punishing effect comes from the inventories of estate of those who died in this era. As a group, decedents among Boston's lowest 30 percent in the first fifteen years of the eighteenth century left much smaller estates than did their counterparts in the last fifteen years of the seventeenth century. In the earlier period, personal wealth at death ranged between £2 and £70 sterling, or, with real property added, from £2 to £86. But those who died during Queen Anne's War left only £1 to £33 personal wealth and £1 to £55 total wealth. The same trend can be observed farther up the ladder, with inventoried estates at death shrinking in the first quarter of the eighteenth century from those left by Bostonians in the closing fifteen years of the previous century. But the most disproportionate decreases occurred at the bottom, among mariners, laborers, and lesser-paid artisans such as tailors, coopers, and shoemakers. Only the top 5 percent of Bostonians, which included some merchants who had turned war to their advantage, left larger estates than had been accumulated at a comparable level in the late seventeenth century.

One of the corollaries of decreasing material wealth was decreased property ownership and the consolidation of urban real estate holdings in the hands of a rentier class. The rate of real property ownership declined nearly 25 percent in Boston from 1685 to 1725, and by the latter date at least the bottom four-tenths of society did not hold property.

The financial status of two kinds of Bostonians who figured importantly at the bottom of Boston's social structure—mariners and widows—reveals some other effects of the war years. Merchant seamen were by far the largest occupational group represented in the bottom 30 percent of the seaport's inventoried decedents. Their wages were notoriously low, probably no more than £10 sterling per year. In 1713–14 ordinary seamen on private vessels received about £2.5 per month Massachusetts money, which, when adjusted for currency depreciation, would have come to about £12 to £14 sterling per year. With wages at this level it is not surprising that the inventories of men such as Samuel Pell, Daniel Blin, and Nathaniel Fox included only the clothes on their back, a sea chest, and occasionally a set of knee buckles or an extra pair of shoes.

Some mariners were able to work their way up from ordinary seaman to second mate, and then to first mate and captain. Wages rose accordingly, although by unwritten rule captains were paid no more than twice as much as ordinary seamen. But this edge, when combined with a marriage that brought a bit of investment capital, enabled some captains and mates to purchase partial shares in a voyage and thus lift themselves above the ruck of mere subsistence. The inventories show that about one in five mariners (roughly the ratio of captains to crew) left more than £400 at death until 1716–1725, when the percentage dropped sharply. Another one-quarter to one-third left between £101 and £400. In the wake of Queen Anne's War, however, almost two-thirds of Boston's mariners died with estates worth £100 sterling or less, and not even one in five managed to leave over £200 in possessions.

The second-largest group in the bottom 30 percent was widows. Many of them were undoubtedly war widows, and their numbers, as a proportion of all decedents at the bottom of Boston society, slowly increased in the early eighteenth century. Cotton Mather reckoned in 1718 that one-fifth of the communicants in his church were widows.[11] Widowhood would continue for decades to be one of Boston's gravest social problems.

Although Boston had not suffered direct attack, war profoundly affected the town—snuffing out the lives of hundreds who participated in a generation of fighting in Canada and along the eastern frontier; driving up taxes to levels that were particularly onerous to the lower and middle classes; requiring the issue of huge amounts of paper money that through depreciation ate into the real wages of laboring people and others on fixed salaries; and leaving in its wake a new class of dependent poor. For some merchants and for many master artisans the wars generated substantial profits. But for Boston as a whole the war was a disaster, producing, in its pamphleteers' words, "The Present Melancholy Circumstances" and "The Distressed State of the Town of Boston."[12]

The War Years in New York

New York's fortunes were also intimately connected with war for the first two decades of the eighteenth century, but in ways that differed strikingly from Boston. The Hudson River entrepôt never grew to more than two-thirds of Boston's size in this period, and the volume of shipping usually ranged from one-third to one-half that registered in the Massachusetts port. Nonetheless, shipping was the mainstay of New York's economy, and although it was often disrupted during Queen Anne's War, the overall volume of trade increased substantially. New York, like the colony it served, was never drawn into the actual fighting. It raised money for the defense of its northern frontier, but the amount appropriated was less than one-eighth of what Massachusetts spent. Consequently, paper money issues in New York were far smaller—about one-tenth of those in the Bay colony—and inflation was largely avoided. Moreover, New York contributed only token numbers of men to the expeditions against French Canada, despite shrill calls for intercolonial cooperation from officials in London and northern colonial governors. New Yorkers even refused to attack the French across their own frontier, partly because the Hudson River town of Albany had established a profitable illegal trade with the French in Montreal and also because in 1701 the powerful and strategically located Iroquois tribes had adopted a policy of neutrality in the growing Anglo-French rivalry. Overland attack without Indian assistance was regarded in New York as unthinkable, and trading with the enemy was clearly preferable to fighting him. Simply by not participating in the futile attempts to drive the French from Canada, New Yorkers avoided most of the problems that affected Bostonians so severely from 1689 to 1720.

During King William's War, New York benefited as one of the main suppliers of foodstuffs to the British fleet in the Caribbean and to the Spanish colonies in the West Indies. Its own fleet almost quadrupled, growing from about 35 vessels in 1689 to 124 in 1700. During Queen Anne's War, however, Spain outlawed the American foodstuffs trade with her Caribbean possessions, depriving New York of one of its best markets, and the French navy wreaked havoc on the town's merchant fleet. By 1704 the French had destroyed almost one-quarter of the fleet that had existed four years before. Trade with London plummeted, and the war-buffeted economy languished until the mounting of the 1711 Canadian expedition. With New York sharing the role of provisioner with Boston, an infusion of English money began to pull the seaport's economy out of the doldrums.

Piracy also figured prominently in the effect of the wars on New York's economy. Pirates needed a home port where booty could be exchanged for provisions and durable goods. After 1690 New York became their favorite American port.

Piracy was wholly illegal and condemned by every European government. English governors in the American colonies were strictly enjoined to offer no succor to pirates. But from the colonial viewpoint pirates served a crucial economic function: they brought in much-needed hard coin. Each time a pirate ship sailed into a colonial seaport, tavernkeepers supplied liquid refreshment, ship carpenters refitted their vessels, shopkeepers sold fine goods, provisioners resupplied the ships, and merchants and government officials gave covert support from the top. Governor William Markham in Philadelphia was so little offended by pirates that he married his daughter to one of the most notorious of the day, Captain John Avery, who was known to all seafaring men and was even celebrated as the hero of Daniel Defoe's *King of Pirates,* published in London in 1720. Governor Benjamin Fletcher of New York offered pirates commissions to sail as privateers and promised them immunity from prosecution. He received handsome rewards for his hospitality, as did two members of his council, William Nicolls and Nicholas Bayard, who acted as intermediaries between the governor and pirate captains. Many of New York's mercantile fortunes took a sharp upward turn during the 1690s as a result of complicity with the pirates. Nicholas Bayard, Frederick Philipse, Stephen DeLancey, Gabrielle Minvielle, William Nicholls, William "Tangier" Smith, and Thomas and Richard Willett were only some of the town's leading merchants who engaged in this early American version of white-collar crime.

The pro-pirate Fletcher was replaced in 1698 by Richard Coote, earl of Bellomont, and when the new governor announced a crackdown on pirates he found plenty of support among the Leislerians, many of whom came forward to implicate those in the anti-Leislerian party who had abetted the pirates. Hard money was something all New Yorkers needed, but the vigorous Leislerian support of Bellomont's campaign against the oceanic freebooters suggests that the rewards of the piratical connection were by no means uniformly distributed. Because they were not equal beneficiaries, the Leislerians opposed smuggling and piracy, "the beloved twins" of the seaport's Anglo-Dutch mercantile elite.[13]

The risks of wartime shipping, the benefits of smuggling and piracy, the use of larger vessels, and the increasing complexity of New York's trade seem to have consolidated economic power in the hands of a small class of wealthy merchants. Among these fast-rising merchant princes, none was more successful or more representative of the character of late seventeenth-century mercantile life than Holland-born Frederick Philipse, who had married the wealthy widow Margaret Hardenbroeck de Vries and had parlayed his newfound wealth into one of the Manhattan seaport's greatest estates by the time of Leisler's rebellion. Some of this fortune came from his position as New York's largest importer of African slaves. By the 1690s Philipse calculated that he could make several thousand pounds' profit on a single voyage to Mozambique and Madagascar, where slaves that fetched £30 on the New York market could be obtained for less than £2 and where rum that cost 2 shillings a gallon in New York could be sold to pirates for 50 to 60 shillings per gallon.

In the early 1690s, when Governor Fletcher openly welcomed pirates in New York, Philipse was a member of his council and a willing mediator between the marauders and the royal governor. Fletcher's replacement by Bellomont required Philipse to alter his mercantile activities slightly. Trading with pirates in New York now became impossible. But great profits could still be reaped from combining the Madagascar slave trade with the supplying of pirates outside New York. One could provision the Red Sea and Indian Ocean pirates from New York and then load up with Madagascar slaves for the return voyage. Philipse had made about £2,000 sterling on a previous voyage of this kind, bearing out Govenor Bellomont's assertion that supplying pirates could be even more profitable than turning pirate oneself.

In 1698, however, Parliament imposed tight restrictions on trade east of the Cape of Good Hope, and thus virtually sealed off Philipse's avenue for amassing wealth. When he was caught red-handed attempting to smuggle a cargo from the Indian Ocean, his only loss was forfeiture of the smuggled goods to the crown. At his death four years later, he left to his only son one of the great American estates of the time, including more than 90,000 acres in the Hudson River Valley, several hundred tenant farmers and slaves, a small fleet of ships, and a fortune in Manhattan real estate.

The wars had differential effects on New York society, benefiting large merchants more than small and bringing intermittent economic stagnation and uncertainty to parts of the community. New York contributed far fewer men to the war effort in proportion to its population than did the Bay colony capital; it generally escaped price inflation and rising taxes; and its postwar economic recovery was faster than Boston's. Pauper lists for New York make the contrast with Boston clear. The first surviving list, from January 1700, names only thirty-five persons receiving aid. Almost all of them were orphaned, crippled, or aged. Another census of the poor, taken near the end of Queen Anne's War, in 1713, lists only sixteen persons, including two children, one soldier's wife, and only two adult males. Throughout that year only twenty persons were aided by the churchwardens, who directed the care of the needy, and in 1714 their charges numbered twenty-eight. Expenditures for poor relief, though rising from £219 in 1698 to £454 in 1714, were still lower on a per capita basis than in Boston, which had spent about £500 in 1700 and about £1,000 in 1713.[14] Much of New York's 62 percent increase in per capita expenditures on the poor between 1698 and 1714 resulted from the yellow fever epidemic of 1702, which swept away about 10 percent of the city's population and probably hit the laboring classes with unusual severity. According to a household census taken just after the epidemic, 130 households, or one-sixth of all families in the town, were headed by females. This substantial widowing of New York obliged the assembly to double the poor rate. But impoverishment did not become widespread, for although smallpox was fatal, its victims were not so concentrated in the lower ranks as were the several hundred Bostonians who had succumbed in army encampments and on naval vessels during the years of miscalculated adventuring against French Canada.

Philadelphia Rides Out the Storm

Of all the northern seaports, Philadelphia was least affected by the turn-of-the-century wars. The Quaker-controlled government argued shrewdly that the immature state of the colony, the pacifist beliefs of most of its inhabitants, and its greater distance from the zone of Anglo-French rivalry made Pennsylvania's participation unfeasible. So Philadelphians contributed virtually no men to the war efforts and had to tax themselves only lightly to provide token support for what were supposed to be intercolonial campaigns. On a per capita basis they contributed less than one-twentieth as much as Bostonians did in town and provincial taxes in this era. Spared military expenditures, Pennsylvania never had to print paper money; Philadelphians therefore experienced none of the price inflation that depleted the pocketbooks of Bostonians.

Philadelphia's immunity from the dislocating effects of the wars is evident in its poor relief and tax records for 1709. Only fourteen city dwellers, including three men and four widows, received aid from the

Overseers of the Poor in that year. Total expenses for subsidizing the indigent were only £153. The tax list of 1709 also shows that only 5 percent of households were headed by women, less than one-third the proportion in New York and Boston.[15]

Although Philadelphia was spared the unsettling effects of the wars that especially affected the laboring classes, the city's trade, upon which economic conditions in general hinged, swung back and forth between bursts of activity and periods of recession. During the first half of King William's War, when French privateers played havoc with English shipping on the Spanish Main and off the coast of North America, Pennsylvania's trade slumped badly and land prices in Philadelphia spiraled downward in response. But when the French marauders were contained in the closing years of the war, Philadelphia merchants reaped handsome profits from the West Indian trade. In the brief interwar period the city remained prosperous.

Similarly, in the early years of Queen Anne's War, French privateers infested the Caribbean waters, and the Pennsylvania grain market, the underpinning of the economy, was badly shaken. Conditions improved after 1706, and as the war drew to a close Philadelphians flourished. Population growth, spurred by the beginning of heavy Scots-Irish and German immigration after 1715, continued into the early 1720s. Per capita imports from England, which can be taken as a crude measurement of economic conditions, rose from 9 shillings annually in 1701–1710 to 12 shillings 6 pence in the next decade, a 47 percent increase. With shipping routes cleared of enemy ships, a new period of growth and prosperity came to Philadelphia.

Philadelphia's probate records for the years before 1720 yield some interesting indications that in the Quaker capital, comparatively untouched by the two major conflicts of this era, ordinary artisans and shopkeepers did better than their counterparts in Boston. The pattern of wealth left by Bostonian and Philadelphian decedents in the last fifteen years of the seventeenth century was very similar. But in the first quarter of the eighteenth century the pattern differed markedly. Median wealth at death among all but the top 10 percent dropped significantly in Boston, while in the Quaker capital it remained about the same among the bottom third and rose considerably among the top 40 percent. By 1725 the median wealth left by all Bostonians except the upper tenth was half or less of that left by Philadelphians.

This difference probably reflected not only Boston's greater involvement in the Anglo-French wars but also Philadelphia's more productive hinterland and its greater proximity to West Indian markets. Wealth in the Quaker town was also much more evenly distributed than in the Puritan capital. In Boston, the top 5 percent of those who died between 1700 and 1725 possessed 40–49 percent of all inventoried wealth, compared with 25–37 percent possessed by their counterparts in Philadelphia. In the Quaker town, population growth and eonomic development, carried out without significant involvement in war, was leading only slowly toward a less even distribution of wealth; the average carpenter, shopkeeper, or mariner was leaving at death as much as or slightly more than his counterpart of the previous decades. In Boston, ordinary men left less personal wealth than those of a generation before, and the concentration of wealth accelerated.

To what extent urban artisans and others understood the scope and meaning of the changes wrought by war is not easy to say, for they left in writing almost nothing of their thoughts. But the political behavior of these seaport dwellers provides ample clues that they were not insensitive to the transformation of their world and did not passively accept new conditions.

The Rise of Popular Politics in Boston

Between 1688 and 1693 each of the northern seaports had been shaken by a political disturbance that revealed the fragility of traditional beliefs that the well-born and wealthy should lead, the commonalty should follow, and everyone's eyes should be firmly fixed on the public good rather than on private interests. Each town had witnessed some degree of turbulence, crossing of traditional lines of authority, denunciation of established leaders, mobilization of ordinary town dwellers, and development of loose political interest groups, if not parties. The cause had differed in each town: in Boston it was disillusionment with royal authority; in New York, ethnic tension mixed with economic grievances; in Philadelphia, opposition to a proprietor and local rulers whose use of political power was thought to be highhanded.

It is not accidental that social disruption and political innovation proceeded fastest and furthest in Boston, where economic dislocation was more severe, and lagged far behind in Philadelphia, where economic problems were least felt. Of the three northern ports, New York had been the most buffeted by political storms in the 1690s; there the overthrow of James II in England had brought to a head a decade of interconnected economic and ethnic grievances. In the next quarter-century Boston, its economic and social life disrupted by war, was the most politically volatile.

During Queen Anne's War and its aftermath, Boston weathered three controversies that reveal the changes overtaking urban society. The first began in 1710, when Andrew Belcher, Boston's largest grain merchant, personally created a bread shortage in the town. Belcher had the contract to supply 400 royal marines who were joining the Massachusetts militia for another attack on Port Royal. In his capacity as the grain merchant he bought up most of the wheat supplied to Boston from the countryside, held it while prices rose sharply under the pressure of new demands, and sold it to himself, in his capacity as commissary general, at a handsome profit.

War profiteering was one thing, but a shortage of bread was another. When Belcher began to export grain from Boston to other colonies, the townspeople took to the streets, exercising what one historian has called "the right to be fed."[16] Under cover of night a group of marauders descended on one of Belcher's ships, about to sail from the harbor with 6,000 bushels of grain, and sawed through the rudder. The next night a crowd of about fifty Bostonians commandeered the disabled vessel and tried to run it aground. The selectmen, whose pleas Belcher ignored, petitioned the General Court to stop the export of grain. Apparently convinced by the direct action of the townspeople, the legislature complied, although it exempted the grain already on Belcher's ship.

Though restricted from exporting more grain, Belcher continued to buy it up and hold it in his warehouses while prices rose. In 1713 grain shortages in the West Indies gave Belcher another opportunity to offend his townsmen. Rather than sell flour to hungry Bostonians at a modest profit, he chose to export grain to Dutch Curaçao in the Caribbean. The selectmen pleaded in vain with him to halt the shipment. But a crowd of about two hundred took matters into their own hands, attacking and emptying his grain warehouses.

The behavior of the Boston crowd in 1710 and 1713 illustrates the determined resistance of ordinary people to those with great economic leverage who used it in disregard of the traditional restraints on entrepreneurial activity. Some of Boston's merchants, anticipating a new era, were attempting to forge a fresh set of economic relationships that promised greater flexibility and higher profits. The old political economy, medieval in origins, rested on a view of the world as made up of many semiclosed economies, each operating in a nearly self-sufficient way. Boston, according to the model, was connected to its hinterland, with each part of the system serving the other to some degree while remaining semiautonomous. But by the early eighteenth century Boston had become a part of a far wider commercial network that linked the town not only to England and other mainland colonies but also to Newfoundland, the West Indies, Portugal, and even Africa. This wider market was indifferent to individuals and local communities; the flow and price of commodities, as well as of labor and land, were dictated by the invisible laws of the international marketplace. If grain fetched 8 shillings a bushel in Curaçao and only 5 in Boston, then the merchant was entitled, according to the emerging ethic, to ship to the more distant buyer all the grain he could procure from the countryside.

Economic decisions made in consonance with this version of a freer and more international market ran squarely against the precepts of traditional economic thinking. For decades Bostonians had lived with the understanding that the government was obliged to provide for the general welfare by licensing certain economic activities, prohibiting others, and overseeing prices, wages, quality controls, and many other aspects of daily economic life. Serving corporate needs required deference from common citizens. But it also imposed obligations on those at the top. Transactions or contracts that militated against a person's right to subsistence, however arrived at, were unjust and invalid. For most people the ultimate appeal in disputed dealings was to social, in contrast to economic, duty.

For decades, however, the new values had been intruding upon older mores. In terms of this shift the American colonies probably lagged behind England. But change was in the air on both sides of the Atlantic. Not until a genuine crisis occurred did the full extent of the conflict between the new entrepreneurial freedom and the older concern for the public weal become manifest. Such crises arose almost exclusively during periods of war, for food shortages were never a problem in colonial America unless external demand grossly depleted homegrown supplies. During the later years of Queen Anne's War, such a conflict developed between the profit orientation of Boston's largest grain merchants and the needs of local consumers, who demanded to be fed at prices they could afford.

Boston's common folk did not stand by impassively when the town's merchants attempted to substitute the laws of supply and demand for the older ethic. They did not hesitate to take direct—even illegal—action to compel the engrossers, hoarders, and exporters to back down.

What is more, they not only halted Belcher's grain exports but also escaped punishment for taking government into their own hands. After the 1710 incident the Boston grand jury, made up of substantial members of the community, returned a writ of *ignoramus* rather than indict the rioters who had attacked Belcher's ship. In effect, they acknowledged that the ruling elite possessed neither the power nor the moral authority to restrain or punish the crowd leaders. Boston's conservative elite probably applauded Ebenezer Pemberton, who in 1710 ranted that it was "not God's people but the Devil's people that wanted Corn. There was Corn to be had; if they had not impoverished themselves by Rum, they might buy Corn."[17] But many Bostonians believed that Belcher's actions justified breaching the law in order to uphold a more fundamental, if unwritten, principle. It is not clear whether the looting of the houses of some wealthy Bostonians during a major fire in the following year was a populist act of retributory justice, but it set the clergy to exclaiming about the "Monstrous Wretches" and "Monsters of Wickedness" who were abroad.[18]

The second controversy that enveloped Boston in the era of Queen Anne's War concerned the reorganization of town government. At issue was the viability of the town meeting and the wisdom of electing a wide range of public officials, the hallmarks that distinguished Boston's municipal government from all others in colonial America. In 1708 a plan to dismantle the town meeting system was introduced by some of the selectmen, who argued for converting Boston into an incorporated municipal borough to be ruled, as were most English towns, by a mayor and board of aldermen who would appoint most local officials. The change was needed, argued some, because Boston's town meeting was too unwieldy and turbulent to make decisions efficiently and wisely.

At the time this proposal was made the town was already divided into two factions, one supporting the royal governor, Joseph Dudley, still hated by many for his autocratic tendencies in the Andros government, and the other supporting Elisha Cooke, a doctor, lawyer, and landowner who was the leader of the "popular" faction. The two groups were not split strictly along class lines; well-to-do merchants and shopkeepers were numerous in each. But the Dudley party, led by Boston's wealthiest merchants, was strongly oriented toward the growing Anglican church, whose pews were filled with conservative men who looked toward England and the world outside Massachusetts. Cooke's group included many younger and less established merchants but also made a strong appeal to artisans. Every spring for thirteen years, beginning in 1703, Governor Dudley stoked the fires of animosity between the two factions by vetoing Elisha Cooke's election to the council.

When the proposed reorganization of municipal government came before the Boston town meeting in 1708, it was rejected. Six years later, proposals for municipal incorporation were brought forward again, this time in the midst of a controversy concerning the issue of paper money. A group of investors closely associated with the Cooke faction, now under the leadership of Elisha Cooke, Jr., who had inherited the role of opposition leader from his father, wanted to create a private bank that would issue £300,000 in paper money. Subscribers could mortgage their property to the bank in return for private bills of credit issued in the amount of two-thirds of the value of the borrower's land. The proposers hoped to relieve the severe shortage of circulating hard coin in Boston and also to return a profit to the organizers. The bank would also have given Cooke and his associates important leverage in their private economic struggles with Boston's more established merchants.

In the midst of the battle over the private land bank, the plan to reorganize Boston's government came to a head. The Cooke faction, in appealing to the voters before the town meeting, published two pamphlets carefully demonstrating the connection between the plan for a municipal borough and the economic divisions that were separating Boston into two communities. One blasted the plan as an oligarchic plot because it would allow only men worth £1,000 to qualify as aldermen. Its advocates were likened to "the Great Fish" who wanted to be "lords over the Small."[19] The second pamphlet charged that the proponents of incorporation were plotting to strip Bostonians of their most precious rights. "Then Farewell to all Town-Meetings," warned the author, "and to the Management of the Town Affairs by the Freeholders, Collectively; Rich & Poor Men then will no more be jumbled together in Town Offices, as they are in the Grave, no more Mobb Town-Meetings of Freeholders, (as some are pleased to call them)." Under the proposed reorganization, "The Rich will exert that right of Dominion, which they think they have exclusive of all others . . . and then the Great Men will no more have the Dissatisfaction of seeing their Poorer Neighbours stand up for equal Privileges with them."[20] The plan was rejected by a large majority.

Though successful in saving the town meeting, the Cooke faction failed to obtain approval for the private bank scheme, which was vigorously opposed by the mercantile elite surrounding Governor Dudley. At the largest town meeting in Boston's history, a majority of voters opted to issue bills of credit by a public bank under the management of the General Court rather than incorporate a private bank. They had chosen a public solution to the problem, approving the printing of more paper money and keeping the management of the money supply in the hands of the court.

For six years after the defeat of the private bank proposal of 1714, Boston politics centered on paper money, the third source of controversy in the era of Queen Anne's War. Annual elections for selectmen and representatives to the General Court were contests between the Dudley and Cooke groups, and the rift between them widened. The issue was what to do when the large emissions of public bank bills, issued by the colonial government from 1714 to 1716, were retired in 1720. The value of Massachusetts currency fell sharply after 1715, dropping 44 percent in the next six years. The soundness of paper money came into grave doubt at the same time that the town was suffering a postwar recession.

Modern economists use the term "stagflation" to describe the phenomenon of recession accompanied by inflation. Bostonians had no name for it and were unsure of the cure, but they could see its effects in idled ships, rising prices, and widespread distress. Historians have disagreed on what was happening to the Massachusetts economy, but two tendencies are generally acknowledged. First, the excess of imports over exports kept hard money flowing from Massachusetts to England; second, the sterling exchange rate, which measured the amount of Massachusetts currency required to purchase a pound sterling, inched upward. Various remedies were proposed, but nobody fully understood the colony's ailment or had a comprehensive program for dealing with it.

As in most recessions, those with the smallest margin of security were hit hardest. As trade declined, sailors could not find berths, shipbuilding slumped, and house construction must also have suffered, leaving many laborers and artisans without work. Price increases struck at wage earners and people on fixed incomes such as clergymen, artisans whose wages were regulated by the town, and widows living on stipends set by probate courts. Also affected adversely were lessors tied to long-term leases, lessees whose landlords raised rents faster than their wages rose, and anyone indebted to a shopkeeper or merchant who demanded repayment in specie when it was in scarce supply. Even the fiscal conservatives opposing Elisha Cooke's popular party recognized that the inflationary trend had "so raised the price of necessaries, that *Tradesmen and Labourers* can scarce subsist."[21]

The popular party of Elisha Cooke was nurtured amid this economic dislocation, and Bostonians were exposed for the first time to an extended published argument on an issue that concerned everyone's daily existence. In more than thirty-five pamphlets published from 1714 to 1721 the Cooke and Dudley factions traded blows. To state their case the merchant-dominated "court party" relied heavily on conservative clergymen such as Cotton Mather, Edward Wigglesworth, and Thomas Paine, who charged "the Ordinary sort" of people with a "foolish fondness of Forreign Commodities & Fashions," excessive tippling in the taverns, laziness, sottishness, and a hunger for things above their station in life.[22] Cotton Mather admonished: "It is to be demanded of the Poor that they do not indulge in an Affectation of making themselves in all Things appear equal with the Rich: but patiently submit unto the Differences, which the Maker of you Both, has put between you."[23] Boston's poor might well have cheered the night marauder who, shortly after this nostrum to the suffering, threw a bomb through Mather's window.

It is unlikely that those without work or caught in the inflationary squeeze were deceived by such rhetoric. Some pamphlet writers strongly defended the industriousness of laboring men, and, as the debate grew more shrill, explicit warnings of class conflict rang out. A mean spirit was loose, charged a pamphleteer in 1720, whereby those with power studied "how to oppress, cheat, and overreach their neighbours." Gathering great estates and scattering "a few of their mites among the poor" for show, "the Rich, Great, and Potent, with rapacious violence bear down all before them, who have not wealth, or strength to encounter or avoid their fury."[24] Picking up the thread, the egalitarian Congregational minister from neighboring Ipswich, John Wise, wrote that the people "are fully Resolved [that] it is in their own Power to Remove those who stand in their way, and supply themselves."[25]

The economic malaise that swept Boston in the wake of Queen Anne's War had profoundly politicizing effects. On the one hand, Boston's local trade seemed to be hampered by an inadequate circulating medium; and on the other hand, the addition of more paper money seemed likely to erode the value of Massachusetts currency, and with it the buying power of wage earners. Few Bostonians were immune from the monetary difficulties, and neither class nor occupational lines were tightly drawn on the issue. But it was clear that some Bostonians suffered more than others, that the fiscal conservatives were the town's wealthiest merchants, and that they were closely tied to the conservative clergy, who counseled the poor to rest content with their lot. Those who led the opposition to the court party of Governor Dudley and his successor, Samuel Shute, did not come from the ranks of artisans themselves and were not without their own axes to grind. But they recruited support among laboring men and confronted the elite in language that must have resonated deeply in the homes of mechanics and laborers. Some men, declared Oliver Noyes, an important member of the Cooke party, would "like a design to inslave a People and make a few Lord's and the rest Beggars."[26] Such language, and the attention paid them by popular party leaders, made ordinary townspeople feel that some of Boston's best were responsive to their needs.

Political controversy led to the emergence of a political press. Before 1714 campaign literature appealing directly to freemen at election time and polemics pitched to the public at large were uncommon. But in the eight years from 1714 to 1721 economic dislocation brought forth a rush of pamphlets, which were printed at the expense of political factions and often distributed free. These pamphlets were intended to make politics everyone's concern, and they "accustomed people of all classes, but especially of the middling and lower estates, to the examination and discussion of controversial issues of all sorts."[27] Those whom even the most liberal politicians would not have formally admitted to the political arena were drawn into it informally.

In the troubled years after 1714, one man in Boston worked so diligently on broadening and organizing the arena of politics that he created "America's first urban political 'machine.' "[28] There was nothing plebeian in the background of Elisha Cooke, Jr. Rather, his politics were "popular" because he came from a family with a strong tradition of entrepreneurship combined with a concern for the common people. When the elder Cooke died in 1715, his son, a Harvard graduate and physician as well as a considerable landlord, took up where the father had left off. Stung by the defeat of the land bank on his first appeal to the electorate, he set about to mold a political organization that could capture the town meeting and penetrate all aspects of town and provincial politics. Temperamentally, Cooke was well suited to the task; he was "genial, generous to needy people of all classes, and a drinking man without equal."[29]

Beginning in 1718, when he was elected to the General Court, Cooke undertook to mobilize broad-based support in Boston through a political club later known as the Boston Caucus, formed under his direction in about 1719. Its goals were to draw up slates of candidates for selectmen and General Court elections; to mobilize the voters, using the town's taverns as political nodes; and to disseminate political literature in the community. It operated secretively, dispensed quantities of free liquor in order to win votes, and was carefully managed by a small clique, in contrast to the town meeting, which was open, participatory, and sober. But the goals of the Caucus were definitely populistic. Strongly oriented toward the artisans and shopkeepers, it was managed by large landlords in the South End who also had extensive contacts with laboring people, thus already exercising a degree of power over them. These leaders assumed that the political interests of the artisans and laborers were well served by the same measures from which they hoped to benefit—an increase in the supply of paper money, a strict hedging of the governor's patronage and prerogatives, and the promotion of public works projects such as the construction of a bridge across the Charles River and a canal across Cape Cod. It was not against material gain that the popular leaders inveighed, but against privilege and narrowly concentrated power.

Governor Samuel Shute's supporters complained bitterly of "that Incendiary" Cooke, who tried "to poyson the Minds of his Countreymen, with his republican notions."[30] But this "republicanism" was no more than an expression of the legislative power of the people at the provincial level and the maintenance of the town meeting system of politics at the local level. Much later, a prominent Boston Tory would claim that the Cooke machine controlled the elections by spending nearly £9,000 sterling in the 1720s, dispensed in the form of bribes and election-time liquor treats. The striking decrease in the turnover of Boston's selectmen, tax assessors, and representatives to the General Court in the 1720s attests to Cooke's success in maintaining control.

In creating a distinctly modern political organization, Cooke's accomplishment was not to expand the electorate but to organize and politicize it. The center of political gravity did not move downward, either in terms of the kinds of people who were elected to town office or in terms of those who went to the polls. Well-to-do Bostonians continued to fill the positions of representative and selectman, and the number of voters seems to have decreased, despite the increase in Boston's population. It is possible that the party of Cooke and his associates, strengthened by effective pamphlet writing and the creation of a disciplined organization, may have so overwhelmed the opposition that many who adhered to the conservative court faction simply stayed away from the polls. This effect is also suggested by the fact that in the decade after 1719, when the Caucus probably formed, fewer than one-third of the Boston elections for representatives to the General Court were contested. By making his party responsive to the public will, exemplified by regularizing the practice of voting comprehensive instructions to the General Court representatives at the town meeting, Cooke proved that a popular party could also be a carefully managed party, maintained in power by the annual endorsement of a small fraction of the community's adult males.

Political Factionalism in New York

In New York the fires of ethnic politics were damped for a few years after the hanging and beheading of Leisler and Milbourne in 1691. But the bitterness of the Leislerians, who were strongly Dutch and predominantly artisan, was unassuaged. Oligarchic rule and ethnic aggression had been at the heart of the Leislerians' disaffection, and the public execution of their leader could only increase their alienation. So despite the fact that New York suffered few of the economic difficulties that plagued Boston during the three decades after 1690, the town's politics remained unstable, factional, and highly inflamed. The trade recession, inflation, and spread of poverty that colored Boston politics had no real equivalent in New York. Instead, more subtle economic issues and crosscutting ethnic hostility shaped political life. Nonetheless, urban politics evolved in New York in the same direction as in Boston. Politics became a clash between factions functioning like parties.

The merchant elite—the DeLanceys, Van Cortlandts, Schuylers, Livingstons, and Philipses—enjoyed the support of Governor Fletcher, who took office in 1693, and this advantage was quickly converted into the appointment of a set of sympathetic sheriffs, grand jurors, justices of the peace, militia officers, and other officers of government. Their economic power could also be converted to political advantage because those dependent upon them for jobs, such as shipwrights, coopers, and retailers, ignored their "advice" at considerable risk. Even so, the opposing faction, the Leislerians, had carried New York City in the assembly elections of 1695. Determined to regain control of the town's delegation to the assembly, the anti-Leislerians convinced the magistrates on the night before the election to grant "freedoms" to dozens of New York mariners under their control, thus entitling them to vote. On election day, orders were sent to the captains of English ships in the harbor to send their sailors to the polling place so that the Leislerians, who were heavily represented in the laboring class, would believe an impressment was imminent. This ruse proved successful, sending the Leislerian candidates down to defeat.

From 1698 to 1702 political chicanery proliferated. In April 1698 Richard Coote, earl of Bellomont, arrived to replace Governor Fletcher. In England the Whig Coote had been a bitter opponent of the Tory Fletcher. If that was not enough to align him with the Leislerians, the Whig-controlled Parliament had provided an added incentive by reversing the bills of attainder against Leisler and Milbourne. Bellomont at first appointed a bipartisan council composed of deposed Leislerians and some of Fletcher's favorites. But in initiating legal action to repossess huge tracts of land that Fletcher had generously conferred upon his favorites and in cracking down on smuggling and piracy, he bitterly offended the merchant elite, whom he soon dismissed from the council. Then, in an event of tremendous symbolic importance, Bellomont authorized the reburial of Leisler and Milbourne in the Dutch church. The governor reported that twelve hundred people, about one-quarter of the seaport's population, turned out in the pouring rain for the disinterment and triumphant march from the potters' field, where Leisler and Milbourne had been buried in ignominy, to the Dutch church, the main ethnic symbol in the town. Nothing could have signified more pointedly the vindication of the Leislerian movement or the return of its supporters to political power.

For the next four years elections in New York were hotly contested, and new techniques of political management were introduced. Political clubs, the first to appear in any of the seaports, were formed to coordinate and plan electoral strategy. Aristocratic anti-Leislerians carried petitions for the ouster of Bellomont about the streets and solicited votes. Election pamphlets, virtually unknown in New York until this time, were printed and handed about. Each side formed a "ticket" of four men whom the voters were asked to elect en bloc.

These daring innovations defied the traditional understanding of the proper relation between officeholders and the electorate. Political clubs and tickets were explicit admissions of factional politics. Instead of going to the polls to select virtuous and wise men who would serve the public interest, the voters were urged to elect a set of men who would serve the interests of one group within the body politic. The open solicitation of votes also reversed the conventional view, which held it inappropriate and demeaning for those virtuous and eminent enough to occupy positions of public trust to scramble for votes.

It was because two distinct and inveterately opposed interest groups emerged earliest in New York that the organization and dynamics of politics changed there first. Ethnic hostility, strongly linked with class interest, was largely responsible for producing an inflammatory political situation in which the leaders of both factions sought to broaden their political bases. When the upper layer of society split into competing factions, each was obliged to recruit the support of those previously inert or outside the political process. At that point politics became open, abusive in tone, and sometimes violent.

The shattering of the political ethic that had damned parties and factions as conspiracies had dramatic effects on the elections in New York from 1698 to 1701. In a burst of pre-election activity in 1698, 289 men, most of them artisans, paid the required fees and obtained freemanship so they could vote. In Boston, by contrast, with about 40 percent more adult males, the largest turnout in this period was 459. In the New York municipal elections of 1701 the turnout was even more spectacular, exceeding in some wards the number of legitimate voters. A subsequent investigation by specially appointed boards found that women, indentured servants, transients, minors, and the propertyless had illegally voted.

The revival of Leislerian popular politics reached its peak in 1702, when an attempt was made to avenge the executions of 1691. The archenemy of the Leislerians was Nicholas Bayard, who had played a leading role in the judicial murder of Leisler and Milbourne and had continued to direct the anti-Leislerian opposition during Bellomont's governorship. Learning that Edward Hyde, Lord Cornbury, had been named as Bellomont's successor, Bayard gathered signatures for a congratulatory message. He also circulated two petitions to the king and the House of Commons that contained wide-ranging criticisms of the administration of the outgoing governor. When the Leislerians discovered that a number of soldiers had been induced to sign the petitions, they used this opportunity to charge Bayard and his henchmen with "incitement to mutiny and conspiracy against the government."[31]

The extended and highly public trial that followed was carefully staged as a replica of the infamous Leisler-Milbourne trial—with the sides reversed. Bayard and John Hutchins were convicted of treason and sentenced to death. Several other prominent anti-Leislerians were convicted of complicity in the "plot" against the government and banished from the colony. In the end, however, the Leislerians were content to allow Lieutenant Governor Nanfan to reprieve their opponents and request a royal pardon in England. Nevertheless the Leislerians drove home the point that power, arbitrarily employed, could cut both ways.

Cornbury's arrival in New York in 1702 reversed the tables of partisan politics once more. Leislerian appointees were swept from office; most of the legislation passed by the Leislerian legislature was quickly reversed; and suits were brought against the Leislerian leaders. In new assembly elections the anti-Leislerians allowed English soldiers stationed at Fort James to vote, and, according to the Leislerians, they voted as instructed by their officers. The assembly passed revenue bills favoring the largest merchants and repealed laws enacted under Bellomont to vacate the huge grants of land made under Fletcher. Thus the politics of plunder and reprisal continued.

Ethnic and class division gradually faded during Queen Anne's War, and by the time Governor Robert Hunter arrived in 1710 a measure of stability had returned to politics. During the next decade, while the temperature of factional politics rose in Boston because of serious economic difficulties at the end of the war, New York's politics cooled off. Historians usually explain this trend in terms of the exhaustion of the contending factions or the adroit conciliatory skills of Robert Hunter. Another important factor, however, was the general prosperity that returned at the end of the war. Unlike Boston, New York was obliged to issue only small amounts of paper money, beginning in 1709, and inflation never became a problem. Moreover, New York enjoyed an expansion of trade in the postwar period, whereas Boston suffered a contraction of trade. Finally, after 1710 New York lacked a popular leader such as Elisha Cooke, Jr. In fact it was left to the governor himself, Robert Hunter, to assume the role of political manager. Unlike the governors appointed in Massachusetts, Hunter shunned the wealthy mercantile elite of the seaport and instead developed a program that had broad appeal among the artisans and shopkeepers. Under his leadership, a series of laws was enacted that fixed the legal rate of interest, established protective duties to encourage local industries such as linseed pressing and lampblack making, and promoted shipbuilding. Allying himself with Lewis Morris, a large landowner in Westchester

County, Hunter built a political machine responsive to the needs of the community at large.

Economics and Politics in Philadelphia

While Boston's politics were conditioned by grave economic problems that at the time seemed almost insoluble and while New York recovered from a period of immoderate factionalism, urban politics in Philadelphia from 1690 to 1720 involved conflicts over William Penn's proprietary control of his colony. At first glance the struggles that developed between proprietary and antiproprietary factions appear to have been purely political in nature, a struggle at the top for the fruits of office. Closer examination reveals that the distribution of political power was interwoven with access to economic opportunity. Philadelphia was spared the economic misfortunes that struck Boston, but nonetheless political life changed, in both style and organization, even if not nearly so drastically as in the other seaports.

Oppositional politics, originating in Philadelphia's early years as a response to proprietary prerogatives and propelled to new heights in the early 1690s by the Keithian schism, continued in the last decade of the seventeenth century. When Benjamin Fletcher, who assumed the governorship of New York in 1693, was also given administrative command of Philadelphia following the king's suspension of Penn's proprietary charter, the old faction led by Thomas Lloyd did everything possible to cripple his attempts to rule. Fletcher's authority lasted only until early 1695, when word arrived that Penn's charter had been restored. For the next four years, until Penn's return in 1699, sparring persisted between the proprietor's lieutenant governor and the principal Quakers in the assembly.

Penn remained in Philadelphia for less than two years, and much of that time was spent in hammering out new articles of government. In these matters he found himself opposed by men of substance who wished to limit his proprietary prerogatives—the right to impose quit-rents on land, to control the judicial process through proprietary appointment power, and to intrude upon the legislative process by denying rights to the assembly that were customarily allowed in other English colonies. At the same time he was able to gather around him merchants and landowners whose support guaranteed them important places in the government after his departure. Compromise was the result of this struggle to determine the locus of power.

In the modified court system greater power was given to the county courts, appointed by the assembly, especially in equity cases, which dealt with most economic disputes. In the legislative system Penn's appointed council was stripped of much of its power, and the elective assembly won many of the privileges that Penn had steadfastly denied the body for years. In land affairs, Penn retained his right to quitrents, thus guaranteeing great wealth to his heirs, but land disputes were assigned to ordinary courts of justice rather than to his appointed Board of Proprietary. Finally, Penn approved a new charter for Philadelphia that increased the powers of the municipal government and tightened the qualifications for freemanship.

A major part of what Penn consented to as he left the colony in 1701 had already been accomplished piecemeal without his approval during the years of his absence. By cultivating the support of a powerful phalanx of placeholders he hoped to preserve what was left to him in 1701. But these men already knew that they would have to vie for political supremacy with those who dominated the county courts and the legislature.

The leader of the emerging antiproprietary faction was David Lloyd, a Welshman who had arrived in Philadelphia in 1687 bearing Penn's commission as attorney general. A brilliant orator, a gifted student of the law, an unequaled legislative draftsman and parliamentarian, Lloyd became the Elisha Cooke of Philadelphia in the first quarter of the eighteenth century. Like Cooke, his brilliance was matched with pride, volatility, and ambition. In the early 1690s he had directed his talents to opposing the king's authority in Pennsylvania, but after Penn removed him from public and proprietary offices in 1699—at the crown's insistence—he lapsed into deep resentment of Penn and the proprietary interests. When his only child died in 1701 he sank into despair, but soon emerged to lead the antiproprietary struggle with passion for the next ten years—and to some degree for the rest of his life. Government must exist not as an extension of proprietary authority, he said, but as the instrument of the people's will. He articulated this philosophy with a power and clarity that made it resonate with new force in Philadelphia.

Pitted against Lloyd was the young Ulsterman James Logan, whom Penn had brought with him as a personal secretary in 1699. Eighteen years Lloyd's junior, Logan was as controlled as Lloyd was volatile and as imperious as Lloyd was gregarious. Like Lloyd, he was brilliant. Understanding this, Penn conferred upon him the offices of provincial secretary, clerk of the council, receiver general, commissioner of pro-

2. *Southeast Prospect of Philadelphia ca. 1720 by Peter Cooper*

priety, and proprietary secretary. This concentration of political and administrative power contradicted the Whig philosophy of government to which Penn the political theoretician could never have subscribed but which Penn the beleaguered proprietor readily accepted. Lloyd could match these powers, however, for by 1704 he was speaker of the assembly, justice of the Philadelphia county court, president of the city court, and recorder of the Corporation of Philadelphia.

Control of the city courts and the assembly provided two vital staging grounds from which to launch further attacks on the machinery of proprietary management. When the Philadelphia county court authorized Logan's quitrent collectors to put liens on the property of tax delinquents, for example, the city court asserted its authority in such matters and annulled the decision. Controlling the assembly proved more difficult, but Lloyd's group carried every election in the decade after Penn's departure except in 1706 and 1710, and Lloyd was chosen speaker of the house in five of those years.

For eight years—from late 1701, when Penn embarked from Philadelphia, until December 1709, when James Logan took ship for England to report to Penn—Philadelphia was the center of political controversy between the proprietary and antiproprietary factions. No element of government was immune, and every component of constituted authority was challenged or deprecated. At moments, such as in 1703 and 1708, government virtually ceased to exist as the proprietary governors gave up residence in the town, the courts lapsed for want of legislative backing, and the council was unable to act.

This decade of strife was a response to a number of factors: Penn's tangled affairs in England, the economic dislocation of the early years of Queen Anne's War, the incompetence of Penn's governors, and the personal feud between James Logan and David Lloyd. To some extent also, the factional struggles can be seen as the culmination of the attempts of first-generation Quaker immigrants in Pennsylvania to assume the mantle of political responsibility. Many comments in the early eighteenth century about the endemic prickliness of Penn's colonists and their love of pitting themselves against any kind of authority, however mild its exercise of power, are reminiscent of similar descriptions in the 1680s and 1690s. Isaac Norris, one of the wealthiest merchants of Philadelphia and a staunch supporter of Penn, wrote of the "strange, unaccountable humour (almost a custom now) of straining and resenting everything, of creating monsters and then combating them."[32] Whatever the causes, they had a lasting effect on Philadelphia's political life. For in promoting the powers of the assembly and the Corporation of Philadelphia, Lloyd and his party employed strategies and rhetoric that expanded the consciousness and power of ordinary Philadelphians.

The interminable battle of words, the taking of extreme positions for the purposes of bargaining, led both antagonists farther afield than they initially wished to go. Logan grew increasingly distrustful of the people and by 1704 was declaring that the Quakers were "unfit for Government by themselves, and not much better with others."[33] He would grow even more pessimistic as the battle wore on. Lloyd too developed myopia, convincing himself that Logan and Penn intended the destruction of representative government in Pennsylvania. For those in Philadelphia who listened to the two leaders, it must have seemed that there was no middle ground, as one city dweller wrote, "between arbitrary power and licentious popularity."[34]

Lloyd's struggle against proprietary authority ultimately led to a major shift in political power. He did much to undermine deferential attitudes toward established authority, and in so doing he developed a firm confidence in the ability of the common people to think rationally and act responsibly. He pitched his appeal in Philadelphia to those who worked with their hands and was especially successful in garnering the support of the common people, who had joined Keith in significant numbers in the early 1690s.

The popular party introduced various techniques that helped to cultivate the support of the laboring classes. An election law passed in 1700 had already initiated the publicizing of writs of election by requiring the sheriff to read the call to the polls in Philadelphia and to post it on the doors of every county courthouse, church, and meetinghouse in the colony. In 1704 the Lloydian assembly authorized for the first time the publication of a part of the assembly's proceedings. Two years later printed copies of the minutes of legislative proceedings and the votes of the assembly were ordered sent to the coffeehouse in Philadelphia where the legislators often met and to other counties for public display. This practice was an important step in the development of the idea that the freeholders were entitled to more than an annual opportunity to reelect or remove from office their representatives. They were to be regularly informed of what took place in the legislative chamber so that their opinions could be immediately brought to bear upon those they had elected.

In 1706 the Lloydian assembly passed an election law that further developed the notion that society was divided into interest groups and that members of the electorate must decide wherein their interest lay. The law provided for presenting slates of candidates, who presumably held a unified view on certain issues of concern to the people. Slates of candidates meant tickets, which could be distributed before the election and brought by the people to the polls for deposit in the ballot box. This discovery of the electorate was accompanied and facilitated by new methods of political organization that effectively mobilized the support of lesser men within the body politic against merchants and large landowners. "We will never obtain a good election," Logan wrote in 1709, "until the recent voting law be replaced."[35]

In expanding the politically relevant sector and introducing organizational strategies that encouraged the commonalty to think in terms of interest groups, Lloyd had launched a kind of politics in Philadelphia that Penn and the original promoters of the colony had never anticipated. The proprietor had envisioned an annual gathering of the colony's most substantial men, who would deliberate for a few days and pass such laws as were required for the common interest. New government seemed to consist of long verbal battles between the assembly and the governor, extended legislative sessions that sometimes ran to seventy or eighty days a year, published remonstrances and accusatory letters to Penn, invective and recrimination, and long harangues on the rights of the people. For ten years Lloyd cried out against proprietary prerogatives and upper-class privilege. The result was a chronic feeling of resentment against authority of any kind. "There is a general infatuation . . . got among us," wrote Logan, "as if we were all in a ferment and whatever was impure among the whole people rose in its filth to the top."[36] Letter after letter reached Penn regarding Lloyd's success in stirring up the people, of a populace "drunk with wide notions of privileges."[37]

Although political contention in Philadelphia became heated in the first decade of the eighteenth century, it never reached the boiling point as in Boston and New York. No angry crowds took to the streets; the art of pamphleteering never reached the heights it had in Boston; rampant factionalism did not turn into political violence and judicial murder as in New York; and at no time did artisans assume places of power in municipal government as in that town. As in Boston, the electorate continued to install men of substance in high offices. But often they were men who spoke the language of the lesser sorts, listened to their pleas, and responded.

For more than a decade after 1701 a calm descended over Philadelphia politics that paralleled the situation in New York but contrasted strikingly with that of Boston. Philadelphia, like New York, emerged from a decade-long slump in trade at the end of Queen Anne's War and entered a period of general prosperity. As in New York, the value of annual imports from England doubled in the second decade of the eighteenth century. Shipbuilding flourished and the town enjoyed full employment. Popular politics under these conditons withered, and the Lloydians were almost always outnumbered in the assembly from 1710 to 1720. The return of economic prosperity cannot wholly explain the exhaustion of the politics of discontent in Philadelphia, but the marked contrast between that city and Boston, where deepening economic woes were accompanied by Elisha Cooke's rise to power and the creation of the Boston Caucus, makes clear the importance of economic distress to the continuation of popular politics. In both Philadelphia and New York, political activism in the lower ranks vanished after 1710; in Boston it increased as the town wrestled with economic problems.

By 1720 the political influence of the wealthiest Philadelphia merchants was stronger than ever before. This new degree of political control did not mean that the groups that Lloyd had so effectively mobilized earlier fell into a permanent political sleep or that factions forming around interest groups had been eliminated from urban politics. In fact the political calm was soon to be shattered.

Urban Change in an Era of Peace

F OR MOST OF the period from 1720 to 1740 peace reigned in the maritime centers. But peace brought no guarantee of prosperity and stability. In Boston, problems created by war did not disappear merely because European diplomats had signed articles of conciliation. All three towns learned that the vicissitudes of the peacetime international marketplace could disrupt the economy as much as did international war. Boston expanded while experiencing chronic economic difficulties; New York prospered, then stagnated and recovered; and Philadelphia burgeoned during an era of economic prosperity interrupted by one brief but wrenching period of recession.

The third and fourth decades of the eighteenth century brought unprecedented economic problems to the seaports. Although they varied in duration and intensity in each town, these difficulties threw the interests of different social and occupational groups into sharp conflict and set the stage for further mutations in the practice and ideology of politics. The politics of deference grew shakier, artisan participation increased, important campaigning innovations tied holders of political power more closely to their constituents, and the ideology of Whig republicanism, with its emphasis on the public good, yielded further ground to the outspoken defense of private interests.

Reshaping the Urban Population

Other factors, largely unaffected by peace and war, were also reshaping the contours of urban society in this period. Population was one of these. Each seaport town grew more rapidly than it had from 1700 to 1720, and New York and Philadelphia demonstrated a special vigor, narrowing the gap between themselves and Boston. By 1740 New

York and Philadelphia had grown to more than 9,000 and Boston to nearly 17,000.

Two major elements affecting the composition of population in the three ports and thus the composition of the urban labor force were immigration and epidemic disease. Boston's labor force remained the most ethnically homogeneous, composed mainly of free, native-born persons, supplemented by a modest number of slaves. New York and Philadelphia relied increasingly on immigrant slave and indentured labor respectively. Following Queen Anne's War a large surge of migrants, mostly German, Scots, and Scots-Irish, poured into the port towns. The first of the Palatinate Germans came to New York in 1710, but the main German immigration after 1715 came through Philadelphia, the portal to the rich Pennsylvania hinterland. Many of these sojourners, especially artisans from Rhineland towns, stayed in the Quaker city. A few Scots and Scots-Irish (with the latter far more numerous) came to Boston, more to New York, but most to Philadelphia, where immigrants had learned beforehand that taxes were lowest, good land most readily available, and military service unheard of because of the Quaker commitment to pacifism.[1] From 1720 to 1740, when ten to twenty shiploads of immigrants arrived each year in Philadelphia, Pennsylvania's population increased from 34 to 57 percent of that of Massachusetts. Largely as a result of this immigration, the city became the administrative and marketing center for the entire Pennsylvania region: more Pennsylvania farmers meant more Philadelphia shipwrights, coopers, blacksmiths, carpenters, shopkeepers, and merchants.

Epidemic disease particularly affected Boston's population. Until about 1700 Boston, like most other New England towns, had been far freer of epidemics than had European urban centers. But the increase in population density meant that diseases spread more rapidly, and Boston's mortality pattern came to resemble that in English or continental towns. A raging epidemic of smallpox in 1720 infected almost 6,000 Bostonians and killed about 850, almost one of every twelve inhabitants. The smallpox returned in 1730; and although the acceptance of inoculation helped contain its sweep, about 400 fatalities were recorded. From 1735 to 1737 diphtheria afflicted Boston along with other New England towns. By 1736 burials were exceeding births, and many families were quitting the city from fear of disease.[2] They migrated to satellite ports such as Salem, Newbury, and Marblehead.

Philadelphians and New Yorkers also suffered epidemics. Philadelphia's high volume of immigration sent its death rate soaring. Typhus, typhoid, and other "shipboard fevers" contracted on the transatlantic voyage were spread to the host population when infected immigrants stepped ashore. By the late 1730s Philadelphia's overall mortality rate was higher than Boston's, although an unusual number of those who died were recent immigrants.

Because of its economic difficulties, Boston lagged far behind New York and Philadelphia in recruiting bound laborers. But in all the towns householders increasingly signaled their gains by acquiring human property as well as personal possessions. Indentured servitude was closely linked to immigration, since very few native-born persons were either voluntarily or involuntarily bound out. The courts sentenced a handful of criminals and debtors to servitude, and the binding out of pauper children for a period of years was fairly common. The number of bound white servants in Boston and New York remained small because the German and Scots-Irish immigrants who provided the vast majority of these went to Philadelphia.

Indentured servants became a fixture of Philadelphia's social structure in the second quarter of the century because they were in great demand and could be readily supplied. James Logan had noted as early as 1713 that in return for their passage most of the arriving poor Germans and Scots-Irish bound themselves out to ship captains, who auctioned them off to the highest bidders when they entered the port or sold them as a lot to a merchant dealing in human merchandise.[3] In 1732 and 1733 a total of eighteen ships arrived carrying German immigrants. After a brief decline, ship arrivals from Germany averaged eleven per year from 1737 to 1754, peaking in 1749, when twenty-four ships arrived from the Rhineland.[4] Of about 40,000 German immigrants arriving during this period probably one-half to two-thirds were redemptioners or indentured servants. Although most of them made their way to rural areas north and west of Philadelphia, a substantial number remained in the city.

A heavy volume of Irish and Scots-Irish indentured servants also arrived, although their number is less certain. The most informed estimate puts the total Scots-Irish immigration at about 30,000 from 1730 to 1750, and the total for the first half of the century might be twice that high. Many of the Scots-Irish indentured servants were sold to farmers outside Philadelphia; but hundreds were purchased by Philadelphians who put them to work not only as domestic servants but also in ropewalks, shipyards, bakeries, shoemakers' shops, cooperages, and liveries. The average length of service was about three and a half years. By the mid-1740s indentured servants probably constituted more than one-fifth of Philadelphia's total white male work force.[5]

Another immigrant group that altered the composition of the urban labor force was slaves, most of them born in Africa. In Boston men with capital to invest in labor began experimenting with Indian slaves captured in South Carolina. The number sold in Boston probably reached the hundreds, but by 1715 the truculence of these Native Americans caused Massachusetts, Rhode Island, and Connecticut to pass laws forbidding further importations from Charleston, the center of the Indian slaving activities. The preamble of the Massachusetts law spoke of the "malicious, surly and revengeful" behavior of the southern tribes and justified the abolition of the trade because of "divers conspiracies, insurrections, rapes, thefts, and other execrable crimes [which] have been lately perpetrated in this and the adjoining colonies."[6]

In contrast, the supply of black labor to the American colonies increased enormously in the first half of the eighteenth century, and slaves became available in every seaport town, including the northern maritime centers. Boston's slave population rose from about 300–400 in 1720 to 1,374 in 1742, a fourfold increase in a period when the white population doubled. The town meeting had expressed opposition to slavery as early as 1700, a duty of £4 per slave had been passed to discourage importation as early as 1705, and white artisans had intermittently complained about the competition of black labor; but Bostonians continued to import slaves and stepped up the pace after 1720, when the supply of Africans became more plentiful. Slaves became commonplace, especially in Boston's shipyards and on ships at sea. By 1742 black slaves represented at least 8.5 percent of Boston's population. Inventories of estates indicate that by the second quarter of the eighteenth century about one-fifth of all Boston families owned slaves.

While Bostonians accumulated slaves slowly, New Yorkers scrambled headlong into the acquisition of human property. After Queen Anne's War, when the heaviest two decades of slave traffic during the colonial period began, importations often exceeded two hundred slaves a year. Slave auctions were held at least once a week during the trading season at the Merchants' Coffee House, Proctor's Vendue House, and other locations. By 1731 black slaves formed more than 18 percent of the town's population, and by 1746 the percentage had risen to 21. By that time at least one-half of the households in the city owned a slave. Census lists indicate that slaves made up about 15 percent of

New York's male manual labor force in 1703 and about 30 percent in 1746.[7]

Slavery thus increased despite white anxiety over the threat of bloody rebellion. In April 1712 some twenty slaves set fire to a building and then lay in wait for the white men who came to extinguish the flames. Wielding knives, axes, and guns, they killed nine whites and injured others before making their escape. After the rebellion had been suppressed, about seventy slaves were taken into custody. Forty-three were brought to trial and twenty-five, including several women and Indian slaves, were convicted. The terror of black insurrection was evident in the sentences imposed: thirteen slaves died on the gallows, one was starved to death in chains, three were burned publicly at the stake, and one was broken on the wheel. Six others committed suicide to escape the medieval tortures prepared by the white community. The assembly quickly passed a new slave code, which strictly regulated the slaves' freedom of movement and stripped away most of their rights. Thereafter the legal lot of New York's slaves was scarcely distinguishable from that of slaves in the southern colonies.[8]

A generation later a wave of black unrest swept the seaboard and in 1741 hit New York. A rash of fires and thefts was attributed to slaves. New Yorkers became convinced that a large part of the slave population was involved in a plot to take over the town and kill all its white inhabitants. Under threats of torture and execution, sixty-seven confessions were extracted from terrified slaves, and in the conspiracy trial that followed eighteen slaves and four whites were sentenced to be tortured and hanged, thirteen slaves were condemned to burn to death at the stake, and another seventy were transported to the West Indies.[9]

New York's slave trade persisted, although it slackened after 1733. White artisans complained of the extensive use of slaves as skilled craftsmen, but the objectors were probably those who could not yet afford a slave themselves. Slave occupations frequently identified in newspaper advertisements included cabinetmaking, silversmithing, coopering, sailmaking, and carpentry. The growth of slavery in New York thus created divisions between artisans who had prospered sufficiently to substitute slaves for apprentices and those who saw their own opportunities blocked by the growing number of black artisans.

In Philadelphia, where white bound labor was used more extensively than in any other seaport, slavery also took deep root. Frightened by the New York slave revolt of 1712, the Pennsylvania assembly imposed a stiff import duty on slaves that slowed the traffic for several years. In 1729, however, the duty was reduced to £2 per slave, and by 1731 it lapsed altogether. A decade later about 10 percent of the town's population was black.

After a period of relatively heavy importation in the early 1730s, the traffic in slaves slackened considerably in the Quaker town. This leveling off reflected the availability of German and Scots-Irish redemptioners and indentured servants who flooded into Philadelphia after 1732. The apparent preference for white indentured servants may have become more pronounced after Philadelphians heard of the New York slave plot of 1741 and other insurrections up and down the coast. By the mid-1740s more than two of every five male laborers were either slaves or indentured servants.

The full meaning of the increased demand for unfree labor in New York and Philadelphia and the much smaller demand in Boston can be appreciated only in its wider economic context. Did a peculiar ideological animus against slavery and servitude exist in New England, retarding the growth of an unfree labor force? Undoubtedly not, for Boston, like her southern rivals, had experimented from an early date with slaves and indentured servants.

The crucial distinction among the three towns was one of demand, which itself was closely tied to general economic conditions. Boston's economic difficulties were becoming chronic in the second quarter of the eighteenth century, while New York and Philadelphia were better off. Even with their considerable natural increase in population, New York and Pennsylvania could not internally fill the demand for labor in their expanding economies. So capital was mobilized for the importation of an unfree labor force to serve ambitious men of the middle and upper ranks. New England, in contrast, was already tasting the first bitter fruit of overcrowding, the result of an expanding population competing for the resources of a relatively unproductive region. Hence less capital was available to invest in bound labor, and those who could afford additional workers could hire willing hands from the steady stream of migrants into Boston from outlying towns. In the northern ports those who were most free of economic difficulties were the likeliest to purchase women and men who were unfree.

Boston's Economic Distress

For Boston there are contradictory economic indicators for the period 1720–1740. Some suggest that the town's economy was active and healthy. Population grew from about 11,000 in 1720 to almost 17,000 in 1742; the port continued to dominate shipbuilding in New England; the physical volume of imports and exports rose; the fish market prospered, especially after New England traders were allowed access to the French West Indies in 1717; and the construction trades thrived. The addition of some seven hundred houses and the erection of several large churches and public buildings gave employment to housewrights, plasterers, painters, masons, glaziers, and laborers. Yet other indicators reveal that Boston was not unable to solve the difficulties deriving from the war years and, more fundamentally, from New England's inability to produce a staple crop. Poor relief rose, as did the number of people relieved of taxes because of poverty; the levels of wealth indicated in the probate records suggest that many struggled merely to maintain what they had; property values did not rise; and per capita imports and exports dropped. Boston was not in a chronic depression during all of this period, and some inhabitants reaped handsome material rewards; but for those at the lower end of the economic order, life remained as precarious in peace as it had been in war. Many in the middle ranks also were squeezed by economic forces beyond their control.

Boston's immediate problem was the depreciation of the paper notes that were used as substitutes for regular money. In 1709 total face value of paper money in circulation had been about £66,000. It rose to £217,500 in 1718 and to almost £358,000 by 1726. Paper money issued in Connecticut, New Hampshire, and Rhode Island also circulated freely in Boston because trade among the four New England colonies was so extensive that none could afford to refuse the others' currency. So while Massachusetts tried hard to combat currency depreciation by retiring much of its paper money after 1730, neighboring colonies, as Governor Shirley wrote in the latter years, flooded Massachusetts with their paper money "to the great profit of themselves but to the greater detriment of our community."[10] In 1730 it took 20 shillings of Massachusetts money to purchase an ounce of silver, compared with 12 shillings 4 pence a decade before. By 1739 the price of silver had reached 28 shillings per ounce.

The problem of currency depreciation was itself a symptom of an even more fundamental difficulty—Boston's deteriorating position in relation to rival northern seaports as the center of the coastal and West Indian trade. New York and Philadelphia possessed richer hinterlands and were blessed with shorter turnaround times to the Caribbean. Hence they undercut Boston's former preeminence as the chief supplier of British goods to the American colonies and as the main provisioner of the sugar islands. Boston's gradual eclipse hinged, above all, on the marginal productivity of its entire region. The thin soils of New England were not renewed by sufficient manuring or crop rotation, and the problem of agricultural underproduction continued to grow. The related problem was making returns to England to pay for imports. Issuing paper money was a way of maintaining a circulating medium, but in the long run large issues of paper money compounded the problem because currency depreciation added to the economic insecurity of particular groups in the society.

Laboring-class Bostonians suffered from the escalating cost of living. In 1725, even before the inflationary trend had become very pronounced, one writer to the *New-England Courant* grieved at the "many flourishing Familys . . . [that] have been oblig'd to fall below such as they once look'd down upon with the utmostly furnish'd tables, [and] have been reduc'd to such a humble Temper, as to be glad of plain Fare and homespun Apparrel."[11] Fourteen years later William Douglass, a staunch opponent of paper money in the 1740s, ranked laboring Bostonians first among the victims of price inflation. He pressed the point home by demonstrating that artisans' daily wages in 1712 had purchased fifteen pounds of butter but by 1739 bought only seven pounds.[12]

Mariners suffered even more. Their wages did not rise until the 1740s, with ship captains receiving £6 per month through 1735 and then £8, and seamen about two-thirds of that. But these increases were proportionately less than even the building tradesmen received and could in no way meet the added expenses that inflationary price increases had fastened on the laboring classes. With seasonal unemployment, ordinary seamen averaged about 20 shillings per week, less than one-third of the household expenses for a laboring-class family of six in 1728.

Most of the pamphleteers of the 1730s and early 1740s beamed their arguments at the middle and upper elements of society, focusing on the sufferings of those with fixed incomes, such as teachers, clergymen, and widows. These people were undoubtedly pinched by the adverse wage-price trends, and one of their kind may have been the wit who sent a cow draped in silks and laces meandering through the streets in 1735 to dramatize the high cost of meat. But artisans, mariners, and day-laborers constituted a much more numerous class that suffered far more, scrimping on their diet and going cold in the winter when they could not afford wood.

As inflation worsened in Boston, bringing many artisans and laborers to the brink of crisis, the elected tax collectors, who were acutely aware of the needs of families in their wards, began removing householders from the rolls or entering them as nonratables—persons with insufficient means to pay even the smallest tax. The population of colonial Boston reached its peak of nearly 17,000 in the early 1740s. But beginning about 1735, when the number of ratable polls was 3,637, the assessors dropped poor Bostonians from the tax rolls in sizable numbers. From 1735 to 1741, while the town's population grew, the number of taxpayers declined by 665. More than one of every six taxpayers was stripped from the rolls as elected officials pragmatically acknowledged that blood could not be wrung from a stone. Others who were retained on the tax rolls were reckoned too poor to pay anything or had their taxes reduced when they satisfied the collectors that they were unable to pay the assessed amount. By the early 1740s roughly one of every four Bostonians had been released from tax obligations.[13]

Not all Bostonians fell upon hard times in the interwar period. The inventories show that many merchants and urban landowners prospered. Peter Faneuil, the son of a Huguenot immigrant who had arrived in Boston in 1691 from Rochelle, France, died in 1743 with a fortune inventoried in Massachusetts currency at the impressive figure of £44,453, which converted to sterling was still £7,557. Jonathan Waldo, merchant and land speculator, died in 1731 with an estate of £9,606 sterling, including mortgages on dozens of Boston properties. Other merchants and landowners, such as William Clarke, Simon Stoddard, John Mico, James Townsend, and Elisha Cooke, Jr., left more than £3,000 sterling in real and personal property. But the broad mass of laborers, artisans, small retailers, and professionals, not these few wealthy merchants, provide the best indication of the community's economic health.

How did lower-class Bostonians cope with shrinking real wages and economic uncertainty? The answers are not readily available in the surviving records, but the classic alternatives from which laboring people in hard times have always chosen are postponement of marriage, limitation of family size, reduction in the standard of living, acceptance of public and private charity, and craft organization. All of these responses seem to have occurred in this period to some degree. Craft organizing took some halting steps forward when barbers and booksellers met as groups to raise prices in 1724 and caulkers refused to take "shop notes"—drafts on particular shops that employers issued at rates above current prices—in 1741.[14] "Intention to marry" statements decreased proportionate to population.[15] Postponement of marriage, which was also occurring in the towns around Boston, meant fewer births per marriage, since young men and women were starting families at a later age. Coupled with this trend may have been a decision to have fewer children. The birth rate, as measured by baptisms in the town, followed a downward trend from the 1730s on.[16] Most of all, laboring Bostonians simply tightened their belts, borrowed from friends and relatives, and hoped for better days.

Economic Cycles in Philadelphia and New York

While Bostonians struggled with economic hardship and the deranging effects of currency depreciation, New York and Philadelphia forged ahead amid general price stability. Neither colony issued paper money in amounts reaching even 2 percent of the bills issued in Massachusetts, and the price level for the two decades following 1720 remained fairly steady. Imports from England nearly tripled in Philadelphia and more than doubled in New York. Given a population increase of 73 percent in the colony of New York and 177 percent in Pennsylvania, these figures cannot be taken by themselves as evidence that boom times were benefiting all inhabitants of the seaports. But the long-range level of economic activity was relatively high, and neither town faced the dogged problem of declining real wages that beset Boston.

The interwar period was not, however, one of uninterrupted prosperity in either town. Beginning in 1720 Philadelphia suffered a serious depression, probably largely the result of a sharp drop in grain prices in a glutted West Indian market. Wheat prices fell, cutting sharply into farmers' profits, which in turn affected urban artisans and mariners. The assembly reported work stoppages in the shipyards, the disappearance of specie with which to carry on local trade, and falling property values. "How deplorable are the Lives of the Common People," cried one pamphleteer in 1721, who called for paper money to remedy the situation.[17] In the next year the governor described a seaport in distress: "The ship Builder & Carpenter starve for want of Employment . . . the Interest on Money is high, and the usurer grinds the Face of The Poor so that Law suits multiply, our Gaols are full, and we are justly apprehensive of falling into debt."[18]

To some extent the economic recession of the early 1720s was cushioned for Philadelphia's artisans and laborers by a decrease in rents and food prices, although this was small solace to those with no employment at all. The sting of the recession was relieved by the emission of £45,000 in paper bills in 1723 and 1724, to be lent at 5 percent interest and secured by mortgages on land and houses. These bills, according to the law, were "chiefly intended for the benefit of the poor, industrious sort of people," and although they could not improve the West Indian grain market, they at least kept debtors out of the clutches of the town's wealthiest merchant-moneylenders, who "exacted Bonds of every Body at 8 per Cent."[19] When grain prices began to rise in 1724 and merchants opened new markets in Spain and Portugal, trade picked up and shipbuilding revived.

A second trade recession struck Philadelphia in 1728. Convinced from the experience of 1723–24 that a moderate issue of paper money was the antidote, the assembly issued £30,000 in paper bills. Within two years the trade doldrums had blown away. Paper money, issued in large amounts as a cure for fundamental economic problems in New England, had magnified the plight of Boston's wage earners. Issued in small amounts in Pennsylvania to combat trade recession, it had proved Philadelphia's salvation.

In the 1730s Philadelphia entered a period of economic prosperity that contrasted sharply with the situation in Boston and New York. The rate of shipbuilding almost doubled from the previous decade, while population increased by nearly one-third. The average annual tonnage clearing the port rose from 4,914 in the 1720s to 9,563 in the 1730s, and the value of English imports almost doubled. The layover time between voyages dropped by about 15 percent. Finally, a series of fine harvests, coupled with sustained overseas demand for grain, created good years for farmers. The results were full employment for mariners, shipwrights, mastmakers, sailmakers, coopers, and other artisans who depended on maritime trade for their livelihoods, and increased demand for the products of other artisans.

The favorable condition of the artisan class in Philadelphia after the depression of the 1720s is reflected in the life stories of a few of those who had come to the port town in the previous decades as inconspicuous individuals and flourished during the second quarter of the eighteenth century. Such a man was Cesar Ghiselin, a Huguenot silversmith who arrived in Philadelphia in the 1680s. In 1693 he was able to purchase a slave. By 1709 he was assessed for an estate of £40, which placed him midway in the hierarchy of wealth. When he died in 1733 his personal estate was inventoried at £609 sterling, which put him in the richest tenth of Philadelphia society.[20]

Many of the city's most prosperous merchants in the 1730s had begun as artisans: Lionel Brittain had come to Philadelphia about 1704 as a blacksmith; Thomas Coates had begun as a brickmaker; John Palmer started as a bricklayer; John Warder as a pipemaker; and William Parsons as a shoemaker.

Benjamin Franklin came to Philadelphia from Boston in 1723 as a printer's apprentice. In the late 1720s and 1730s Philadelphia was filled with ambitious young artisans like himself, and a number of his early friends, such as his Junto compatriots Nicholas Scull, Thomas Godfrey, and William Parsons, made it to the top, though not quite so spectacularly and stylishly as Poor Richard. Franklin became the hero of the "leather apron men" in Philadelphia. Their glory in his success reveals much about their pride of class.

Artisans in Philadelphia were far likelier than those in Boston to attain a level of wealth that entitled them to think of themselves as middle class. About one-third of Boston artisans who died between 1700 and 1745 reached this level, compared with 60 percent of those in Philadelphia. The chances of doing even better—of leaving personal wealth in excess of £300 sterling—were also far higher in Philadelphia than in Boston: about one in six during the first half of the eighteenth century, compared with scarcely one in twenty in Boston. The Philadelphia artisan was eating from pewter, his Boston counterpart from wood. In Philadelphia he was more likely to have a "seven-day clock" hanging from the wall, a few pieces of mahogany furniture in the parlor, a better quality of linen on the table, and perhaps a somewhat larger house.

These differences in material achievement are best explained by the failure of wages in Boston to keep pace with increases in the price of household consumption articles—an adverse wage-price trend that struck hard at laboring people. In Philadelphia the wage-price ratio remained nearly constant in this period, so that in an era of growth it was possible for many to save and invest. Many Philadelphia artisans were investing profitably in urban real estate while their Boston counterparts were stricken by heavy taxes and the shrinking value of wages.

The winds of economic fortune that blew so frigidly on Boston during the interwar era and so favorably on Philadelphia by the late 1720s swept New York with alternating fair and foul gusts. After the Peace of Utrecht in 1713 Manhattan residents prospered for nearly two decades, except for a short trade recession in the early 1720s that was much less severe than in neighboring Philadelphia. But in 1729 New York entered an eight-year period of serious economic stagnation.

By 1734 Governor William Cosby was searching for remedies that might "give life to the expiring hopes of ship carpenters and other tradesmen, recall their unwilling resolution to depart the Province, and encourage others to come into it."[21]

Some of New York's problem apparently stemmed from the competition in the trade to the British West Indies, where most of New York's meat, grain, and wood products were marketed. Probably more important in the shipbuilding slump, however, was the decision of New York's wealthiest merchants to abandon this enterprise as a field of investment in favor of lending their surplus capital at 8 percent interest. In 1734 only one or two ships per year were being built in the town, and unemployment was widespread among the shipwrights and others associated with maritime construction. "John Scheme" wrote in the *New-York Weekly Journal* that "the Baker, the Brewer, the Smith, the Carpenter, the Ship-Wright, the Boat-Man, the Farmer, and the Shopkeeper" had all been hurt and "our industrious Poor [forced] to seek Other Habitations so that in these three years there has been above 300 Persons who have left New-York."[22] Houses stood empty and rents fell. New York's merchant fleet, which had numbered 124 ships in 1700 and 67 in 1715, dropped to 50 vessels by 1734. The importation of slave labor declined sharply, and the town's white population also declined after a half-century of continuous growth—almost certainly the result of outmigration because of unemployment. Per capita imports for the colony from 1728 to 1736 dropped about 11 percent below the levels of the previous decade.

The shipbuilding slump was not the only factor in the prolonged recession. Contributing to the decline was a serious shrinkage of trade, aggravated by the lack of a sufficient circulating medium. Ignoring the example of Pennsylvania, where modest issues of paper money had helped cure a recession, New York issued no paper money between 1724 and 1734. In the face of the scarcity, interest rates climbed to 8 percent. When £12,000 in paper money was finally issued in 1734 and £48,350 added in 1737 to repair "the Decay of Trade & other Difficulties which this Colony has the Misfortune to have Laboured Under," the end of the economic drought was in sight.[23] The value of English imports began to rise in 1734 and showed a 56 percent gain in the next five years from the levels recorded for 1729 to 1733. By 1739, outbound shipping had increased to 10,012 tons and inbound shipping to 9,738.

Although the eight-year depression must have caused hardship, the plight of laborers in New York was not nearly as serious as it was in Boston. Probably a greater part of the work force had been idled in New York than in Boston for at least part of the interwar period, and for these people the situation was very bad. But in New York rents and food prices declined, taking the bite out of underemployment and perhaps even increasing the real income of those who managed to remain fully employed. The common folk of Boston, in contrast, were losers even when trade was good and their services in demand. New Yorkers had suffered in a cyclical slump endemic to market economies, whereas Boston was skidding downward with no end in sight.

The extant data on poor relief in the three towns indicate that Boston's poverty problem was far more severe than Philadelphia's, with New York occupying an intermediate position. By 1730 the number of completely destitute Bostonians had outstripped the capacity of the almshouse built in 1685. Poverty scarred the lives of hundreds in the town. In 1737 Boston spent £627 sterling on poor relief and probably an equal amount was contributed in private charity, both by Boston's churches and by charitable institutions such as the Scots' Charitable Society, the Episcopal Charitable Society, and the Charitable Irish Society.

As poor-relief costs rose in the 1730s, the selectmen and overseers of the poor looked for new solutions to the accelerating rate of pauperism. In 1735 the overseers obtained a new poor law that gave the selectmen the power to eject strangers without appealing first to the county court for a warrant. The law also authorized the erection of a separate workhouse on the Boston Common, where the able-bodied poor would be put to work picking oakum, weaving cloth, and making shoes. The original almshouse would continue to provide care to the aged, infirm, and disabled. The building was completed in 1739 and by 1741 housed fifty-five persons. Although expenses exceeded the income from its occupants' labors, an inspection committee pronounced the experiment a success, since the support of this many people on out-relief would have been far costlier.[24]

Despite the new economies achieved in Boston, the costs of poor relief kept rising. Converted to sterling, expenditures rose from £256 in 1727 to about £600 in 1742. Although the town's population also rose, fewer and fewer taxpayers were shouldering the mounting tax burden. Boston's taxables had paid an average of about 1 shilling 9 pence each for support of the poor in 1727, but the per capita costs rose to 2 shillings 2 pence by 1735 and 4 shillings 2 pence by 1742—a 138 percent increase in fifteen years.

In New York the number of residents requiring public assistance grew slowly after 1720, but expenditures for the indigent did not approach the upward trend in Boston. It is likely that many of those thrown out of work by the severe slump in shipbuilding moved on to other ports, since the town's churchwardens and vestrymen (the counterparts to overseers of the poor in the other towns) were unwilling to levy tax increases for unemployment relief. From 1720 to 1735 the churchwardens and vestrymen relieved from twenty-eight to sixty-eight persons each year. Most of these were crippled, sick, aged, deranged, or orphaned. By building an almshouse in 1736, which admitted only twelve adults and seven children in its first year, the authorities were able to reduce the cost of caring for the poor and to keep annual expenditures under £400 sterling until almost mid-century.

Philadelphia also had its first taste of poverty during the depression of the 1720s. In 1728 the overseers of the poor were petitioning the assembly for funds to erect an almshouse. Money was appropriated in 1729, but by the time the almshouse was completed in 1732 prosperity had returned.

As in New York and Boston, one of the purposes of the almshouse was to reduce the cost of caring for the destitute by sheltering them under one roof rather than supporting them individually as out-pensioners. In 1734 a new poor law was enacted to close loopholes that allowed vagrants to enter the town and become public charges. In all, however, poverty shadowed few lives. In 1739 the overseers of the poor dispensed out-relief totaling £264 sterling to thirteen men and twenty-three women. A handful of others were cared for in the small almshouse, but the institutionalized poor were only a fraction of those in Boston. Philadelphia's poor were still the disabled, aged, and abandoned, and they were still cared for within a thoroughly familial social system. Poverty was not yet a major social problem, as it had become in Boston, and its presence was not yet seen "as symptomatic of a basic flaw in the citizen or the society, an indicator of personal or communal failing."[25]

By 1740 it was apparent that Boston, the oldest and most ethnically homogeneous seaport in British America, was the commercial center of the least productive region on the eastern seaboard. Its hinterland was beset with a serious decline of agricultural productivity that made it virtually impossible for Bay colony merchants to make returns to England sufficient to maintain a balance of payments. Paper money, seen by many as a remedy to the strangling effects of the specie drain, proved to be only a method for placing the burdens of marginal productivity predominantly on wage-earning urban laborers and others tied to fixed incomes. Prosperity drifted southward from New England in the first third of the eighteenth century and did not return.

The Politics of Stagnation in Boston

In Boston two issues dominated politics in the interwar years: the economic malaise, which concerned the colony as a whole, and the question whether Boston ought to establish a regulated market. The idea of a regulated market, where the retailing of farm produce would be closely supervised and controlled, was an ancient one that went to the heart of the concept of what has been called a "moral economy." At issue was whether the supply of food at reasonable prices to the urban laboring classes was so transcendently important that it should never be compromised by either country producers' or city vendors' considerations of private profit. According to traditional, paternalist thinking, the price of country produce entering the city must be strictly controlled, and the conditions under which these necessities of life were retailed should be carefully regulated. Otherwise avaricious traders would intercept perishables en route to the urban consumer in order to create scarcities and thus drive up prices. Equally bad, farmers and merchants alike would take advantage of natural scarcities by charging high prices. In Europe most merchants and agricultural producers had come to favor private marketing, whereby each country farmer was free to sell in open competition to whoever chose to purchase his goods and each merchant was free to buy up and hold for future sale whatever he could. Traditionalists and wage earners, on the other hand, tended to oppose the new laissez-faire approach; they called for the perpetuation of regulated public markets, surveillance of urban traders, and close attention to the needs of the laboring poor.

The elaborate controls over the marketing of food in European cities were breaking down in England in the eighteenth century, and they never existed in colonial American towns because scarcity of food was an occasional rather than an endemic problem. Yet some controls were placed on the retailing of the necessities of life. Boston was unique among the northern capitals in allowing the private retailing of produce by itinerant traders rather than centralizing sales in a public marketplace. Even in Boston, however, the magistrates set the price of bread according to the current price of wheat. But wheat prices fluctuated considerably. Amid rising food prices, Bostonians argued passionately about the advantages and disadvantages of a regulated public market, and the debate reached a violent climax in the 1730s.

Boston had experimented with a public market in 1696, when the legislature ordered a public market and set rules for market hours, weights and measures, and other matters. But many provisions were exempted from the attempt to centralize retailing, and the public market lasted only a few years. It seems to have been backed primarily by merchants who thought they could offer produce at lower prices than the roving peddlers and small retailers who hawked individual cartloads of goods in the town. In 1714 the merchants were arguing again for the public market along with the end of the town meeting system of local government. Their plans were thwarted by those who argued against centralization of power and the restriction of marketing to those who could afford licenses and fees. Thus the European alignment of interests in regard to the public marketplace was reversed in Boston. It was the small retailers and ordinary consumers who preferred the system of open marketing and viewed attempts to establish a public market as part of a movement by Boston's wealthiest merchants to aggrandize power and profits.

The market issue smoldered for almost two decades before coming to a head in the 1730s. The politically conservative merchants affirmed their opposition to engrossing and profiteering but called for carefully regulated markets. Many saw the public market as a design to benefit the few at the expense of the many. Apparently they feared that export merchants would buy up grain and other provisions, shipping them abroad as returns against imports, while laboring families were left to scramble for their food. As recently as 1729 a crowd had gathered at dockside "to hinder the merchants from sending away ye corn as they attempted," and many Bostonians saw similar self-interest behind the merchants' call for public markets.[26] Also, administration of public markets would increase both the tax burden and the likelihood of pricefixing.

The market issue came to a climax when a group of Boston's wealthiest merchants, many of them linked by marriage and otherwise closely allied to Governor Jonathan Belcher, chose to make their move against the aging Elisha Cooke and his popular party. Prominent among them were Thomas Hutchinson, John Colman, George Craddock, and Andrew Oliver. They intended to curb the powers of the town meeting, to strengthen the prerogative party of the royal governor, and to do something about the paper money situation, which continued to plague all mercantile transactions. Instituting a public market was one part of this reform scheme. The selectmen elections of 1732 and 1733 swept all the popular party men from office. Boston's middle-class voters, weary of the gnawing, debilitating inflation, were ready to give fiscal conservatives a chance to apply their solutions. A committee of conservative merchants soon drafted a proposal for three public markets to be operated under the strict supervision of salaried clerks, and the proposal was narrowly approved by Boston voters.

Cooke was a dying man, but he managed to regather his forces and weaken the market proposal so that its purpose was defeated. Every day of the week was declared a market day, and retailers were not restricted from selling in the streets. When the public markets began operating in June 1734, most Bostonians boycotted the facilities and bought their produce as usual from street vendors. Women were the principal marketgoers, and their strong opposition was probably the most important element in the boycott.

In early 1736 it was apparent that the prerogative party's fiscal reforms were not bringing wage-price relief or revitalizing the town's commerce. At the town meeting in March voters eliminated salaries for market clerks, silenced the market bells, and banned paper money at the markets. The markets were in effect abolished.

The final blow came a year later, when, in response to rising food prices, a midnight mob, their faces blackened and some dressed as clergymen, demolished the market house near the town dock and "sawed asunder" the support posts of the market house near North Church "in a great Contempt of His Majesty's Government, in violation of the wholesome Laws of this Province, & in Terror of His Majesty's good subjects."[27] Ritually mocking the conservative clergyman Benjamin Colman, who had written in favor of the markets and whose brother had been a leading member of the original market committee, Boston's ordinary people made their power felt. The anger and determination of the rioters were clear in the public statements they posted on the Town House door and spread through the streets. They had done "what we think proper," they proclaimed. "We are so resolute, that had we any Thing further to do, we would do it, [even if] you loaded your Guns with Powder and Ball; for by the God that made you, if you come to that, we will find as much Powder and Ball as you can."[28]

The antimarket stalwarts also sent a letter to Sheriff Edward Winslow warning him that if the search for the culprits went forward "you will cause them to make a Bloody Ending, and so breed a Civil War . . . If you touch One you shall [touch] All . . . and we will show you a Hundred Men where you can show One; And yet we are Resolved until Death to stand by one another yet for that good Deed."[29] "None of ye Rioters or Mutineers have been yet discovered," wrote the dispirited Colman several months later, "or if suspected seem to [take] regard [of] it, their favourers being so many."[30]

The antimarket mentality demonstrated that the long period of inflation had driven a wedge between merchants and rural producers on the one hand and urban consumers on the other. Moreover, it was well known that the original market committee was made up of the governor's favorites—a group of aristocratic, wealthy, ambitious men who were thought to look down on the common people while enriching themselves at their expense. Governor Belcher in 1733 had called Elisha Cooke, the leader of the popular party, "the late (now abandon'd) head of the scum" and "idol of the mob."[31] Such epithets illustrated the growing class antagonism in the town, which by itself was reason enough for ordinary people to oppose an innovation proposed by those whose "reforms" were seen as schemes that would further concentrate wealth and political power.

The market proposal also went against the deep-running traditionalism of laboring-class Bostonians. They hewed to an older vision of society, which they believed had been more equitable and moral. They attested their belief in an older religion with a stricter code of conduct and resisted the creeping Arminianism of the educated class, which stressed free will more than predestination. Their cultural traditionalism was in many instances antirational, antiscientific, ethnocentric, and moralistic; it was also strenuously egalitarian.

During the market controversy Boston's ordinary people, many of whom were not enfranchised, continued the tradition of voting with their fists. The long struggle over public markets had been carried out in a series of stormy town meetings from 1733 to 1736, and political leaders on both sides had worked hard to turn out the vote. In the 1720s no town meeting had attracted more than 332 voters. But now the number of ballots swelled to 500, 700, and finally, in March 1734, to 916. The fact that even this number was only one-quarter of the taxable polls in Boston strongly suggests that the town franchise was more restricted than is customarily believed. One reason it may have been becoming narrower is that hundreds of taxpayers who had formerly been qualified to vote had been removed from the tax rolls because of poverty. Their worsening economic condition, which relieved them of taxes, simultaneously deprived them of the vote. But their disfranchisement did not keep them out of the streets on the night of March 24, 1737, when the public markets were attacked. Although a majority of those entitled to vote favored public markets and rallied around the prerogative party in the hope of obtaining economic remedies, a minority of voters, allied with those who claimed the streets as their political arena, won the battle.

The highest authorities—the governor, his council, and the sheriff—were obliged to back down in the face of such determined resistance. The public market system could have been maintained only, as has been written in the context of eighteenth-century English society, "if there had been a unified, coherent ruling class, content to divide the spoils of power amicably among themselves, and to govern by means of their immense command over the means of life."[32] Upper-class unity never existed in Boston. Elisha Cooke's faction was led by men of considerable wealth, it enjoyed the support of many lesser merchants and shopkeepers as well as a majority of the town's artisans, and it was backed by a reserve army of disfranchised laboring Bostonians who understood that the ballot was not the only instrument of politics and not always even the most effective.

The second issue on which political controversy pivoted in the 1720s and 1730s was paper money. Massachusetts imported from England more than it could pay for with its exports; it thereby suffered a continuous drain of metallic currency to make up the deficit. It was agreed that some form of substitute currency was essential unless the people wished to return to a barter economy. This need for paper money was compounded by the desire to spread out over several years the costs of a disastrous era of war and to borrow against what proved to be a decreasingly productive future.

Agreement ended here. Debate raged over who should issue paper money, over whether more or less paper money would stabilize prices, and over whether the value of paper money continued its downward spiral because of loss of confidence that the bills of credit were solidly backed or because of manipulations of the money market by avaricious merchants. They also jousted over whether the government, in a time of unemployment and hardship for laboring people, should issue more bills to underwrite public works such as the building of bridges and fortifications.

Almost all who wrote on these subjects, in an outpouring of pamphlets and newspaper articles from 1720 to 1728, were men of the upper class—merchants, clergymen, and officials. None really represented the views of laboring people, although many of them referred to the ill effects of currency depreciation on that part of society. But whatever their views on solving the problem, all shared a class-biased view that it was the indulgence of the common people in buying imported European goods and falling into debt that contributed to the trade imbalance, drained the colony of specie, and thus necessitated issues of paper money, which in turn led to depreciation of the currency. Sometimes the critics pointed their fingers at the well-to-do for living beyond their means, but most often they charged that the ordinary people were profligately spending themselves and their province pell-mell into ruinous stagflation. Paper money, admonished one clergyman in 1726, was meant to gratify the "gay and sensual dispositions" of the people, who were "running mad" in pursuit of "gay and costly clothing from abroad" and other items such as chocolate that only produced more "sensuality, Effeminatness, Unrighteousness, and Confusions."[33]

Actually, Massachusetts people of the middle and lower classes were no more enamoured of English goods than were their counterparts in the middle and southern colonies. Indeed, New Englanders continued to be known for their tightfisted, plain living, particularly in contrast to consumption-minded southerners. That they did not have as much to spend as colonists to the south is evident in the much lower level of imports in New England than in the middle and southern colonies. Massachusetts had the misfortune to be saddled with a heavy war debt at a time when the growing population was placing pressure on the available agricultural resources. Boston had the misfortune to be the commercial center of a debt-burdened, decreasingly productive region.

New York, Pennsylvania, and the southern colonies were spared ruinous price inflation in this period not because they eschewed chocolate, lace, and other luxuries but because they adjoined more productive regions and had not been obliged to engage in massive deficit spending in order to mount military campaigns. The one exception was South Carolina, and it is the exception that proves the rule. Caught up in a decade of war against the Tuscarora and Yamasee, the South Carolina government issued £90,000 in paper currency in 1717, £120,000 in 1723, and £210,000 in 1736. On a per capita basis this was more than even Massachusetts had issued. Just as in the Puritan colony, paper money depreciated rapidly.

In 1730 the Board of Trade in England, determined to stop runaway inflation in Massachusetts and Rhode Island, issued instructions to limit the emission of paper money to no more than £30,000 per year and to retire all paper money by 1741. Recognizing that such a drastic remedy might prove catastrophic for the Bay colony, Governor Belcher in 1733 permitted a group of Boston merchants to issue privately £110,000 in promissory notes redeemable in silver at the fixed rate of 19 shillings per ounce over a period of ten years. Known as Merchants' Notes, the bills relied for their integrity upon the solvency of the merchants who signed them, and these included some of Boston's largest traders. The notes were intended to increase the supply of circulating money while maintaining a sound, stable medium of exchange, but they could not hold back the inflationary trend. Bearing a promise to pay at a fixed rate in silver, they were quickly hoarded as a hedge against inflation while bills continued to drop in value.

By 1736 it was clear that the prerogative party's fiscal reforms, especially the Merchants' Notes scheme of 1733, had failed to stabilize the currency. Many viewed the notes as one more manipulative stratagem by which the people who could least afford it were oppressed by the richest members of society. Pamphleteers again took up the issue, arguing about how to comply with the English demand for the end of paper money. Some simply cried out for delivery of "the poor oppressed and distressed People out of the Hands of the Rich and Mighty."[34] Compromise positions were hammered out, most of them aimed at stalling on the 1741 deadline and hoping for a change of mind in England. Although most people supported the continuation of paper money, there was yet no consensus on how to stop its depreciation. By June 1739 Massachusetts paper money had lost about four-fifths of its face value.

The controversies over public markets and fiscal management during the 1720s and 1730s furthered the transformation of urban politics that had begun a generation before. Leaders of Elisha Cooke's popular party reiterated the argument that men of wealth were not necessarily men of wisdom or even men animated by concern for the welfare of the community. Although Cooke was one of the wealthiest men in Boston and most of his followers who were elected as representatives or selectmen were also merchants or shopkeepers, they were careful not to parade their wealth. They dispensed money liberally to the poor, and they steadfastly maintained that the people, not a privileged elite, should manage civil affairs. No evidence exists to suggest that they wished to broaden the electoral base in a town where only one-quarter of adult males went to the polls even in the most heated elections. But they wanted to mobilize fully this part of the community, and in special circumstances they countenanced street activities by those not entitled to vote.

The popular party placed increasing emphasis on the use of the printing press. Pamphleteers analyzed public issues and attacked those whose positions they opposed—a tacit admission of the legitimacy of oppositional politics. After 1715 the legislature published its debates and votes at the end of each session. Boston's newspapers increased from one to four in the 1720s and devoted plenty of space to discussion of politics. Executive censorship of the press was now virtually dead, and its absence created the opportunity to convert formerly subdued political literature into fiery tracts. Elisha Cooke's party did not really have any answers to Boston's economic problems, but its members could at least remind the people that not everyone was affected equally by the derangement of the currency.

Recession Politics in New York

The highly vocal form of popular politics in Boston in the 1720s found no parallel in New York, where for the most part the governorship of William Burnet from 1720 to 1727 was placid and the laboring classes were quiescent. To be sure, the old debate over distributing the tax burden continued, with the urban-based mercantile interests pressing for land taxes and the rural-based landowning interests favoring commercial taxes such as import duties. Assembly elections were held infrequently—only three times in the 1720s—and common council elections regularly returned the same men to office.

The assembly election of 1727 saw a flurry of activity. Both factions, one led by Lewis Morris and Cadwallader Colden and the other by Adolph Philipse, appealed to artisans and shopkeepers by promising to replace taxes on household commodities such as rum, salt, and molasses with taxes levied against the rich. But all these political leaders were aristocrats. The working people were content to defer to the elite, for as yet they did not feel the need—or possess a supporting ideology—for a permanent class-based political pressure group.

William Cosby's arrival as New York's new governor in 1732 abruptly shattered a generation of relative political calm. The next half-dozen years witnessed political infighting that brought significant innovations in the relationship between governors and governed.

The first sparks ignited by Cosby's arrival concerned the question whether the Dutch merchant Rip Van Dam, who had been acting governor for the previous thirteen months, should pay half his salary to the incoming governor. Cobsy brought suit to recover the money, and Lewis Morris, chief justice of the [provincial] court, ruled against him. Cosby promptly suspended Morris, setting off a new brushfire regarding the constitutional right of the governor to interfere with the courts. When the Morrisite faction took the case to the people in a new paper, which attacked Cosby with unprecedented vitriol, the government indicted its printer, John Peter Zenger, for libel. Freedom of the press was now at stake, and the ensuing trial became world famous.

Although constitutional questions, family politics, and high principles all contributed to the highly inflamed state of politics in the 1730s, three other factors played a role. First, these battles coincided with the most serious economic depression ever known in New York; second, both elite-led factions, but especially that of Lewis Morris, James Alexander, and William Smith, set aside personal preferences for hierarchy and narrowly based politics in order to launch a program designed to attract wide popular appeal. Finally, the artisans, who were suffering from economic depression, were moving determinedly on their own behalf to bring about change.

As never before in New York, the press became indispensable in the political warfare of the 1730s. About forty pamphlets and broadsides were published from 1732 to 1736. The *New-York Weekly Journal* was founded in November 1733 specifically to break the monopoly on communication held by William Bradford's *New-York Gazette*. Bradford was tied to the governor's party by his job as official government printer and was "not Suffered to insert any Thing but what his Superiors approve of" in his paper.[35] The Morris party therefore hired Bradford's apprentice, young John Peter Zenger, to print a paper beamed specifically at the artisans, shopkeepers, and laborers. The *Journal* became the mouthpiece for the antigovernment faction of Morris, Alexander, and Smith, who as its principal spokesmen left little unsaid in accusing the governor and his circle of "tyrannically flouting the laws of England and New York and of setting up personal henchmen with unlawful powers to control the judicial system of New York."[36] Although Zenger was acquitted of the government's charge of seditious libel, the jury's decision did not really change the libel law in New York. It did, however, establish that the "government was the servant of the people and that open criticism was one of the important ways in which magistrates could be kept responsible to them."[37]

The Morrisite party also recommended annual assembly elections as a safeguard against entrenched political power and called for voting by secret ballot. These measures had long been established in Boston and Philadelphia. Further calls went out for making the offices of mayor, recorder, and sheriff elective. In 1731 a new charter had made assessors and collectors elective for the first time. Now it was urged that this democratization be taken a step further. More and more was heard about the accountability of legislators to their constituents.

Woven into the political literature of these years, especially in the direct appeals for electoral support that first appeared then, were promises to the artisans, whose security had crumbled as depression gripped the town. Evidence that laboring men were not passive in this era indicates that what they received was no more than what party leaders knew they must give in return for support from below. In the heated municipal elections of 1733 and 1734 the Morrisite party called for the erection of a new almshouse and poorhouse and the issuing of £12,000 in paper money, to be used primarily for construction of fortifications in the port. These attempts to stimulate employment were abetted directly by Morris, who persuaded his son-in-law, Captain Matthew Norris of the royal navy, to bring his ship into New York rather than Boston for repairs. Norris arrived conveniently just before the September 29, 1734, municipal election and gave orders for refitting his vessel at the expense of £900.

Political literature, signed pseudonymously "Timothy Wheelwright" and "John Chissel," urged artisans to "assert their rights and liberties."[38] Wheelwright made the class appeal unmistakably plain in a public letter that distinguished between the good, honest men of the town and the dishonest, avaricious men. It was "Shuttle" the weaver, "Plane" the joiner, "Drive" the carter, "Mortar" the mason, "Tar" the mariner, "Snip" the tailor, "Smallrent" the fair landlord, "John Poor" the tenant, and more of their kind who represented the sinews of New York. Pitted against them were "Gripe" the merchant, "Squeeze" the shopkeeper, "Spintext and Quible" the lawyer.

The rich were publicly attacked, and those with their backs to the wall were urged to combine against them. "Timothy Wheelwright" revived Leislerian admonitions such as "A poor honest Man [is] preferable to a rich Knave." Another writer asserted that "people in Exalted

Stations" who looked with contempt on "those they call the Vulgar, the Mob, the herd of Mechanicks" ought to be thrown out of office.[39] Governor Cosby and his allies were shocked by such leveling language, but the artisans were tired of being told that the proper remedy for a bare cupboard was prayer.

In the municipal election of 1734 laboring-class New Yorkers turned out in great numbers to elect men of their own kind. New York artisans had always held offices at this level more frequently than in Boston, but in the decline of political activity after 1710 the municipal corporation had come under the control of the town's merchants. In 1734, however, the merchants on the common council were defeated en masse by a slate of anti-Cosby men that included a painter, three bakers, a bricklayer, a bolter, and a laborer. Of the seventy-five men elected to municipal offices in 1733 and 1734, twenty-eight were not even freemen. Election of this many artisans was possible only because the franchise extended far lower in the social structure than in Boston and Philadelphia.

In the 1736 municipal election it was advocated in election broadsides for the first time that aldermen and councilmen act according to instructions from their constituents. This notion that "in the Multitude of Counsel there is safety"[40] would have shocked nobody in Boston, but in New York it was a new step toward admitting explicitly that interest groups were legitimate in politics and should be admitted as such. A further move in this direction came in the next year, when the assembly agreed to record divisions on specific votes, which were then promptly reported in the newspapers so that all could know how their representatives stood on a particular issue.

The feverish activity and leveling spirit that marked the elections in this era were long remembered. In 1737 money was flung "from the windows of the house to the rabble in the streets, with a tempestuous festivity and joy."[41] The next morning, wrote Cadwallader Colden, "the sick, the lame, and the blind were all carried to vote. They were carried out of Prison and out of the poor house to vote. Such a struggle I never saw and such a hurrahing that above one half of the men in town are so hoarse that they cannot speak this day. The pole lasted from half an hour after nine in the morning till past nine at night."[42]

In the 1739 assembly election one slate of candidates published its stands on the issues involved and challenged its opponents to do likewise. The construction of party platforms as a basis for election appeal was accompanied by other concessions to popular politics: the revival of party "tickets," not used apparently since the Leislerian era; the first public appeals for votes in the newspapers, where candidates modestly announced that "your vote and interest are desired"; and the first exercises in admitting the entire electorate to the nomination of candidates.[43] All of these devices, so characteristic of modern political parties, were accompanied by attacks on the rich, who, it was claimed, were riding out the depression while artisans and laborers suffered.

The corollary of attempts to place in office men responsive to the middle and lower classes was the enactment of laws for the latters' benefit. In 1737 the first assembly to be elected in New York in a decade passed a bundle of popular laws, including ones for remodeling the militia, holding triennial elections, establishing public schools, reducing the legal interest rate, and issuing paper money. Other laws, passed but vetoed by the governor's council, provided for more careful regulation of elections, restraint of liquor sales to apprentices and servants, reduction of officials' fees, and the appointment of an assembly agent in England. Even this spate of laws, according to New York's foremost contemporary historian, was "inadequate to the elevated expectations of the multitude and short of the intentions of their leaders."[44]

The transformation of politics in New York can also be seen in the response of Governor Cosby and his successor, George Clarke. They fumed privately and publicly about the Morrisite attempts to "inflame the Minds of the People," but in the end they had to fight fire with fire.[45] They too resorted to the press and sought to mobilize voters. Even the haughty Cosby learned to put aside lifelong habits in 1734; he "became more familiar with the people & invited many of low rank to dine with him such as had never pretended or expected so much respect."[46]

Amid such politicization it is not surprising that the legitimacy of factions and private interest groups was at last openly stated. In an essay that frontally attacked the notions that parties and factions were cancers on the body politic and that all holders of political power should serve only one master, the indivisible "publick good," the *New-York Gazette* pronounced the inevitability of "Parties, Cabals and Intrigues" and argued that "Parties are a Check upon one another, and by keeping the Ambition of one another within Bounds, serve to maintain the public Liberty."[47] Bostonians had been exposed to a similar theory, indirectly stated by John Wise in 1721. Now New Yorkers heard it squarely asserted that private interests, separate from those of the community, not only were legitimate but also might in the end be harnessed to produce the greatest public good. Such a notion abandoned the concept of the town as an organic unit in which individual needs could be harmonized and in which consensus would prevail over rancorous conflicting interests.

Political mobilization occurred in New York in the 1730s because specific grievances were widely held and were not redressed by those in power. Some of the complaints were constitutional and ideological, as in the removal of Lewis Morris from the supreme court and the prosecution of Zenger for libel. But the grievances of ordinary people, who were striding to the forefront of politics, more often concerned their day-to-day welfare. Upper-class lawyers and merchants could join middle-class shopkeepers and laboring-class artisans and mariners in an opposition party. Each group held its own interests, but to promote them each could form a pragmatic alliance against a common opponent.

Political Awakening in Philadelphia

In Philadelphia, where the economic depression afflicting the seaports during the interwar period was briefest, a radical ideology stressing opposition to the wealthy and the necessity for common people to organize in their own behalf flowered most fully. The leader of the movement, paradoxically, was an ex-Jacobite Tory, Scottish baronet Sir William Keith. He arrived in the town as William Penn's governor in May 1717. Within a year, Penn was dead and Keith was accountable to his widow. By 1722, when the economic winds began to blow cold on Philadelphia, he was thoroughly alienated both from her and from the loyal proprietary circle led by James Logan. The reasons for Keith's change of heart have never been clear, but whatever they were he suddenly abandoned the propriety group and joined forces with the aging David Lloyd, the popular leader of an earlier era.

By mid-1721, with trade stagnating and unemployment rising, the demand arose for paper money. For the next five years the question how to lift Philadelphia from the economic slump was aired in broadsides and pamphlets, as well as in the streets and taverns. The debate quickly leaped from a discussion of economic remedies to the accountability of representatives to their constituents, the organization of politics, and the nature of the body politic itself. In the 1690s George Keith, a Scottish outsider, had been at the center of a religious controversy strongly conditioned by economic considerations. In the 1720s

William Keith, a Scottish insider, became the center of a political controversy that sprang directly from economic grievances. From 1721 to 1729, in a town where not a single political tract or election appeal had been issued since 1710, at least forty-six political screeds, many of them highly inflammatory, rolled from Philadelphia's two printing presses.

The assembly permitted the printing of £15,000 of paper money in 1722 and £30,000 the following year. Fiscal conservatives such as Isaac Norris groused about "this Vile paper Currency," but they seemed even more concerned by the specter of a political world turned upside down—a vision promoted by no less a man than the governor.[48] In his opening address to the assembly elected in October 1722, Keith had set aside his class upbringing and harangued the legislators: "We all know it is neither the Great, the Rich, nor the Learned, that compose the Body of the People; and that Civil Government ought carefully to protect the poor laborious and industrious Part of Mankind."[49] He returned later with a program that included legislation not only for issuing paper money but also for reducing the interest rate, curbing lawyers' fees, and restricting the imprisonment of debtors. Adding insult to injury so far as the elite was concerned, Keith expressed doubts that the welfare of the entire community was best served by those with the greatest wealth and education.

James Logan took up the defense of hierarchy, social order, and wealth. Arguing in embryonic form what two centuries later would be called the "trickle-down" theory of prosperity, Logan cautioned Philadelphians that their leveling tendencies were self-destructive, for rich men were essential to the prosperity of any country. Without the rich, he argued, the poor would always be poor, for it was the rich alone "who are in a condition to assist them."[50] Philadelphia's unemployment and newfound poverty were the products, he argued, of laboring-class perversity. It was idleness and fondness for drink that made men poor, and the charging of high wages that drove away employment. Those who tried "new politics" and invented "new and extraordinary Measures" such as paper money misunderstood the roots of economic distress. The rich were rich because of their "Sobriety, Industry and Frugality"; the poor were poor because of their "luxury, Idleness and Folly."[51]

Logan's analysis bore a striking resemblance to arguments published in Boston in the decade after Queen Anne's War. How unemployed artisans and debt-ridden retailers reacted to this formulation of the problem can best be judged by their reelection in the next few years of the paper money legislators opposed by Logan and Norris. Their spokesman, the governor, was joined by David Lloyd, who came out of political retirement to participate in a broadening public controversy. Whereas Keith had hinted that men of wealth were not the "honestest Part of Mankind," Lloyd flatly stated that "a mean Man, of small Interest, devoted to the faithful Discharge of his Trust and Duty to the Government" was well enough equipped for high office and vastly preferable to wealthy, self-interested men.[52] An anonymous pamphleteer, styling himself "Roger Plowman" in a "letter" to "Mr. Robert Rich," began to dig deeper into the economic motives of those who opposed paper money: "the principal Reason why you are angry with Paper-money, is because People who are in your Debt can raise money to pay you, without surrendering up their Lands for one half of what they are worth." Logan had argued that without the rich, the poor would always be poor. "Roger Plowman" reversed the proposition, suggesting that because of the rich, the poor would remain poor. "It is an old Saying with us," he wrote, "that we must never grease the fat Sow in the Arse, and starve the Pigs."[53]

Keith's campaign to shatter the notion that the wealthy were entitled to rule was accompanied by an unprecedented effort at political mobilization among laboring Philadelphians. By 1723 Keith had organized two political clubs, the Gentlemen's Club for his more substantial supporters, and the Leather Apron Club for the artisans. The Palatine Germans who were flooding into the colony were another obvious source of support. By 1725 Keith was sponsoring bills to naturalize them almost upon arrival.

Critics such as Isaac Norris and James Logan continued to insist that mercantile opulence was indispensable to the economic health of the community and that only the "Sot, the Rambler, the Spendthrift, and Slip Season" were in economic straits.[54] In a strict sense the conservatives were correct in arguing that Philadelphia's leading merchants had not caused the depression. But unemployed and debt-ridden Philadelphians were not mistaken in their understanding of who was profiting from the situation. Nor did they fail to see that those who benefited were also those who sanctimoniously charged that the poor had dug their own hole and now could only hope that the rich would generously pull them out. Logan paid a price for this kind of arrogance. His house was attacked by an angry mob, which tore off the window shutters, threw bricks into his bedchamber,and threatened to level one of Philadelphia's most gracious structures. Pamphlets publicly attacked Logan for his contempt of the "poorer sort" and for leading a group of Pennsylvanians who wished to recreate, it was charged, "the Old English Vassalage."[55] Such men dominated the courts, where justice was dispensed according to a man's wealth and status; they ruled the proprietary land office, where land jobbing by the officials was the rule; and they opposed paper money, which offered the best way out of an economic morass that was not of the common people's making.

Unlike the common people of Boston, Philadelphians had not tasted real economic affliction before, and their reaction in the 1720s is therefore of considerable interest. Philadelphia's artisans and laborers looked to upper-class leaders for organizational talent and literary skills, but they were not simply passive toilers who could do nothing for themselves. Two of the first craft guilds in Philadelphia—the tanners and carpenters—were established during the depression, and the timing was probably not coincidental. Leadership developed within these artisan organizations and carried over into politics.

The popular Keithian party dominated politics in Philadelphia from 1723 to 1729 by perfecting organizational and electioneering tactics that were also in use in Boston and New York. The formation of party tickets through caucuses, the recruitment of immigrant German and Scots-Irish voters (the "very scum of mankind" in the view of the conservatives), direct appeals to the electorate though broadside "advice" that announced positions on specific issues and denounced the wealthy, outdoor political rallies that welcomed voters and nonvoters alike—all were part of the new system of popular politics.[56] In 1726, when Logan's efforts to have the governor removed finally bore fruit, Keith ran for the assembly. Amid "Mobs, Bonfires, Gunns, Huzzas" he won a resounding victory, capped by a celebration that ended with the burning of the pillory and stocks—the symbols of authority and social control. For the opening of the new legislative session Keith, according to his enemies, organized a parade through the town, "not of ye Wise, ye Rich or ye learned . . . [but] mostly made of Rabble Butchers, porters & Tagrags." Thus far had politics fallen in Philadelphia, where the ex-governor "made his Gradations Downward . . . to an Equal with Every plain Country Member."[57]

Popular politics took on a new dimension in 1728 and 1729, when economic recession again visited Philadelphia briefly and the Keithians in the assembly pushed for a new issue of paper money. Blocked by rural representatives, the Philadelphia Keithians organized (or tacitly approved) street gangs who intimidated hard-money legislators in the fall of 1728 and spring of 1729. The assembly knuckled under, passing an act for issuing £50,000 in paper currency. When the governor and council announced that they would support a bill for only half this amount, the word quickly spread that several hundred rural people were gathering for an armed march on Philadelphia. Farmers would join urban laborers "to apply first to the Assembly and then Storm the Governor, but with the Council, at least some of them it was to have been the hardest."⁵⁸ Keith's successor, Governor Patrick Gordon, judiciously agreed to a compromise paper money bill.

As in the other port towns, the ideal of the common good could no longer be sustained in an era of such political contention. Political spokesmen on both sides continued to inveigh against politicking on behalf of private interests, insisting that the unitary public good should be the transcendent concern. But this was only a ritual affirmation of older principles that many acknowledged were no longer applicable. Whatever they thought about the desirability of serving the common good, Keithian candidates were firmly pledged to follow instructions from their constituents.

In 1730, as prosperity returned to Philadelphia, artisan-oriented politics began to wane. Never in the next decade did political discourse and electoral behavior attain the boiling point reached in the 1720s. As politics in economically depressed New York heated up in the 1730s, they cooled down in prospering Philadelphia.

When political debate did flare up briefly in the 1730s, the ideological legacy of the previous decade became apparent. Laboring men were exhorted to stand up to those who in derision called them "Leather Aprons, the Mobb, the Scum," and to guard against every encroachment on their liberties and well-being, not just on election day but every day. In the clearest enunciation of the interest-group conception of politics yet heard in America, the voters were instructed that "it is your Right, to ask for anything that may be for the Publick Good, or which is the same thing, your own Good."⁵⁹

In 1733, "Z" and "Anti-Z" squared off in the *Pennsylvania Gazette* and the *American Weekly Mercury* in a debate that codified the ripening debate over society and government. Popular government, argued Z, was the best counterpoise to power-hungry, incipient despots. Moreover, voters should cast their ballots "in Favour of themselves," for in pressing their own particular interests, "which is extremely natural," they would advance "the real publick God," which could not be trusted to those who claimed superior knowledge in society. The conservative Anti-Z castigated such a "loose Republican Scheme," advocated a balance between "devouring Prerogatives and a licentious ungovernable Freedom," and argued that people's decisions in favor of themselves were "seditious." Who had truly known oppression? he asked. Rather, under the pretension of wrongdoing by the elite, the "inferior rank" had attempted to "usurp the necessary Prerogatives of their Superiors" and developed "mistaken Notions of their own Powers." Z acknowledged the need to obey magistrates but reminded his imperious adversary that "we are all born naturally equal" and possess the right and the duty to turn out of office magistrates who have not ruled wisely and equitably.[60]

By now Philadelphia had passed from depression to prosperity. But perceptions of how the political process actually worked, as opposed to ideal conceptions of how it should work, had been fixed in people's minds. Z's arguments were part of no new political mobilization for the achievement of specific goals. They were a clarification of changes in political ideology produced by the previous era of dislocation and class antagonism and subscribed to by many in the community. When economic difficulties and political contention returned, a clearer notion of how to respond—and an ideology sustaining the response—would already be at hand. As for the elite, such as Anti-Z, they had discovered the balance theory by now prevalent in England, which formulated a persistent tension among the one, the few, and the many.

Thus in all the seaport towns the economic stress and social tensions of the 1720s and 1730s weakened the conception of an indivisible public good, or commonweal. Henceforth pursuit of the common good was seen as a rhetorical cloak employed by those enjoying elevated status and material wealth to hide their selfish interests. Paradoxically, the only solution to this abuse of service to the community was to adopt the self-interested tactics of one's self-interested enemies. Competition had replaced consensus, and in a competitive world people must look to their own self-preservation.

In Boston, most writers continued to invoke the traditional rhetoric of covenant and commonweal while participating in political partisanship that belied their pronouncements. Lower-class Bostonians, harking to a simpler ethic of what was just and equitable, simply took matters into their own hands when the occasion demanded it.

In New York and Philadelphia, where the secular concept of community was not so massively reinforced by the religious concept of covenant, the ideological breakthrough proved easier. In the 1720s Philadelphia's Francis Rawle, a small merchant and pamphleteering leader of the paper money movement, found it necessary to speak against self-interest as a spring of human action and to warn against the "mis-rule of a Multitude, or a Rabble, as at Naples under Massanello."[61] Within a decade, however, the debate between Z and Anti-Z demonstrated how far not only the rationalization but also the celebration of self-interested behavior had proceeded. In order to dislodge from power or stave off threats from the conservative gentry, who continued to utter phrases about the necessity of an indivisible body politic or attempted to confine the mass of people by assigning them a share of power within a "balanced" system, the popular leaders of the seaport towns had to articulate an ideology that assumed a fractured community and thus legitimated interest-group politics. The militant action of those beneath them required no less.

War, Religious Revival, and Politics

Chapter 4

FROM THE LATE 1730s to the mid-1750s the seaport towns experienced the first of two eras of boom and bust that would carry them to the eve of the American Revolution. All three had reached populations of 13,000 to 16,000 by mid-century, all were closely connected to the rapid economic development of England in this era, and all were drawn into a European war that was international in scope and increasingly into worldwide commercial networks. The northern cities were becoming locked into an impersonal market world, which on the one hand promised new opportunities for wealth and material comfort and on the other produced discontinuities in the demand for goods and services, periodic economic dislocation, unemployment more widespread than ever before, alterations in customary patterns of work, and a redistribution of wealth.

Urban dwellers in Boston, New York, and Philadelphia struggled to comprehend the new shape of things, to fathom the advancing market economy, to make sense of the way that urban growth and economic development were altering their lives. Part of the adjustment to change was a halting acceptance of a new system of values that legitimated private profit seeking, rationalized the abandonment of economic regulation, and projected a future economic world in which men's energies, cut loose from age-old mercantilist controls instituted to promote the good of all, would produce a common good far better.

The new economic order had already taken root in England, and nowhere was its dark side more visible than in London. The capital city that rose from the ashes of the disastrous fire of 1666 was unmistakably a flourishing place by the early eighteenth century. But it was also a city of Hogarthian misery, where by 1750 less than one-third of the babies born to laboring people survived infancy; where disease, alcoholism, and prostitution were rampant among the lower classes; where starvation was common; and where the unemployed numbered in the tens of thousands. Personal ambition and the acceptance of profit seeking had replaced the rule of the magistrate as the primary incentive to economic activity, and the "liberalized" economic relations that now held sway produced a material utopia for some but a living hell for many more.

In the American coastal towns, adherence to the older notions of public-spiritedness and common goals lasted much longer than in England. But the seaport dwellers could not avoid being drawn into the expanding English commercial system. The development of intensive sugar agriculture based on slave labor in the West Indies provided a growing market for North American fish and agricultural products; the growth of the colonial population magnified the demand for English consumer goods; and the increasing importance of the North American colonies in the British empire swelled the intrusion of English credit, English traders, and English officials on local economies. By the second quarter of the eighteenth century the commercial penetration of the market was well advanced. In one way the American colonists had far less reason to resist the new economic thinking, for the abundant blessings of their environment gave rise to the optimistic notion that private acquisition might be pursued at nobody's expense. One man's gain need not be another man's loss. Yet the traditional communitarian thinking hung on stubbornly in Boston and Philadelphia, the centers of two of the boldest utopian experiments in modern history.

This older view would on occasion receive a kind of negative support from occurrences in England. One such event was the South Sea Bubble of 1720. Organized by a group of shrewd financial capitalists, the South Sea Company had embarked on a series of financial manipulations that by 1720 put it at the center of the speculative mania overtaking France and England. In that year the company's directors announced audacious plans to take over the entire national debt and expand their operations to Africa. Shares in the company soared in price, from about £128 in January 1720 to more than £1,000 in August. England was caught up in a frenzy of speculation, which lasted, however, only until August 18, 1720. On that day the collapse began. For many Americans, the bursting of the South Sea Bubble was a sober warning that the new economic spirit was a national disease instead of a formula for national prosperity. Speculating, stock-jobbing, and unbridled economic ambition were revealed as forms of a public-be-damned mentality that led to chaos and corruption.

As the two conceptions of economic life contended for ascendancy in England, the merchants, shopkeepers, land speculators, and some artisans of the American seaport towns hewed more and more to the new economic dictates, although they continued to mouth the old precepts of the corporate community. Speculation on the English scale was hardly possible, but on a smaller scale the integration of the seaport economies into a more international and more volatile network of commercial transactions had the same effect—the creation of a market- and profit-oriented world. *"Let no man seek his own, but every man another's wealth,"* Cotton Mather had preached in 1710. "For men to *overreach* others, because they find them *ignorant,* or screw grievously upon them, only because they are poor and low, and in great necessities; to keep up the *necessaries* of human life . . . at an immoderate price, merely because other people want them . . . *'tis an abomination!"*[1] By the 1740s and 1750s the modernized clergy of the urban centers could rarely be heard enunciating such thoughts.

The Plague of War in Boston

In the period from 1739 to 1754 war was the most powerful engine of change in all three seaports, whereas earlier in the century it had mainly touched only Boston. The renewal of international conflict began formally in October 1739, when England declared war on Spain. England wanted to stifle the trade of its European rivals and to gain commercial hegemony in the Atlantic basin; thus it was not surprising that the Anglo-Spanish War should merge five years later into a much larger war between England and France.

In Boston, the advent of hostilities provided an immediate tonic to shipbuilding and shipfitting, since much of the commercial war against Spain was to be fought by privateers—ships with commissions called letters of marque and reprisal, which authorized them to attack enemy shipping and bring captured vessels into port for condemnation and sale. Boston's shipyards hummed with activity, and full pay was the rule. According to one report, 164 ships were on the stocks in 1741, in contrast to some 40 to 50 constructed annually in the late 1730s.[2]

Wartime privateering not only benefited artisans associated with ship construction but also held out the possibility of spectacular rewards for the most impoverished in society. The letter of marque and reprisal transformed the pirate into a legal plunderer of vessels belonging to the enemy of the government that commissioned him. Through the agency of the privateer, profits could be reaped on a scale that was unthinkable in the realm of mundane business transactions.

The pot of gold at the end of every privateer's rainbow proved agonizingly elusive, however, for most Boston buccaneers. The mortality rate on all seagoing vessels was extraordinarily high in the eighteenth century, not so much from enemy fire as from shipboard epidemics. Many would-be overnight fortune builders never saw their home port again. Even when rich prizes were captured, the dividend for the ordinary sailor was surprisingly small. In the most spectacular capture of the war, the seizure in 1746 of the 400-ton French *Soleil,* which was carrying a cargo valued at £30,000, the share of the prize for each ordinary seaman was only £78.[3] Obtaining prize money often took months or even years. Cases were frequently contested, and sailors who had little capital to live on while awaiting a court decision were often obliged to sell their claims to prize money at a discount in order to meet current expenses. Finally, because most seamen received no wages on privateers, but signed on solely for shares in any prize taken, many came home empty-handed after a year or more at sea.

The rewards of privateering seem to have fallen chiefly to the mariners who resisted the main chance and contented themselves with berths aboard merchant vessels. Privateering created a temporary boom for merchant seamen because a heavily armed privateer needed a crew of a hundred men or more, whereas merchant ships usually sailed with crews of five to ten. This enormous enlargement of demand for the services of seamen brought a rapid rise in wages. By 1745 merchants were offering more than double the prewar pay, and the next year, according to the selectmen of Boston, mariners' pay was at "an Extravagant height."[4] Less unpaid layover time in port also aided seamen. In peacetime mariners often had to wait weeks for a ship to obtain a full cargo. Now the situation was reversed; fully loaded ships waited for crews, sometimes, as one Boston merchant complained, until "their Cargo have been almost or quite Ruined."[5]

The risks and rewards of wartime entrepreneurial activity operated at a different level for members of the merchant community. Those with only small amounts of capital to invest could realize decent returns from small-scale war contracting. But if they were caught short when their creditors made demands or if their ships fell prey to Spanish or French privateers, they could plummet from the heights and live out their days in bankruptcy. Such was the case with Benjamin Colman, a shipbuilder, who was in financial difficulties by the end of the war.

For the shrewdest men, war offered incredible opportunities. In Boston one of the masters of the new era of economic opportunism was Thomas Hancock, upon whose war-built fortunes his less commercially astute nephew, John, would later construct a shining political career. Hancock, a minister's son, began his career modestly as a bookseller. Marriage to the daughter of a well-to-do Boston merchant provided a toehold in the larger commercial arena, and he soon became one of the town's most successful traders.

When war came, Hancock invested in privateers, supplied military expeditions, and increased his profits on the inflated prices that usually went with wartime demand. And so long as enemy privateers did not infest the northern waters, which were controlled by France rather than by Spain, Hancock's usual trading voyages returned excellent profits.

The entry of France into the war in 1744 made European and West Indian trade far more risky, filling the seas with French privateers that harassed Anglo-American shipping. Patrolling the northern Atlantic waters from St. Lawrence ports, the French intercepted Boston shipping, sent the cost of imported goods soaring, and vastly increased the risk of all oceanic voyages. But for well-connected merchants such as Hancock, these importunities of war were more than offset by military contracting on a level never before known in the colonies. In the contest against the French, the British shored up their military outposts in Newfoundland and Nova Scotia, and then in 1745 planned the largest assault ever attempted on the fulcrum of France's North American empire—the fortress of Louisbourg on Cape Breton Island, guarding the approach to the St. Lawrence River. Winning contracts to supply the army depended on the quality of one's connections in London. Bribes, hours of letter writing, and lavish entertainment of those in strategic positions to influence English officialdom were a part of the game, but the stakes were so exceptionally high—£200,000 sterling for the Louisbourg expedition alone—that Hancock and other Boston merchants were willing to play it as never before.

By the end of the war Hancock had amassed profits that probably exceeded £12,000 sterling. It was not coincidence that in 1754 the three wealthiest men in Boston—Hancock, Charles Apthorp, and John Erving—were the town's three largest war contractors.[6]

At the other end of the economic scale, among roughly the bottom quarter of society where economic dislocation and price inflation had impoverished many in the prewar years, the war promised one main opportunity—service in the cause against Spain and France, either by shipping out on privateers or by enlisting for the volunteer army. More than a thousand men were recruited in and around Boston in August 1740 for the naval expedition against Portobelo, Panama, and Cartagena, Colombia, and, according to Thomas Hancock, "had 2000 been wanted wee could have had 'em."[7] That so many men of eastern Massachusetts were available at low pay indicates how effectively war could serve as a sponge, absorbing the unemployed and underemployed. Another 500 men were recruited for Caribbean service in 1741, and 1,000 more were added between 1742 and 1744 for campaigns against the Spanish and on the northeastern frontier. An even larger number found themselves involuntarily serving the king after being caught in the impressment dragnet that the royal navy threw over Boston during these years. Of some 3,500 Massachusetts men recruited during the Anglo-Spanish War, it is likely that one-sixth were drawn from the streets of Boston. Many of them were apprentices, servants, and underage sons, but hundreds of others were men from the laboring classes.

When the Anglo-Spanish War widened into conflict with France in 1744, a second phase of military recruitment began. Once the decision had been made to unleash a mighty expedition against the massive French fortress at Louisbourg, the "Gibraltar of the New World," Massachusetts supplied its quota of 3,000 volunteers for the combined New England forces. The pay was less than ordinary seamen received in peacetime, only 25 shillings per month and an enlistment bounty of £1. In 1746 attempts were made to raise still another 3,500 men for an overland expedition against Quebec, but by this time most of the available manpower in the lower levels of eastern Massachusetts society had been exhausted. War had temporarily solved the problem of underemployment in maritime Massachusetts but in a way that was to compound prewar difficulties.

The recruitment for the 1745 Louisbourg expedition and the fate of its participants and their families provide an important demonstration of the differential effects of war on urban society. From the very beginning there was strong opposition to the expedition because it was seen as the brainchild of the ambitious militarist governor William Shirley and was thought to be beyond the human and financial resources of Massachusetts. Only after considerable lobbying by Boston's merchants and by the fishermen of Marblehead, Salem, and other coastal towns, whose trade had been interrupted by French privateers, was the plan narrowly approved. Primarily, they saw the expedition as an opportunity to drive the French from the lucrative cod fisheries off the Newfoundland coast, thus guaranteeing a New England monopoly in that area.

Although Louisbourg was not quite Havana or Cartagena, Governor Shirley and his supporters promised recruits that there would be riches aplenty for all. By February 1745 about 3,000 Massachusetts men had been enlisted for the expedition. Now it was necessary to recruit 1,000 seamen to man the transports that would carry them to Cape Breton Island. At first, £8 per month "old tenor" (worth £1.1 sterling) was proposed, slightly under the pay offered the land troops. But the recruitment of soldiers and naval impressments had so depleted the poorest ranks of eastern Massachusetts society that, according to the chairman of the General Court's Commission of War, "we are put to it to get 'em" for double the pay.[8] Finally the mariners were rounded up and fifty-one transports and armed sloops weighed anchor from Boston on Sunday, April 4, 1745, in the largest expeditionary force ever launched from the American colonies.

All New England rejoiced in June 1745 when news arrived in Boston that the impossible had been achieved: a six-week siege of the French fortress had brought surrender by its commander. Boston's ministers saw God's guiding hand at work, maritime men smiled at the prospect of an American monopoly of lucrative northeastern fisheries, and all New Englanders rejoiced that the Indians allied with the French would no longer attack the New England frontier. Once the flush of victory passed, Boston confronted the costs of war. Long before the Louisbourg expedition sailed, it was known how staggering the losses could be in protracted amphibious operations, for of the 3,600 Americans recruited for the Cartagena expedition in 1740–41 not more than one-fifth had returned. Among the 500 Massachusetts volunteers, only about one-tenth survived yellow fever, dysentery, and outright starvation.

Massachusetts' losses in the campaigns of 1745–46 can be estimated as at least 8 percent of the colony's males age sixteen and older. It seems likely that Boston, which contributed more heavily to the war in proportion to its population than inland areas, lost at least 400 men. There can be little doubt that this loss of life struck a punishing blow to the colony's productive capacity, for such casualty rates exceed the accepted statistics for the death rate in the colonies during the American Revolution and in the Union during the Civil War.

The social ravages of war are evident in a number of surviving records. A census taken in Boston in 1742 reported some 1,200 widows, "one thousand whereof are in low circumstances."⁹ If these figures are accurate, then 30 percent of Boston's adult women were widowed, many by the disastrous Cartagena expedition. The Louisbourg campaign added hundreds of new widows to the town's poor rolls. Even three years after peace was declared, Boston's tax assessors reported 1,153 widows in the town, "of which at least half are very poor."¹⁰ Taxable polls fell from 3,395 in 1738 to 2,972 in 1741 to about 2,660 in 1745. War had shortened the list of taxable inhabitants and lengthened the list of those requiring poor relief. The expedition had triumphed, but hundreds of Boston families were fatherless, husbandless, and dependent on charity for food and fuel. Even among those who returned there was little to celebrate, for the promised plunder never materialized and Louisbourg itself, earned with the blood of several thousand New Englanders, was promptly handed back to the French at the end of the war.

For a large number of Bostonians the Anglo-French conflict meant full employment and steady income. But high wages were offset by the imposition of hefty war taxes and the last reeling stages of the currency crisis. Taxable Bostonians had paid an average of about 12 shillings annually from 1730 to 1734 and about 20 shillings sterling from 1735 to 1739. From 1740 to 1744, as the costs of war sent provincial expenditures soaring, the burden per taxable averaged almost 33 shillings. In the next five years, at the height of war economy, it rose to 50 shillings—a fourfold increase in fifteen years. Tax arrearages grew, and the selectmen sighed that taxes were "so very Burthensome, that many, even of the Richest of the Inhabitants are groaning under the Weight of them."¹¹

Coupled with taxes was the continuing depreciation of Massachusetts currency. By 1741 it took 28 shillings of Massachusetts money to purchase one ounce of silver. When the Anglo-French war began in 1744, all pretenses of limiting the supply of paper money were laid aside, for nothing less than running the printing presses could finance the war. Between 1744 and 1748, £700,000 in "new tenor" (or £2,800,000 old tenor) bills of credit were issued. Faith in the new currency was badly undermined; its value continued to plummet until by 1749 it took 60 shillings in provincial bills to buy a single ounce of silver. The sterling value of Massachusetts currency had fallen to less than one-tenth of its face value.

This hyperinflation distributed its burdens unequally. Those on fixed incomes, such as clergymen, schoolteachers, and sometimes widows, were usually heavy losers. An anonymous clergyman wailed publicly in 1747 that although his congregation had tripled his salary, prices had gone up ninefold. Wage earners also suffered, though not quite so heavily, since they demanded wage increases to match rising prices. Anyone who ran into debt, however, was assured that the longer he postponed payment, the more he had to gain. It is impossible to analyze precisely how the price inflation of the 1740s redistributed wealth in Boston, but it is generally assumed that those whose income goes almost entirely for the necessities of life are the most likely to suffer in such a situation. Even further up the social scale, Boston's selectmen warned, "the Middling Sort of People are daily decreasing, many of them sinking into extream Poverty."[12]

A partial indicator of the plight of those in the lower ranks of Boston society is the price of bread, the most important single item in their diet. The price of wheat rose from 14 shillings per bushel in the late 1730s to 29 shillings by June 1741 and to 40 shillings by late 1747. Not until it topped 50 shillings per bushel in 1749 did the upward trend subside. Profits for grain producers and merchants rose handsomely, but for Boston's laboring poor the situation was vastly different. A penny bought six ounces of household bread in 1740, four ounces in 1745, three ounces in early 1747, two ounces by November 1747, and hardly an ounce in 1749.

In the closing years of the war Bostonians struggled to understand the forces that had been unloosed in their society. Nathaniel Appleton, a Cambridge clergyman, was certain that "oppression" against the many had been perpetrated. How had it come to pass? Unlike ministers in the aftermath of Queen Anne's War, he did not attribute it to the profligacy of ordinary people who consumed more imported luxury goods than they could afford. Perhaps it was the "Merchants and other Traders" who "ran down" the intrinsic value of the paper bills, thus causing them to decline in value. Or perhaps it was the fault of the common people who purposely went into debt, hoping to pay off their obligations at a later date in depreciated bills. Whoever was to blame, one thing was clear. The long experience with paper money and the era of war had shattered all sense of community and commonweal. "A covetous selfish Spirit" now ran through the people, and "every Man looks at his own Things, and not at the Things of others." Gone was a "publick Spirit," and in its place stood a "greedy Desire of Gain."[13]

The Boston clergy, of course, had been decrying the decline of public-mindedness for generations. What was new in Appleton's jeremiad was the vision of a society in which interest groups pitted against each other produced not only moral decline but also economic distress. Clergymen had long warned that for lack of a "publick spirit" the people of Massachusetts would lose their souls, prosper as they might. Appleton warned not only of spiritual decay but of economic oppression as well.

Secular writers in the Boston press portrayed the same vision of society coming unhinged in its economic relations. In the *Boston Evening Post* in 1748 an anonymous writer analyzed the rapid rise of food prices.[14] He noted that prices had been driven up by the heavy demand for provisions to supply the large Anglo-American garrison at the captured Louisbourg fortress and argued that the problem was compounded by the heavy loss of life among Massachusetts soldiers, which had drained off agricultural manpower and thus cut into farm production. Alongside these uncontrollable effects of war he identified two ghastly examples of economic self-interestedness that also played a role in the rising cost of food. All around Boston, he charged, men were turning from their professions to become buyers and butchers of livestock. They understood that by intercepting Boston's supplies and holding them for a time, they could drive up prices and take over the function of the town's butchers and hucksters. A thousand men in adjacent towns were practicing this kind of forestalling in a sort of economic warfare between rural and urban society. The war against the hated French had not unified Massachusetts but had set one element against another in the pursuit of private gain.

The breakdown of an interdependent economic community was equally visible in the actions of merchants in other colonies. Foodstuffs exporters in New York and Philadelphia piled up profits by engaging forty or fifty ships to sail under flags of truce in an illegal trade with the French and Spanish in the West Indies. Bostonians paid more for their food because of shortages that could have been alleviated by grain and livestock from the middle colonies. Instead, merchants there diverted commodities to the Caribbean, primarily to feed the enemy's slave populations. Here was the ultimate betrayal of the public good by private economic interest, a betrayal reflected in the food bill of every Bostonian.

The Profits of War in New York and Philadelphia

In both Philadelphia and New York the Anglo-Spanish and Anglo-French wars brought prosperity that spread downward through the urban ranks, making their experience far different from Boston's. As in the wars of the previous generation, neither colony contributed much money or manpower to the expeditions against the Spanish Main and French Canada. Instead, they concentrated on privateering and trade.

In New York, the Anglo-Spanish War also spurred the economy. New York emerged as the premier North American port for privateering and illegal trade. More than 60 privateers were commissioned between 1743 and 1748. In August 1744 4 of them returned with 6 prizes worth £24,000 sterling. The fever of instant wealth swept the city; shares in privateering voyages were traded in the coffeehouses, in a kind of early stock market, where prices rose and fell on rumors of fabulous captures of enemy ships or losses to the enemy. From 1739 to 1744 New York's Admiralty Court condemned 32 prizes sold at vendue for about £167,000 sterling. In the next four years 213 prizes, worth £450,000, were condemned and sold in the city. New York, as one historian puts it, was the "grand beneficiary" in the wartime sweepstakes.[15]

The profits of legalized piracy were handsomely supplemented by the rewards of illegal trade. A "Fair Trader" of the port complained in 1748 that hardly a week went by that illicit traders did not sail with supplies for the enemy.[16] Illegal trade with the French and Spanish kept shipbuilding craftsmen, merchant seamen, ship chandlers, bolters, coopers, and others humming at their daily work. They could not expect to reap the kinds of profits that fell to well-connected New York war contractors such as John Watts, Peter Livingston, and James Alexander, but they could take satisfaction in full employment and steady income.

When the call came from Massachusetts in 1745 for aid in raising expeditionary forces against Louisbourg, the New York assembly refused to raise troops and appropriated only a token £3,000 for supplies. In a rage, Clinton dissolved the assembly and called new elections, but he was only able to persuade the new legislature to cough up the not very impressive sum of £5,000—less than 1.5 shillings per inhabitant. In 1746 New York was more generous. Spurred by the devastation of the frontier town of Saratoga in November 1745, the legislature committed £40,000 and raised 1,600 men for the overland Quebec expedition.

New York's stinginess was wholly related to its legislators' perception of their economic welfare. They knew that if New York were drawn into the war the pipeline of profits from Montreal to New York would be smashed. The larger economic motive, however, was simply the desire to avoid heavy war taxes and to concentrate on the private war at sea against French shipping.

Philadelphia's prosperity in the 1740s was not so closely linked to the war as New York's. Many of the town's merchants were Quakers, whose consciences did not permit them to participate in any kind of violence. So warfare by privateers was left to those with fewer scruples. A small number of men made fabulous fortunes, such as Captain John Sibbald, whose ship brought in prizes worth £135,000 sterling. But Philadelphia had far fewer privateers than did New York. In fact the town's merchants may have lost more ships to French and Spanish privateers than they captured. But the intensified demand for bread, flour, and meat in the West Indies drove prices to all-time highs and brought exceptional profit margins. Mariners' wages also rose sharply because privateers had scoured the waterfronts clean in all the port towns. Increased demand along the normal lines of commerce, bolstered by illegal trade with the French West Indies, kept the town alert to the advantages of war while politicians shielded it from the adverse effects.

The other source of Philadelphia's prosperity during the war came from the building boom associated with the continuing heavy immigration of Germans and Scots-Irish. The Anglo-Spanish and Anglo-French wars coincided with the greatest influx of immigrants in Philadelphia's history. Along with natural increase, this influx swelled the city's population from about 8,000 in 1734 to almost 14,000 in 1751. In a period when Boston's population remained static and New York's was slowly recovering from the slump of the 1730s, Philadelphia's increased by fully 75 percent. The population boom meant full employment for brickmakers, carpenters, masons, bricklayers, painters, plasterers, glaziers, joiners, carters, stonecutters, and laborers—almost everyone associated with the building trades.

The contrast between Philadelphia and Boston is plain in their tax and poor relief records. While Boston was losing nearly 1,000 taxpayers from the rolls between 1735 and 1745, the number of Philadelphia's taxables increased from 1,420 in 1734 to about 2,075 in 1746. Conditions in Boston by 1742 led the overseers of the poor to put 146 persons in the almshouse and workhouse and left hundreds of others on out-relief. Philadelphia, in contrast, had only a few dozen out-reliefers and perhaps 30 persons in the small almshouse during the era of war.

Postwar Economic Conditions

The postwar peace, which was to last for only six years after the Treaty of Aix-la-Chapelle in 1748, had widely varying ramifications. Philadelphia was afflicted by a business slump beginning late in 1749, which sent an unusual number of merchant houses reeling into bankruptcy. In 1753–54 another cyclical downturn slowed commerce there and hit New York even harder. In 1754 New York imported the lowest level of English goods in nearly a decade. These trade fluctuations were basically caused by falling demand in the West Indies and southern Europe for the foodstuffs that made up the bulk of the New York and Pennsylvania export trade, and thus primarily affected merchants and country farmers.

For the laboring classes of the Middle Atlantic port towns the level of ship and house construction was far more important to full employment. In both cities, shipbuilding rose dramatically. House construction followed a similar trend to accommodate substantial population increases. The building trades in Philadelphia constructed about eighty houses a year as urban settlement began to spread rapidly to the adjacent areas of Southwark and the Northern Liberties. This high volume of construction brought the largest rewards to urban landowners, who could sell lots at prices unheard of in the 1720s and 1730s, and to those with capital to build and rent new houses. Edward Shippen, for example, who had plunged more than £4,000 into Philadelphia real estate during King George's War (1744–1748), sold off lots at gratifying profits in the years following the peace treaty. When real estate tycoon Samuel Powel died in 1755, he left his son more than ninety houses with a rental income of several thousand pounds per year.[17] But almost all artisans benefited to some degree, for when the building trades flourished, business also hummed for tailors, shoemakers, cabinetmakers, and many others.

New York and Philadelphia found peace almost as prosperous as war because they were centers of trade for rapidly growing hinterlands. Boston, however, had hardly completed its celebrations of the fall of

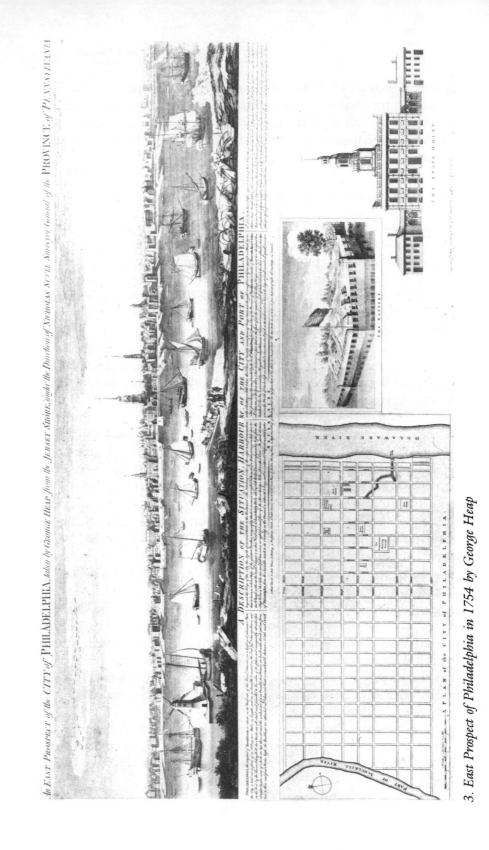

3. *East Prospect of Philadelphia in 1754 by George Heap*

Louisbourg when it began to slip into a commercial decline that compounded all its other troubles. At the root of this decay was the loss of much of the shipbuilding and distilling business—keystones of the town's economy. Shipbuilding in New England had been centered in Boston since the seventeenth century. By the 1730s the annual tonnage built often reached 6,000, about four times the volume in Philadelphia, and during one twelve-month period near the end of the war, 10,140 tons slid off the ways.

At the end of King George's War, however, Boston shipbuilding was struck by what one citizen called "a galloping consumption."[18] In 1749 only fifteen ships totaling 2,450 tons were built. Satellite ports in eastern Massachusetts were cutting deeply into Boston's hold on New England shipbuilding. By 1753 it was claimed that Boston produced only one-quarter of the region's shipping;[19] two years later only 2,162 tons of shipping came out of Boston's yards.

Compounding the loss of shipbuilding was an exodus of butchers, bakers, tanners, distillers, and glovers. Distilling and sugar baking in 1756 had fallen to half the level of eight years before, and coopers' work had fallen by two-thirds.[20]

The selectmen specifically blamed rising taxes for the exodus and argued that "unless the heavy Burthen be lightened there will be no such Town as Boston."[21] Many had viewed the Louisbourg expedition as a way of recouping their fortunes, but military success had further impoverished a large part of the town. Poverty bred poverty, for as the number of poor who had to be maintained rose, officials were obliged to levy heavier taxes upon the remaining taxables. In this situation, many artisans apparently decided to try their luck in outlying towns, where the selectmen claimed tax rates were sometimes only one-fifth those in Boston.

Peace also brought a tapering off of military supply contracts, which had provided gunsmiths, bakers, coopers, shoemakers, and tailors with work, and less demand for merchant seamen, who experienced a drop in wages and an increase in dead time between voyages. Wages for mariners, which had risen as high as 90 shillings per month in 1746, were back down to 42 shillings by 1754. Added to all this were high food prices, caused by a drought in 1749–50 so severe that, in a reversal of the normal flow of the grain trade, Boston merchants were ordering wheat and hay from London.

As if its economic problems were not enough, a smallpox epidemic struck Boston in January 1752. By March the General Court had moved to Cambridge, and by May nearby towns were flooded with refugees. In the seaport "all business is laid aside . . . the streets desolate, many of the shops shut up, and the people universally spend their time to attend to the sick."[22] By the end of July 5,566 Bostonians had contracted the dreaded disease and 569 had succumbed. Some 1,850 inhabitants fled as the death toll mounted. Many apparently never returned. They had had enough of heavy taxes, sporadic employment, and disease. The loss of many substantial taxpayers inevitably increased the burden on the rest of the community.

The final factor that drove shipbuilding craftsmen and mariners from Boston to neighboring ports was the fear of impressment on British ships. Royal navy captains were chronically short of crew because of the high number of desertions that occurred in American harbors. They tried to make up their losses by raiding the streets and taverns of the port towns, not always staying within the law that allowed impressments only with the consent of the provincial governor and carefully exempted mariners already in service on privateers, merchant ships, or coastal vessels.

Bostonians fought press gangs with a passion throughout the war years of the 1740s. But impressment continued, and by 1745, when every mariner in Boston was shipping out for high wages on merchant vessels and every fortune-seeking country stripling had been recruited for the Louisbourg flotilla, press gangs began scooping artisans into their nets. Impressment on a ship of the royal navy was regarded as approximating a death sentence because of the miserable conditions that prevailed, and according to the town meeting in 1746 it was this fear that drove many shipwrights and other artisans to satellite ports.[23]

This almost biblical series of misfortunes explains why the population of Boston dropped from nearly 17,000 in 1742 to less than 16,000 a decade later. Both war and peace had delivered crushing blows. By the end of the interwar period the Massachusetts seat of government had unparalleled numbers of impoverished inhabitants, the heaviest taxes in its history, and little notion of how the decay of shipbuilding and other industries could be remedied.

Boston's War on Poverty

Unable to reach the roots of the malady, Bostonians focused on the symptoms, in particular on the problem of poverty. The remedies they devised involved a transformation of thinking about indigence and its amelioration that had profound implications for the future.

Boston tried five expedients to grapple with its soaring poverty rate in the difficult years between the end of King George's War and the outbreak of the Seven Years' War. One was to bind out the children of the poor. Since 1704 the poor had been legally defined as persons who were not rated for town or provincial taxes. Their children could be taken from them and bound out to other families in the town in the manner of indentured servants. Taxpayers would thereby be relieved of the expense of maintaining the children of the indigent. After 1735 it was the responsibility of the overseers of the poor, appointed for each of Boston's twelve wards, to take poor children from their parents and indenture them to taxpayers. The practice was never extensive, however. In the 1740s, 178 Boston children were bound to other families, most of them outside the town. The number decreased slightly in the 1750s, indicating that even in worsening times the overseers were reluctant to separate parents and children, especially in families who had long lived in the community.

A second attempted remedy was to "warn out" the hundreds of sick, weary, and hungry souls who tramped the roads into the town. This device dated back to the general Indian war of 1675, when refugees from outlying towns had streamed into Boston. Warning out relieved the town of any obligation to support newcomers who were in need or might become so in the future. From 1721 to 1742 the authorities had warned out about 25 persons per year. But the "Warning Out Book" that begins in 1745—a remarkable register of human misfortune during this period—lists an average of 65 persons per year fom 1745 to 1752, rising to 222 in 1755.[24]

Most of the transients were part of a growing class of the strolling poor, who had taken to the roads in search of jobs or greater opportunities. Family holdings had been broken up into smaller and smaller parcels as each generation produced more children to be provided with land. Declining crop yields, the result of overutilizing available acreage, and the depletion of the supply of arable land set hundreds of people on the road each year. By mid-century the warning-out system in eastern Massachusetts towns was processing people in merry-go-round fashion. Boston authorities warned out families coming south from the Essex County towns of Salem, Marblehead, Newbury, Beverly, and Ipswich. The authorities in these towns, in turn, warned out Bostonians who were headed north. Each town tried to spare itself the burden of the other's poor at a time when its own swollen relief rolls were driving taxes skyward.

A third palliative employed by Boston's leaders was to exhort the affluent members of the community to greater charitable contributions in order to alleviate the distress of the poor. Wealthy Bostonians who had amassed great fortunes during the war years gave large amounts to ameliorate the condition of the town's poor.

At mid-century Boston's leaders tried one other expedient for relieving economic adversity: they appealed repeatedly to the General Court for tax relief. Pointing out that Boston groaned under the heaviest taxes in the colony because of its poverty problems, they argued that the city should pay a smaller percentage of taxes. But the General Court, dominated by rural interests, mostly turned a deaf ear in the 1750s.

None of these tactics was equal to the problem at hand, and more and more Bostonians were caught in the web of poverty. So finally the community's leaders turned from the benevolent desire to help the poor to the idea that the poor should help themselves.

The roots of this self-help approach to poverty are very tangled. New England Puritans, like their Elizabethan forebears, had always maintained a hearty distaste for the dependent poor, especially those who were thought to prefer public alms to hard work and self-support. Cotton Mather reflected this attitude perfectly when he wrote that "for those that Indulge themselves in *Idleness,* the Express Command of God unto us, is *That you should Let them Starve.*" As late as 1721 Mather was complaining that in the salubrious "Hive" of New England it was lamentable that there should be "any Drones."[25]

Many English writers at this time began to blame the poor themselves for their plight. The lower class, it was said, was naturally lazy and would work only when forced to by hunger and extreme poverty. Therefore, well-intentioned lawmakers who passed relief statutes were only cultivating dependency and encouraging sloth.

Out of this new climate of thought came the public workhouse movement. By 1723, when workhouses were operating in almost every sizable English town, thousands of impoverished persons were taken off out-relief and forced to move from their homes to the workhouses. There they were set to spinning flax, weaving linen, and picking oakum. It was hoped that through hard labor the poor would pay for their own support and in the process gain a taste for the rewards of industry and frugality. The workhouse would benefit the middle and upper classes by reducing the poor rates; it would aid the poor by repro-gramming them for a more satisfactory way of life. The English work-house became a cultural artifact of the early eighteenth century, an institution arising from a moral analysis of poverty and committed to reducing the taxpayers' load in maintaining the impoverished. A num-ber of authors with whom Bostonians were familiar, including Henry Fielding, William Temple, William Petty, Charles Davenant, and Ber-nard Mandeville, also plumped for the new system.

In 1735, with poverty spreading, the Boston town meeting decided to build a separate workhouse where the able-bodied poor would be segregated, relieved, and rehabilitated. In 1739 the brick workhouse on the Common opened its doors. Two stories high and 140 feet long, it was one of the largest buildings in Boston, capable of holding several hundred impoverished and unemployed persons. However, it never housed more than fifty-five.[26] The difficulty, apparently, was that many of Boston's poor refused to be taken from their homes. A large number of these were widows with young children who had lived decently, if not handsomely, in the past. It is understandable that they would rebel at the notion of giving up their lodgings, however cramped and cold, and repairing to the workhouse, where poverty was compounded with indignity and their ties with friends, relatives, and neighborhood life would be broken.

The most unfortunate of Boston's impoverished—the aged, sick, crippled, and insane who had no families to care for them—had no choice but to go to the almshouse. About one hundred such Bostonians did so each year in the 1740s. Another forty or fifty persons could be induced to go to the workhouse, especially if they did not have children or had been apprehended for prostitution or other crimes. But most of Boston's poor regarded themselves above such treatment. They re-fused to brook the strict regimen of the workhouse, with its rules against free coming and going and its provisions for gagging and bread-and-water diets for "wanton and lascivious Behaviour." Moreover, they must have found it ungenerous that the selectmen allowed them only one penny out of every shilling they earned—and that "to be disposed of by the Overseers for their greater Comfort."[27] Boston's leaders had erected a substantial building that could not be filled. As in the case of the public markets, the workhouse experiment failed because it underestimated the resistance of ordinary people, who had their ways of defending themselves against attempts to alter their way of life.

In 1748 Boston's leaders made another attempt to deal with the widowed poor and their dependent children, whose numbers had continued to grow during King George's War. If they would not trade their mean lodgings for the workhouse, perhaps they could be persuaded to go to a manufactory during the day, where their labor would contribute to their own support and lighten the taxpayers' burden. Thus was born the United Society for Manufactures and Importation, the first American experiment in female factory labor. Its subscribers intended to put the unemployed poor to work, halt the rise of property taxes, and make a profit from the cheap labor of poverty-stricken women and children. Public authorities had been unable to make the dependent poor self-supporting; now private parties were to have a try.

The Society for Manufactures had in mind a textile factory where flax would be spun and linen cloth woven. Flax grew well in New England and linen was widely imported—to the value, according to contemporary estimates, of £20,000 to £60,000 per year.[28]

Nothing went easily for the organizers. The initial call for investors in 1748 brought only thirty-six subscribers and about £200 sterling. Linen weavers and loom builders were not to be found in Boston and had to be advertised for abroad. Nor were spinners available, for, contrary to the conventional understanding of historians, urban women and children who could spin were the exception rather than the rule. It took until December 1750 to lease a building, set up looms, and open several free spinning schools for teaching pauper children the art of the distaff and wheel. By this time the United Society for Manufactures and Importation had reorganized and changed its name to the more benevolent-sounding Society for Encouraging Industry and the Employment of the Poor.

The manufactory opened its doors in 1751, and six months later the society reported that Bostonians were producing 5,000 yards of linen per year, two-thirds of it woven by women working for the society.[29] This output of only about sixteen yards per workday, however, was not very impressive for a town whose pauper population approached a thousand souls.

At the very time when the society was reporting limited progress in putting the indigent to work, smallpox struck so severely at the lower class that it "entirely destroyed the Linnen Manufacture."[30] Undaunted, the society redoubled its efforts when the epidemic passed. A campaign for subscriptions to erect a large new building began, and some of Boston's most prestigious ministers, including Samuel Cooper at Brattle Street Church and Charles Chauncy at First Church, were enlisted in the cause. The latter argued that because of the society's praiseworthy efforts "some hundreds of Women and Children have . . . been kept at Work, whereby they have done a great deal towards supplying themselves with Bread, to the easing the Town of its Burthen in providing for the poor."[31] Cooper, who was Boston's most articulate exponent of the increasingly popular philosophy of economic self-interest, observed that Bostonians could indulge their natural and legitimate "self-love" while subscribing to the new enterprise, because the manufactory was designed to "advance our private interest" by lowering taxes and turning a profit while giving employment to the idle.[32]

Ministerial urgings, however, could not unlock Boston's mercantile wealth. Unable to attract enough private capital, the society's officers turned to government and got the response they sought. In March 1753 the town meeting voted to lend £130 sterling toward the construction of a new building, and in June Boston's representatives persuaded the General Court to impose a luxury tax on coaches, chariots, and other wheeled vehicles for five years in order to raise £1,125 more. Newly capitalized, the society started afresh. By fall the Linen Manufactory House on Tremont Street was ready to open. To whip up enthusiasm the society staged a spinning exhibition on the Common in August. "Near 300 Spinsters, some of them 7 or 8 years old and several of them Daughters of the best Families among us," reported the *Boston Gazette,* "made a handsome Appearance on the Common."[33] High upon a stage erected for the occasion sat a number of weavers, one at work at his loom.

All the bright hopes that the new linen manufactory would rid Boston of poverty were shattered within a few years. By 1758 its operations were grinding to a halt. The next year the General Court ordered the building sold at auction in order to recover the costs. But who would buy a linen factory that would not work? No bids were made, and all the government could do was lease a part of its white elephant to two Boston weavers who wanted to try their own textile experiment. Not until the British troops eyed it as a barracks in 1768 could anyone think of a use for the manufactory.

Why had the linen manufactory failed? Cheap labor, sufficient capital, and technology were the prime factors that led to success in Scotland and Ireland. All were available in Boston. During its existence, in fact, the society produced more than 17,000 yards of cloth. The enterprise failed because it could not produce linen as cheaply as it could be imported. One reason may have been, as the society claimed, that the government did not provide subsidies as in Ireland. There were also problems of synchronizing labor and procuring ample supplies of flax. But much of the manufactory's failure must be charged to the resistance of the intended recipients of the society's efforts. As in the case of the workhouse, women and children showed great reluctance to toil in the manufactory. They would spin at home, working as time allowed to produce what they could within the rhythm of their daily routine and accepting small piecework wages. But removal to an institutional setting, even for daytime labor, involved a new kind of labor discipline and a separation of productive and reproductive responsibilities that challenged deeply rooted values.

As the wives of artisans, mariners, and laborers, laboring-class women had probably always contributed by helping in their husbands' shops, taking in washing, serving as seamstresses for middle- and upper-class families, and doing daytime domestic labor in the houses of the well-to-do. After the 1720s, when the economic security of laboring-class families was steadily undermined, supplemental income from wives and older daughters probably became even more imperative. Domestic service may have been particularly important because Boston lacked the substantial labor pool of female slaves and indentured servants who performed household work in Philadelphia and New York. Much of the demand for domestic labor in Boston must have been filled by young, unmarried women and by the wives of lower-class men, especially if they were childless.

Older women with young children may have taken in boarders as a second major way of supplementing the family income. The striking difference in this period between the number of people per house in Boston and in the other two port towns indicates either that Boston families were larger or that many householders rented rooms and furnished board to transients, unmarried mariners, and other families from the ranks of the laboring poor. In 1741 Boston had 9.5 persons per house and in 1765 9.3 persons. Philadelphia and New York in the same period had fewer than 7 persons per house. All the data available indicate that the birth rate in Boston was lower than in the other northern ports, for the mid-century wars took a fearful toll on a generation of young males, leaving a surplus population of young women whose childbearing potential was cut short by the loss of a husband or who remained single and childless altogether for lack of marriageable men. Hence it is reasonable to conclude that the large number of persons per house in Boston primarily represents the taking in of boarders. For many Boston women, especially widows, this may have been the main source of family income.

Both in daytime domestic service and in maintaining boarders Boston's poor widows had previously been able to combine maternal responsibilities with intermittent work, which brought a modest income but had to be supplemented with out-relief. Factory labor, however, was far less amenable to the discharge of women's familial responsibilities. Spinning done in the home could be fitted into the maternal work rhythm; in the factory it could not.

The evidence of resistance to the new work system, though fragmentary and sometimes indirect, is compelling. The company's accounts show that in 1757 the manufactory had twenty-one looms and sixty wheels. Hundreds of spinners had been trained in the previous years, and twenty-one looms would have required yarn from the wheels of several hundred of them. Many, it appears, had accepted the society's suggestion that they work at home, or, in a reversal of causality, had obliged the society to accept this modification of the original plan. Many were also spinning for themselves instead of for the society. Several merchants began to purchase privately produced cloth, and apparently most of the poor preferred to work for them, as their domestic responsibilities allowed, rather than work for or in the manufactory. If they had been fully supported by wages, perhaps women and children could have been induced to go to the manufactory. Since they could not live on the wages offered, about 7 shillings per week for spinners, they chose to stay at home, working at their wheels in their free time, selling their yarn to independent weavers, and counting on private and public relief to supplement their wages.

The resistance of these women is all the more remarkable given the pressure exerted on them by the town's leading figures, who were intent on making the manufactory succeed. This upper-class determination is most revealingly articulated in the sermons given at the annual meetings of the society by some of eastern Massachusetts' best-known clergymen. In a sermon launching the society's new subscription drive in August 1752, Chauncy took as his text "Thus we commanded you, that if any would not work, neither should he eat." He lamented the "lazy and indolent, who are both healthy and strong"; and he warned against giving money to the idle poor, because charity of this kind, far from helping, would be "a great Hurt to a Community."[34] Despite such threatening rhetoric, many poor women refused to submit to a work routine that disrupted traditional ways of life and split the dual functions of laboring-class women—work and family—into two separate spheres.

Boston's decline, caused initially by deep-rooted problems of productivity and compounded in the 1740s by war, brought into sharp relief the possibilities and pitfalls of the increasingly pervasive market economy. Entrepreneurial achievement per se in Boston was not resented but was broadly admired, as the repeated election of the town's wealthiest merchants to public office attests. Yet the new system, which promised so much, had not obliterated older conceptions of the community and of social relationships within it. A kind of crisis of belief occurred when war dislocated the economy, brought impoverishment to many, and at the same time elevated a few to unprecedented wealth. It was then that echoes of the traditional social system, in which mutual obligations rather than the free exchange of goods and labor governed behavior, began to be heard.

Resistance to the new order and a longing for a passing system registered most clearly in the lower reaches of the laboring classes, where contributions to the war had been heaviest and inflation pinched most severely. This trend was primarily visible in Boston, where the market economy had distributed its rewards least evenhandedly. It showed itself in resistance to the new methods of poor relief and, even more dramatically, in an evangelical evocation of the lost spirit of community and a rising chorus of voices against entrepreneurial wealth and abuse of power.

It was not all upheaval in Boston and all placidity in the other ports, however. In each town struggles for power within the elite as well as political activity in the plebeian ranks ensured that the hurly-burly of public affairs inherited from the previous generation continued. Moreover, each of the towns was moved by a religious revival that sent hundreds of souls "flying to Christ." In Boston economic decline kept the political cauldron bubbling; in New York and Philadelphia it simmered quietly, occasionally becoming heated but never reaching the boiling point of the 1720s and 1730s. Likewise, it was in Boston that religious revivalism was most intense and manifested itself most clearly as an expression of social discontent.

New Politics at Mid-Century

In each of the northern towns new techniques of political organization that had been initiated in the first third of the century acquired further legitimacy after 1740. Party caucuses drew up slates of candidates, which at least in theory gave voters a real choice at the polls. In New York the private nomination of assembly candidates was replaced in 1739 by an outdoor rally for nominating candidates. Boston's popular Caucus never opened its deliberations to the multitude in this period, but Philadelphia began to follow New York's example in 1754. In that year the conservative proprietary party, yielding to the realities of political life, advertised in the *Pennsylvania Gazette* for a public turnout to choose candidates for the upcoming assembly elections.[35] In another concession to popular politics, candidates publicly advertised for votes.

Even more significant in transforming politics from a private to a public affair was the further development of the political press. By the 1740s the printed word had become an indispensable part both of campaigning for office and of pressuring legislators who were considering controversial bills. In every contested election, pamphleteers industriously alerted the voters to the awful consequences of a victory by the other side. In 1754, as the Massachusetts legislature considered a liquor excise bill aimed at merchants and distillers, seventeen pamphlets appeared in Boston to rally public support against it. The controversy over chartering King's College in New York in 1750–51 provoked several dozen tracts. More and more the urban newspapers, which were increasing in number in this era, were filled with polemical literature and election appeals. In 1750 the leader of New York's popular party exclaimed that the forthcoming election had "produced a violent paper war here [which has brought forth] a dozen different papers."[36] If newspaper articles are included, about forty partisan pieces in all were printed.

Also signaling the widespread influence of the political press were the anguished cries of political leaders about the dangerous implications of this increasingly potent weapon. Most members of the elite, whether they belonged to the popular or the conservative faction, had ambivalent feelings about courting the electorate in print. A few optimists such as Benjamin Franklin and Elisha Cooke looked upon fiery pamphlets and newspaper fusillades as instruments "to prepare the Minds of the Publick."[37] But most leaders assumed that people easily succumbed to their basest instincts and that the "unthinking multitude," which was thought to include a vast majority of the population, was moved by boisterous passion rather than by cool reason. Guided by these views, most of the elite considered exhortatory literature a threat to the social order. Conservative politicians frequently attacked what they called irresponsible attempts "to inflame the minds of the common people" or "to breed and nourish Discontent, and to foment Faction and Sedition."[38] Yet by the 1740s and 1750s even the most conservative leaders had to resort to the press. The same men who earlier had lamented its use, such as James DeLancey of New York, and Richard Peters, a proprietary leader in Philadelphia, eagerly employed scurrilous broadsides and pamphlets by mid-century. Their opponents, long accustomed to wielding the poisoned pen, could only shake their heads in dismay, charging that attempts were being made to propagate "Clamour & Slander" and turn the heads of "ignorant people & others who are not well acquainted with the publick affairs."[39] That said, they again took up the pen themselves.

The critics of the political press were not inventing bogeymen when they expressed fears that bombastic political literature would have a dangerous effect on ordinary people. "When all *Order* and *Government* is endeavoured to be *Trampled on, Reflections* are cast upon Persons of all Degrees, must not these things end in Sedition?" asked James DeLancey.[40] The answer depended upon how one defined sedition. To conservatives it was the erosion of deference and the intrusion of laboring men into politics. Elitists imagined that such people were manipulated by the press into an artificial anger. Cadwallader Colden of New York wrote of the "prejudices & republican notions artfully instill'd into numbers of peoples minds," as if to suggest that ideas could be implanted mechanically though pamphlets and broadsides.[41] While they may have been wrong in their conception of how laboring-class resistance was sparked, they were right about the effect of the burgeoning political press. The printed word sharpened the ability of ordinary people to criticize those above them and strengthened their feeling of power. Thus there was some truth in the equation made by conservatives between "scribbling" and "leveling," although the conservatives too were obliged to scribble in pursuit of votes.

Not only a quantitative leap in the production of political literature but also an escalation of rhetoric made the press a particularly potent weapon by mid-century. As political literature proliferated, the quality of language and the modes of argumentation changed markedly, for a broader audience was being addressed. Many of the early eighteenth-century pamphlet writers, perhaps mindful of the revolutionary potential of the printed word, and beaming their arguments to the upper stratum, had couched their arguments in legalistic terms. Boston readers of the numerous pamphlets on the currency issue in the 1720s encountered nothing more virulent than charges that the opposition view was "strange and Unaccountable," "intolerable," "unreasonable and unjust," or that writers on the other side were guilty of "bold and wilful Misrepresentation." But by 1754 the antiexcise pamphleteers in Boston were painting images of the opponents as "Little pestilent Creature[s]," "dirty miscreants," and unspeakably horrible creatures ready to "cram [their] . . . merciless and insatiable Maw[s] with our very Blood, and bones, and Vitals," while making sexual advances on wives and daughters.[42]

In New York, the appearance in 1752 of the *Independent Reflector,* the first American magazine created for political exposé rather than for amusement, brought vituperative politics to a new height. In the King's College controversy in New York City, the Anglican clergy was bitterly vilified and granted no semblance of integrity. In phrases that made Zenger's *New-York Weekly Journal* of the 1730s seem polite by comparison, "Philo-Reflector" warned his readers of the clergymen's "ghastly juggling, their Pride, and their insatiate Lust of Power" and cautioned them to keep a weather eye out for the "Seduction of Priest-craft," the "dark and horrible Plot for usurping the sole Rule of the College," for "our intended Vassalage," and for "clerical Rubbish and Villainy."[43]

Not even in Philadelphia, the pacifist center of the American colonies, could politicians avoid rhetorical violence. Factional leaders hurled insults at each other, charging opponents with "Inveterate Calumny, foul-mouthed Aspersion, shameless Falsehood, and insatiate Malice." When the imperious Anglican clergyman William Smith attacked Benjamin Franklin, the artisans' hero, his opponents wrote that "the Vomiting of this infamous Hireling . . . betoken[s] that Redundancy of Rancour, and Rottiness of Heart which render him the most despicable of his Species."[44]

In effect, the conservatives' worst fears concerning the use of the press were confirmed as the tactics of printed political discourse changed from attacking the legality or wisdom of the opposition's policies or pleading for the election of public-minded men to assailing the character and motives of those on the other side. The effect of the new political rhetoric was circular; each escalation in the brutality of language brought an equivalent or greater response from the opposition. Gradually the public was given reason to suspect not simply the wisdom or constitutional soundness of one side or the other but also the motives, morality, and even sanity of its leaders. The same high-placed individuals to whom the rank and file was supposed to defer were portrayed as the most corrupt and loathsome members of society.

Another facet of the new politics in the 1740s and 1750s was the growing involvement of religious figures. Most urban leaders, both secular and clerical, deplored this trend but nonetheless caused it to happen. The clergy had never been isolated from political life in the early history of the towns, but their efforts to influence public affairs had ordinarily been conducted discreetly and privately. When clergymen published pamphlets on political subjects, they usually did so anonymously. Traditional belief considered it inappropriate for church leaders to mix religion and politics. Attacks on clerical involvement in politics continued throughout this period, but the urban clergy became more and more politicized as contending secular leaders urged them to enter the arena of public controversy.

To some extent the line between politics and religion became blurred because some of the most burning issues of the period could not be confined to either the civil or the religious sphere. In Philadelphia the issue of war and defense appropriations in 1748 brought the first full-scale exchange on a secular question between opposing denominational spokesmen. In a dozen signed pamphlets, Anglican and Presbyterian clerics took on Quaker leaders in a public dialogue on the necessity of military defense in the face of a threat of French and Spanish invasion. This battle of words thrust the clergy squarely into the political arena. The first sermon given by the fiery revivalist Gilbert Tennent to justify defensive war was published, he claimed, at the request of the leaders of the anti-Quaker party. Before the controversy was over the political role of the Philadelphia clergy had been greatly magnified and the precedent established for their open participation in public affairs. Once the process commenced, churches began to split on political questions. Only a decade after the Anglican church of Philadelphia began to involve itself in the primary political issues of the day, its leaders and laity divided irretrievably on the question whether the vast landholdings of the proprietors of Pennsylvania ought to be subject to the same war taxes as the property of others.

In New York the King's College controversy similarly provided the occasion for the rapid obliteration of the line separating religion and politics. A group of Anglicans who were politically sympathetic to the conservative governor James DeLancey hoped to establish a college supported by public taxes. Although the Anglicans had the backing of much of the Dutch Reformed church, they ran into a hornets' nest of opposition from the Presbyterians, who intended to stop this creeping Anglicanism.

From 1753 to 1755 the issue raged, and the Anglicans even launched a newspaper, the *New York Mercury,* labeled by the opposition the "partial, party, paltry, and priestly Newspaper."[45] King's College was finally chartered and run under Anglican direction without public support. But the controversy had politicized the churches, and politicians had learned to look at religious sanctuaries as new fields upon which to stage political battles. By mid-century church leaders were learning that they need not apologize for "preaching politics," as Jonathan Mayhew of Boston put it.[46]

Awakened Sinners and Political Dissidents

Nowhere did the lines of separating religion, economics, and politics crumble more swiftly or completely than in the experiential and ideological upheaval connected with the Great Awakening—the firestorm of religious enthusiasm that swept the northern colonies in the mid-1730s and continued for almost a decade. More than a religious movement, the Awakening must be seen as a profound cultural crisis involving the convergence of political, social, economic, and ideological forces that had been building for several generations. This was especially true in Boston, where social change had proceeded more swiftly and corrosively than in the other towns and where, correspondingly, the Great Awakening had the greatest force.

At its core the Great Awakening was "a search for new sources of authority, new principles of action, new foundations of hope" among people who had come to believe that "the churches as institutions no longer met the spiritual needs of the people."[47] The Awakeners preached that the old sources of authority were too effete to solve the problems of the day, too encrusted with tradition, self-indulgence, hypocrisy, and intellectualism to bring a sense of hope and faith to a people who were witnessing the rapid transformation of the world of their fathers. At a time of cultural crisis, a new wellspring of authority was desperately needed, and that source, the evangelists preached, was the individual himself. Like the seventeenth-century Quakers who immigrated to Philadelphia, the Awakeners believed that God did not operate though an elite corps of vice-regents composed of the learned clergy and the aristocracy. All individuals, whatever their stations in life, could seek and find God, even though they might lack special learning or lofty status. Like the Quaker inner light, given by God to every man and woman, the new light within the awakened enabled them to achieve grace through the conversion experience. From experiential religion, which every woman, man, and child was capable of achieving, a new sense of community could be forged, a new brotherhood of man achieved, the city on the hill restored.

The urban appeal of the revivalists was apparent from the first American tour of the master itinerant, George Whitefield. A diminutive man with a magnificent voice, Whitefield was the son of an English tavernkeeper who had worked his way through Oxford, converted to Methodism, and become a master of open-air preaching. He crossed the Atlantic to preach briefly in the new colony of Georgia in 1737, returned to England in 1738, and crossed the ocean again in late 1739. Only twenty-five years old then, he began a barnstorming trip that evoked a mass response of dimensions never before witnessed in America.

In his triumphant American tour in 1739–40 Whitefield, as one contemporary wrote, "chiefly confined his Labours to the populous towns."[48] He attracted large crowds in Philadelphia and New York, but it was in Boston in September 1740 that he received his most spectacular reception.

Whitefield preached his first sermon in Boston at Benjamin Colman's fashionable Brattle Street Church. A series of appearances followed at other Boston churches, and then, on a Saturday afternoon, nearly the entire population of Boston flocked to hear him on the Common. Throughout his three weeks in Boston Whitefield drew huge crowds whenever he preached outdoors. His farewell appearance on the Common drew a record audience of at least twenty thousand. When he left Boston, the town was quivering with excitement about the imminent second coming of Christ, and thousands had experienced the desire to be saved. But it was the message as well as the medium that explains why such large numbers of colonial America's urban populations flocked to see Whitefield. He frontally challenged traditional sources of authority, called upon people to become the instruments of their own salvation, and implicitly attacked the prevailing upper-class notion that the uneducated mass of people had no minds of their own.

When Whitefield began his American tour in 1739, the elite did not yet clearly perceive the social dynamite buried deep in his message. After all, his preachings produced thousands of conversions and filled the churches, which had been languishing for more than a generation, to overflowing. To civil leaders, too, he appeared at first as God-sent. Eighteenth-century leaders had long thought of religion as the handmaiden of social control. The master evangelist seemed to be ushering in a new era of discipline, morality, and social harmony.

The enthusiastic reception of Whitefield in Boston, however, did not conceal serious opposition to his preaching. Of the town's fifteen Congregational ministers, three remained cool toward his performances and three opposed him outright. The three Anglican ministers also vocally criticized him because, although Whitefield was an ordained Anglican priest, he was highly critical of the church's policies and seemed to take special satisfaction in attacking the Church of England, praising Puritan religiosity, and berating the bishop of London's policy of sending Anglican ministers to New England to proselytize in a Puritan stronghold.

With Whitefield's departure from Boston in October 1740 and the arrival of his American field lieutenant Gilbert Tennent, enthusiasm for the Awakening diminished rapidly among the clerical and civil establishment. Tennent was "a burly, salty, downright man" who preached, according to one contemporary, "like a Boatswain of a Ship, calling the Sailors to come to Prayers and be damned."[49] Shortly after he arrived on December 13, 1740, it became apparent that he was a different sort of spellbinder from his English mentor. His highly agitated manner of preaching produced emotional writhings and faintings that had not been features of Whitefield's performances. Worse than this, Tennent began to attack the established clergy as unregenerate and to encourage people to forsake their ministers. "The sapless Discourses of such dead Drones" were worthless, he proclaimed.[50] Worst of all, Tennent invested his exhortations with a social radicalism that was frightening to the upper orders of society. Whitefield had taken occasional cuts at aristocratic fashion and criticized the religious lassitude that came, he said, with the accumulation of material wealth. But his American successors, Tennent first among them, adapted his message to the social landscape they knew so well and infused their evangelical preaching with a radical egalitarianism that left many former supporters of Whitefield reaching for their pens. By the time Tennent left Boston in March 1741 the conservative reaction against revivalism was in full swing. Tennent was called "a monster! impudent & noisy," a man whose "Beastly brayings" were having even more dangerous effects upon the humbler people of the town than had Whitefield's preaching.[51]

What had started out in Boston in 1740 as a religious revival that cut across class lines was becoming a class-specific movement. As the social content of the evangelists' message became more explicit, support from the upper and middle levels of Boston society fell away. But the enthusiasm of the lower orders only grew more powerful and ecstatic. Instead of unifying Boston's economically troubled, politically divided society, as appeared possible at first, the Awakening was fragmenting it further.

The growing polarization in Boston became more painfully apparent in 1742, when Tennent was succeeded by the man who became the bête noire of the clerical establishment—James Davenport. A graduate of Yale College and son of the greatly respected pastor of the Congregational Church in Stamford, Connecticut, Davenport had accompanied Whitefield on his tour from New York to Philadelphia in 1740. By mid-1741 his own itinerant journeys were drawing thousands at every stop. Everywhere he went throngs turned out for street singing, all-night revival meetings, and emotional outpourings that often left dozens prostrated on the ground. Congregations split into fervent enthusiasts and antagonists wherever he went, and by the spring of 1742 his incendiary preaching was regarded as so dangerous that he was arrested, tried, and deported from Hartford amid a near riot.

When Davenport reached Boston, clergymen united in denying their pulpits to him and in signing a declaration against his preaching there. This move mattered little to Davenport, for his natural amphitheater was the street or field rather than the meetinghouse. Moreover, to proscribe him from the top of society was to recommend him to the bottom, for deference was crumbling like dry leaves among "God's people," as the radical revivalists called the poor and dispossessed.

Davenport appeared daily on Boston Common, where he proved his extraordinary ability to create religious hysteria and to provoke hatred of Boston's chief figures of authority. The people, he cried, should drink rat poison rather than listen to the damnifying preachments of the corrupt, "unconverted" clergy.[52] The Boston press tried hard to curb Davenport's popularity by characterizing his followers as "chiefly made up of the idle or ignorant Persons, and those of the lowest Rank." In the end it was only by indicting him before the grand jury "on the charge of having said that Boston's ministers were leading the people blindfold to hell" that the conservative leaders were able to get him deported from town.[53] In handing down a verdict of non compos mentis the grand jury gave the conservatives less than they wanted, but it was enough to drive the fiery Davenport from the city.

On the surface Davenport's threat to Boston's leaders was directly related to his attack upon the clergy. His assault may have bruised egos, but it was not in fact the main threat, for the clergy were not losing their flocks as a result of Davenport's preaching. The real danger came from his hot indictments of the rich and powerful, his criticism of the yawning gap between the rich and poor, and his exhortations to ordinary people to resist those who exploited and deceived them. Only then, he cried, would the Lamb Jesus return to earth. Even before his arrival, the conservative press was ridiculing the "new lights" for pursuing "Porters, Cobblers, [and] Barbers"—the bottom layer of the laboring class.[54] After Davenport's arrival, Charles Chauncy, lofty minister of the wealthy First Church and generalissimo of the antirevivalists, expressed the near-hysterical conviction that radical revivalism was making "strong attempts to destroy all property, to make all things common, wives as well as goods."[55] Other critics noted the connection between religious enthusiasm and social leveling.

The strength of feeling Davenport inspired in Boston and his ability to evoke a joyous collective spirit among a mass of common people account for the alarm voiced by his critics. "Were you to see him in his most violent Agitations," wrote the *Boston Evening Post*, "you would be apt to think, that he was a Madman just broke from his Chains; But especially had you seen him returning from the Common after his first preaching, with a large Mob at his Heels, singing all the Way thro' the Streets, he with his Hands extended, his Head thrown back, and his Eyes staring up to Heaven, attended with so much Disorder, that they look'd more like a Company of *Bacchanalians* after a mad Frolick, than sober Christians who had been worshipping God."[56] Masses of people were flocking daily to Boston Common to hear a man whom the established leaders declared insane; they were deriving from him a spiritual satisfaction they had never received before; and they were forging a communal experience that was profoundly threatening to the established culture, which stressed order, discipline, and submissiveness from the laboring classes.

Boston's leaders were probably correct in charging that Davenport had "few admirers among the sober judicious Part of the Town," but by "sober" and "judicious" they meant the middle and upper classes.[57] His people were those at the bottom of the urban hierarchy—laborers, seamen, the impoverished, slaves, indentured servants, and the young— those who in the counterpart Wesleyan movement in England were called "Christ's poor." The street processions, unconventional singing, and emotional outpourings on the Common were displays of folk

solidarity, of egalitarian yearnings, of opposition to conventional modes
of expression, and of the moral superiority common people felt toward
the town's middle and upper classes, who had been inspired by Whitefield but could not abide the more radical preachings of Tennent and
Davenport.

By 1742 Boston had become a magnet attracting a procession of
itinerant gospelers and haranguers, all of them labeled social incendi-
aries as well as religious mystics by the established clergy. Among the
itinerants who torched Boston with the Lord's truth in the spring and
summer of 1742 was Andrew Crosswell, who attracted huge crowds
across the river in Charlestown and triggered a fierce barrage of newspaper criticism. A friend of the dispossessed, Crosswell preached against
cruel treatment of prisoners in the jails and against slavery. To many
"respectable" citizens it seemed as if Boston had turned into a cauldron
of lower-class religious enthusiasm and social disintegration.

Of all the manifestations of social leveling that accompanied the
Great Awakening, the one that summed up the reckless social thrust
of evangelicalism in the view of conservatives was the practice of public,
lay exhorting. Within the structured Protestant churches there was no
room for lay persons to compete with the ordained ministry in preaching the word of God. Nor was there room for "self-initiated associations
of the people meeting outside of regularly constituted religious or
political meetings," for to do so was to relocate authority collectively
in the mass of common people.[58] Lay exhorting was rampant in eastern
Massachusetts by mid-1742. It was deeply hated and feared by the
upper crust, for it shattered the monopolistic hold of the educated
clergy on religious discourse; put all people on a plane in the area of
religion; gave a new importance to the oral culture of common people,
whose spontaneous outpourings contrasted sharply with the literary
culture of the gentry; established among them the notion that their
destinies and their souls were in their own hands instead of the hands
of the elite clergy; and turned the world upside down in allowing those
who had traditionally been consigned to the bottom of society to
assume roles customarily reserved for educated, adult men. Lay exhorting crossed class lines and defied sexual and racial roles. Such
obliteration of hierarchical boundaries gravely undermined the concentration of power and prestige in the elite.

The threat posed by Tennent, Davenport, and other radical evangelists can be fully appreciated only in the context of the political crisis
that Boston was experiencing at this time. Since 1739, the burning
issue had been what to do about the greatly inflated paper currency,

which by orders from England was to be completely retired by 1741. Many believed that Massachusetts would have to defy England, for with its chronic trade imbalance the withdrawal of paper money would leave the colony without a circulating medium. In 1739 two solutions were proposed. One was for a Land Bank, which would issue the equivalent of £600,000 in old tenor bills of credit, secured by land mortgaged to the bank. Any subscriber properly backed by land could borrow as much as £2,000 in paper money and repay the loan in notes or enumerated commodities over twenty years at 3 percent interest. In effect the Land Bank refurbished a proposal for privately issued bills of credit put forward more than twenty years before. Its chief organizer was the same John Colman who had promoted a private bank along similar lines in 1714 for the same purpose—to solve Massachusetts' monetary problem by converting land, the colony's most valuable resource, into a circulating medium.

Rivaling the Land Bank scheme was one for a Silver Bank, organized by a group of wealthy Boston merchants who wanted a far less inflationary solution that would increase the supply of coin, which they needed to balance accounts in London. They planned to issue the equivalent of £120,000 old tenor in bills of credit backed by silver and redeemable in fifteen years, much in the manner of the Merchants' Notes of 1733. Around these competing plans politics reached a fever pitch in 1740 and 1741. The proponents of the Land Bank swept the May 1740 elections, but both banks published their plans and began issuing bills late that summer, even though they had no legislative approval to do so.

Boston's international merchants "damned the [Land] Bank as merely a more invidious form of the soft money panacea typically favored by the province's poor and unsuccessful" and publicly vowed that they would not accept the organization's bills.[59] Land Bank supporters attacked the Silver Bank as another scheme of the rich to throttle the poor. Governor Belcher banned both banks, and the inflationist House of Representatives battled the deflationist governor and council, each seeking ways of outwitting the other. This constitutional chess game was ultimately decided in London, where Parliament in 1741 prohibited all private banks from issuing currency in Massachusetts. News of the decision arrived in Boston in late May, along with the news that William Shirley, a longtime resident of the town and a man known for his skills as a mediator, had been appointed the colony's new governor.

Bostonians responded with widespread defiance of the proclamation against Land Bank bills, while reports circulated that a thousand Bostonians would join thousands of men from the countryside to force the merchants to accept the bills. Grain prices were also increasing alarmingly and wheat was in short supply, giving rise to the report that the angry mobs assembling for a march on Boston would also seize any grain they could find in merchants' warehouses. William Shirley, who succeeded the unpopular Belcher, defused the situation with promises of a new economic policy, but the rancor engendered by the Land Bank controversy persisted for years afterward.

Whitefield's arrival in Boston coincided with the furor over the Land and Silver Banks. He preached his initial sermons only a few weeks after Boston's leading merchants announced that they would not accept the Land Bank bills, and his stay in Boston overlapped the public attacks on the merchants as "gripping and merciless usurers" who "heaped up vast Estates" at the expense of the common people.[60] In this atmosphere, Whitefield's ability to call the masses to worship must have been seen at first by conservatives as a positive gain, for the experience of a common religious exaltation might serve as an antidote to economic tension and incipient class conflict.

The itinerant evangelists who invaded Boston after Whitefield's departure, however, lashed out at wealth and vested authority. Davenport excoriated the rich and powerful, howling at his audiences to "Pull them down, turn them out, and put others in their Places."[61] He preached the gospel of antiauthoritarianism and leveling, and in the context of the Land Bank controversy there could be no strict compartmentalization of religious and economic discontent. By the time he had been banished from Boston, the wealthy opponents of the Land Bank were being cursed openly in the streets as "carnal Wretches, Hypocrites, Fighters against God, Children of the Devil, cursed Pharisees."[62] The religious flavor of such epithets, with which lower-class Bostonians indicted those on one side of the currency debate, demonstrates vividly that economic exploitation and religious degeneracy were linked in the minds of many. William Douglass saw order crumbling as the managers of the Land Bank "spirit[ed] the People to Mutiny, Sedition, and Riots."[63]

Thus the Great Awakening in Boston represented far more than a religious earthquake. For almost all the awakened, but especially for those from the lower echelons, the revival years brought an expansion of political consciousness and a new feeling of self-importance as people took part in spontaneous meetings, assumed more power in ecclesiastical affairs, and were encouraged repeatedly from the pulpit to adopt an attitude of skepticism toward dogma and authority. The leaders of the Great Awakening were preaching a radical message: religion was at a low ebb in America because the clergy were effete, corrupted by participation in creeping materialism, and intellectually bankrupt in their capitulation to Arminian theology, which stressed that individuals could gain their own salvation through good works rather than through God's mysterious saving grace. Ordinary people must take matters into their own hands. The Awakeners thus encouraged doctrinal controversy and sanctioned the casting out of unconverted leaders by the people. It was precisely this message that frightened so many upper-class city dwellers and led them to charge the revivalists with preaching anarchy.

Toward what ends was this new popular power to be employed? The lowliest town dwellers, including slaves, servants, the impoverished, and many who struggled to gain a foothold on the treacherous slopes of economic security, were looking not toward democratic bourgeois revolution, but backward to an earlier age, when, it was believed, individuals did not act for themselves, always striving to get ahead at the expense of their neighbors, but pulled together as a community. The crowds that followed Davenport, Crosswell, and the other radical evangelists seem to have been composed primarily of these dispossessed Bostonians. Charles Chauncy, who defended the profit motive and the pursuit of self-interest and made his church a comfortable gathering place for those with established fortunes and others striving for higher places, called these people the "idle and Ignorant," "the rabble," persons of "the lowest rank." Although some of the terms were derogatory, they accurately described the social position of those who marched through the streets behind the radical itinerants. For these people economic freedom meant little; their struggle was concerned with simple survival. In the Great Awakening, Gilbert Tennent's "common people" not only liberated themselves from "the contumely of their self-appointed betters" but also "glimpsed the possibility of a people's acting to make their united will prevail as the guarantor of the common good."[64]

The concern for social justice permeated the Awakeners' outlook. Jonathan Mayhew, another Congregational minister who spoke for the entrepreneurial fortune-builders of Boston's best-heeled churches, might declare that the "publick happiness is nothing but the happiness of a *number of individuals* united in society."[65] But the Awakeners denounced such an atomistic conception of society and answered that he who was "governed by regard to his own private interest" was thereby committed to "act the part of an enemy to the public."[66]

These two fundamentally different conceptions of society defined the responsibilities of the upper class in sharply different ways. The old light or rationalist clergy (and some of the new light ministers such as Benjamin Colman, who wished to infuse their affluent congregations with new religious energy) pragmatically countenanced the emerging capitalist ethic. The radical Awakeners, on the other hand, were thoroughly uncomfortable with the acquisitiveness of the urban elite. The motive behind such materialism, as Tennent understood it, was the desire "to be a little demigod in the World, a sort of independent Being, by having many depending on thee, courting thy Smiles, and trembling at thy frowns." Of humble stock himself, Tennent heaped scorn on "the Grandees" of America and warned that men "grow in Wickedness in Proportion to the Increase in their Wealth."[67]

The rationalists, speaking for securely positioned Bostonians and those who strove for positions in the competitive world, counseled the poor to be content with their lot and minimized the obligations of the rich toward them. Charles Chauncy warned that charity would encourage laziness. Hence it was best to cut off charity to the laboring poor so they would learn that starvation, not public aid, would be the fate of idlers.

The radical Awakeners and some moderates, in contrast, preached the obligations of the fortunate to the indigent. A "private niggardly spirit," wrote Jonathan Edwards, "is more suitable for wolves, and other beasts of prey, than for human beings."[68] The Awakeners' law of charity demanded that the rich give freely of their wealth and acknowledged that except by the grace of God and human accident they might stand in the places of the poor themselves.

Whitefield, Tennent, Edwards, and even radicals such as Davenport and Crosswell were not preaching class revolt. The seeds of overt political radicalism were still in the germinative stage. But the multitudes who harked to the revivalist message in Boston were strengthened in their conviction that it was justifiable in extraordinary circumstances to take matters into their own hands. This is why even Edwards was seen by the commercial elite and its clerical allies as "the grand leveler of Christian history," even though sedition and leveling were not what he had in mind.[69]

It is no wonder, then, that Whitefield, who had been so enthusiastically welcomed in 1740 by Boston's clerical establishment, received their bitter disapproval when he returned in 1744. By then, however, war with France was imminent. Lower-class religious enthusiasm would shortly be redirected to maiming the Antichrist of the north, and Whitefield would be induced to use his influence with the lower orders to spur enlistments. The "rabble," whose form of religious passion was so greatly feared from above, were now to become Christian soldiers.

The Great Awakening in New England was not caused by economic dislocation, spreading poverty, or currency problems that affected some parts of society more than others. Its roots reached far deeper into the subsoil of Calvinist Puritan culture. But the response to the Awakening was strongly conditioned by these phenomena, as a comparison of the Awakening in Boston with its effects in New York and Philadelphia shows. Neither of the latter experienced the Awakening as enduringly or as messianically. An important reason for this difference was their relative economic prosperity during the previous generation. There were poor and buffeted persons in both New York and Philadelphia, to be sure, but their numbers were small. Large crowds assembled whenever Whitefield or Tennent preached, and they often responded ecstatically. But the more radical exhorters, whose message contained far more social dynamite than Whitefield's, never had the impact in New York and Philadelphia that they did in Boston.

In New York, another factor besides the absence of widespread poverty dampened the effects of the Awakening. The clergy of that city were almost unanimous in their opposition to Whitefield, Tennent, and their followers and did everything possible to close their pulpits to them and to minimize their influence. Whitefield's humanitarian statements on behalf of slaves also offended many New Yorkers, who held in chains the largest urban black population in America. So on his three visits to New York in 1739 and 1740 Whitefield preached in the fields to only moderate crowds and on one occasion to the small Wall Street Presbyterian congregation.

The case was much the same in Philadelphia. During 1741 and 1742, when Boston was seething with lower-class religious emotionalism, Philadelphia was sedate. No street processions, midnight revels, or mass singing occurred. Nor was the Philadelphia press, in contrast to Boston's, filled with attacks on the revivalists for disrupting society, inverting the class order, and kneading the people into a state of radical insubordination.

Benjamin Franklin, who was a friend of Whitefield's but felt no need to be born again, described how in Philadelphia the Awakening worked a kind of reverse magic from what occurred in Boston. "It was wonderful to see the Change soon made in the Manners of our Inhabitants; from being thoughtless or indifferent about Religion, it seem'd as if all the World were growing Religious; so that one could not walk thro' the Town in an Evening without Hearing Psalms sung in different Families of every Street."[70] In Philadelphia the revival remained a cohesive, socially stabilizing force, as leaders hoped it would. Doctrinal controversy rended the Presbyterian church, but in an atmosphere of economic prosperity the Awakening never became invested with the kind of social meaning it held for the laboring poor of Boston.

Just as street religion took deeper root in Boston during the Great Awakening than in the other port towns, so did street politics in the aftermath of the revival. The backdrop for this trend was economic dislocation. Civil war had been rumored during 1741 in connection with the dismantling of the Land Bank, and in the closing years of the decade Boston went twice more to the precipice of wholesale disorder. The first crisis came in November 1747, when Charles Knowles, commodore of the royal navy in North American waters, brought his fleet to Boston for reprovisioning in preparation for cruising to the West Indies. Desertions during the stay in port left Knowles's fleet shorthanded, so on the evening of November 16 press gangs set out to fill the crew vacancies from Boston's waterfront populace.

Knowles was almost within his rights. Ships could not sail unmanned or even seriously undermanned, and ship captains were therefore authorized to impress colonial subjects into service for the crown. But after 1696 captains had to have an order from the provincial governor to send press gangs ashore. A 1707 law, still in force according to Americans but denied by the English, also prohibited the impressment of any mariner, on ship or shore, in American waters. The matter was usually academic except in time of war, because only then was the British navy present in American waters. In dispatching his press gangs Knowles was resorting to a policy that had long been unpopular in the colonies but represented the only alternative at his disposal.

Knowles doubtless knew that his press gangs had their work cut out for them, for lower-class Bostonians had fiercely resisted impressment since 1741. Violence had begotten violence on several occasions in New England's largest seaport, which the man-hunters of the royal navy seemed to have made a special target.

When Knowles's press gangs swept ashore before dawn, gathering up shipbuilders, servants, slaves, and others, while other royal mariners raided the crews of vessels at anchor in Boston harbor, they touched off the most massive civil disobedience in Boston's history. By mid-morning a crowd of Bostonians was sweeping through the streets in search of British seamen. Several officers were nabbed, and when others took refuge in the governor's house a crowd surrounded the mansion and verbally abused Shirley. Attempting to stop the crowd, the sheriff and his deputies were badly mauled. The militia, called to arms by the governor and instructed to "suppress the Mob by force, and if need be, to fire upon 'em with Ball," showed no intention of responding.[71] By dusk a crowd estimated by Thomas Hutchinson at several thousand answered the governor's attempt to issue a proclamation for dispersing the mob by stoning the government house free of its windows. Shirley and his merchant allies did what they could to appease the assemblage, but the throng now surged toward the waterfront to burn a twenty-gun vessel being built for the royal navy. They satisfied themselves with dragging what they thought was a royal barge from one of the ships in the harbor to the courtyard of Shirley's house and burning it there amid cheers. The enraged Knowles threatened to bombard Boston from his warships. Only determined negotiations over several days of tumult led to the release of the impressed Bostonians and averted a showdown.

In the investigations of the impressment riot, Boston's leading citizens pretended that the "Riotous Tumultuous Assembly" was composed of "Foreign Seamen, Servants, Negroes, and other Persons of Mean and vile Condition"—precisely the targets of any press gang.[72] But in this case the dragnet seems to have extended much further, including even a few middle-class Bostonians, and to have evoked a response from more than "the rabble." The governor himself was convinced that the mob had been "secretly Countenanc'd and encourag'd by some ill minded Inhabitants and Persons of Influence in the Town," and Thomas Hutchinson wrote that while "the lower class were beyond measure enraged," the impressment was resented by "men of all orders."[73] The fact that the General Court refused to condemn the riot during the two days when the crowd controlled the town is further evidence that those who were in the streets had the tacit approval of many who were not. Later, after Knowles had released most of the press gang captives and the crowd had dispersed, the middle- and upper-class representatives in the General Court and town meeting expressed their "Abhorence of such illegal Criminal Proceedings" and condemned "this infamous Insult upon the King's Peace."[74] Little, however, was done to indict or prosecute those who had been plainly seen leading the crowd in its assault on the Province House and the royal barge.

The impressment riot extended one of the central social thrusts of evangelicalism. In defying the royal governor and a commodore of the royal navy, ordinary Bostonians engaged in a supreme form of antiauthoritarianism. They demonstrated a consciousness squarely in the tradition of the earlier crowd actions over grain exports and public markets. Such bold defiance of the highest authorities accorded well with the vision that the Awakeners had called forth, of ordinary people rising against constituted authority to redress grievances perpetrated by power-hungry, morally bankrupt figures who misused their power.

Less than two weeks after peace returned to Boston's waterfront, a hard-hitting pamphlet in plain language was on the streets. It vigorously defended the "natural right" of the townspeople to band together for defense against illegal impressments and attacked some of the town's wealthy for defending Knowles's action. "Some of Figure and Interest among us," it charged, "live at Ease upon the Produce" of the lower ranks, whose members had been coerced into service in the royal fleet. These wealthy defenders of royal impressment were "Tools to arbitrary Power . . . Slaves to their present petty Advantages . . . so lost to all Sense of Goodness, and so abandon'dly Vicious" that they should be "obliged to serve, as a common Seaman, for seven Years, on board the worst Ship of War, and under the worst Commander, the King has in his Service."[75]

The pamphlet was the work of a growing anti-Shirley group that was attempting to revive the populistic politics of the Elisha Cooke era. One of its leaders was Samuel Adams, Jr., whose father, one of the principal Land Bankers, had been financially ruined by its liquidation and driven from office by Governor Belcher. As part of its campaign, the Adams group launched an antiadministration newspaper, the *Independent Advertiser,* which first appeared on January 4, 1748. Its pitch to the laboring classes was obvious from the outset. "Liberty can never subsist without Equality," it pronounced, "So when Men's Riches become measurably or surprizingly great, a People who regard their own Security, ought to make strict Enquiry, how they came by them . . . But some will say, is it a Crime to be rich? Yes, certainly, At the Publick Expense."[76] Taken verbatim from *Cato's Letters,* the hard-hitting attacks on Walpolean government and the new capitalist economy in England by John Trenchard and Thomas Gordon, this was the most explicit formulation yet expressed in Boston that the rise of a wealthy elite was causally connected with the miseries of so many in the lower and middle ranks. In language reminiscent of the vitriolic phrases of the radical Awakeners, the *Independent Advertiser* essayists repeatedly played to feelings of social inequity in Boston and explicitly linked the increasing stratification of wealth with growing political despotism.

On the heels of the impressment riot came the dénouement of the currency question that had been in the forefront of Boston's politics for years. After taking office in August 1741, Governor Shirley had been spared by King George's War from the unpleasant duty of enforcing the parliamentary demand that Massachusetts restrict its issue of paper money and withdraw the bills of credit in circulation by the end of that year. Wars could not be fought without the printing of money, and this was the most expensive war by far in the colony's history. By 1747, when England called a halt to further attacks on Canada and ordered demobilization, almost £3 million (old tenor) of paper currency had been issued. Runaway depreciation was the result, with the value of the Massachusetts pound plummeting to about one-tenth of its English counterpart by 1747. In 1748 Parliament granted Massachusetts £183,649 sterling as compensation for the war effort. Silver was to be shipped to the colony and used to sink the massive issues of paper money. It was hoped that Massachusetts could reorganize its monetary system, returning to a hard money currency for the first time in more than half a century.

What at first seemed a boon nearly turned into the colony's bane, for Massachusetts rocked with controversy over how the monetary reform should be accomplished. Governor Shirley and a group of wealthy merchant supporters called for an immediate retirement of all paper bills. Their opponents called for a gradual retirement over several years. If all paper money was abolished at once, they argued, local trade would be disrupted, specie would again flow out of Massachusetts to pay for trade deficits, and the colony would resume the course it had traveled for the past two generations.

Many believed, moreover, that a drastic deflationary policy would enrich some men and impoverish others. Those with the most to gain were wealthy merchants and government officials, who, in anticipation of the redemption of paper money, had been gathering in as many depreciated bills of credit as possible, hoping to exchange them at a rate that would bring fat profits. Even Thomas Hutchinson, who drafted the immediate redemption bill and was known as the leader of the wealthy fiscal conservatives, reported in his *History of the Colony of Massachusets-Bay* that the common people believed the £183,000 of silver would "fall to the share of men of wealth, and would either be exported or hoarded up, and no part of it would go to the labourer, or the lower class of people, who must take their pay in goods, or go without."[77]

The conviction was widespread among ordinary Bostonians that windfall profits at the expense of the masses were what the wealthiest merchants had in mind. The town seethed with resentment against the drastic redemption bill, and Hutchinson and Boston's other merchant representatives who had voted for it were summarily defeated in the May 1749 elections, an indication that opposition to the redemption act reached far into the middle class. In the fall, when the British ship arrived with the silver, crowds roamed the streets, threatening Hutchinson with physical harm and convincing him that he had best retire to his summer mansion in Milton, outside the city, to avoid being mobbed by his townsmen. A rump town meeting in December sardonically elected Hutchinson and fifteen other wealthy merchants as tax collectors, a job that would take them out of their mansions and into the streets, where they might personally see how ordinary Bostonians were faring during hard times. The Boston press spewed forth diatribes against wealthy war profiteers, who had now found a way of turning even postwar depression to their own ends. An anonymous pamphleteer wrote that "Poverty and Discontent appear in every Face, (except the Countenances of the Rich), and dwell upon every Tongue." A few men, fed by "Lust of Power, Lust of Fame, Lust of Money," had grown rich by supplying military expeditions during the war and had now devised a monetary system guaranteed to heap their gains higher. "No wonder such Men can build Ships, Houses, buy Farms, set up their Coaches, Chariots, live very splendidly, purchase Fame, Posts of Honour," railed the author. But such "Birds of prey . . . are Enemies to all Communites—wherever they live."[78]

These expressions of class hostility reflected social reality in Boston. The war and the postwar depression had greatly intensified the problems of Boston's laboring people and had hobbled the middle class while enriching the war contractors and speculators—the vanguard of the new entrepreneurial age. These facts were plain to all Bostonians. In their small city it was impossible to disguise the distress of poor

women and children who were being urged to labor in the linen manufactory, or the plight of unemployed artisans and financially ruined
middle-class families. Equally visible were the wartime gains of the few,
perhaps most grossly registered by the return in 1749 of Edmund
Quincy's privateering vessel. One hundred sixty-one chests bursting
with 300,000 pieces of Spanish gold and silver were trundled under
armed guard from Quincy's wharf to his house.

Divisions within the Elite

There were no comparable expressions of antipathy toward the wealthy
or evidence of street politics in either New York or Philadelphia during
the 1740s. To a large extent, politics in Manhattan centered on James
DeLancey and his opposition to New York's participation in a land
war against the French in Canada. Heir to one of the city's great
commercial fortunes, DeLancey received an English education at Cambridge and the Inns of Court, was appointed chief justice of the colony
in 1733, and became a member of Governor William Cosby's inner
circle. DeLancey faithfully served Cosby and his successor George Clarke.
But when George Clinton replaced Clarke and advocated throwing
New York's resources into the war against French Canada, a policy
that seemed to the mercantile interests to promise only heavy taxes,
economic disruption, and the risk of unraveling a half-century of stable
Indian relations, DeLancey switched sides and became the leader of
the antiadministration party that controlled the New York assembly.

In the ensuing political contests, New York City produced the clearest case that had yet emerged in urban politics of a bifurcated elite,
both halves of which worked to mobilize popular support. DeLancey
used the *New-York Evening Post* to reach the electorate; Clinton used
the *New-York Post Boy*. Political pamphlets cascaded from the presses
by the dozens in the four assembly elections held between 1745 and
1752. Each side courted the middle and lower classes, accusing its
opponents of representing wealth and privilege to the detriment of the
common people. At the same time each blasted the other for demeaning
politics by hobnobbing with the poorer sort and soliciting their votes.

Despite these rousing attempts to mobilize the people, election turn-
outs were very low and radical street politics conspicuously absent.
Only 176 votes were cast in the city in the assembly election of 1745.
The primary explanation must be that laboring men were willing to
allow the nabobs of the DeLancey party to control politics in an era

when economic prosperity was widespread, a costly war had been avoided, and no specific economic grievances were present. The governor's party had to seek assembly seats primarily outside New York City, so strong was the merchant-led DeLancey party in the town.

Only once in this era did laboring-class New Yorkers take to the streets. In 1753, at the instigation of about fifty merchants, the legislature considered a law for devaluing the English halfpence from twelve to fourteen to the shilling. Because pennies were commonly used in payment of artisans' wages, the effect would have been a substantial decrease in wages. A riot protesting the proposed change broke out, and one newspaper proclaimed that "all Labouring Men" were hurt by the impending measure.[79] DeLancey, whose well-oiled political machine had relied heavily in the 1740s on laboring-class support, showed his true colors by suggesting that the way to quell the riot was to shoot people down in the streets. By this time he had been appointed lieutenant governor, and the grand jury's report assured him that the riot was the work of ignorant people, many of them not inhabitants of the city. Nonetheless, the riot was a small and isolated disturbance in comparison with those in Boston, where the issues of economic depression, currency reform, and impressment kept the town in turmoil for most of the 1740s.

In Philadelphia, where economic conditions were more favorable than in any other port town in the 1740s and early 1750s, politics were generally unmarked by the violence and polarization that prevailed in Boston. Only King George's War seemed to provide a basis for challenging the dominant Quaker party in the assembly. Officeholders and friends of the proprietary governor attempted to fashion a political party that would break their long domination, but the party's only issue was military preparedness, and unless the threat of French invasion was more than theoretical, they had little hope of success at the polls.

The one bloc of potential voters they might exploit was the Germans, who by 1740 made up about one-third of the population. But the Society of Friends had long before wooed the Germans successfully, promising that Quaker pacifism would keep them safe from military conscription and onerous taxes, which had plagued their existence in the home country. For the Quakers the problem in the 1740s was to maintain influence in a society in which they were fast becoming a minority. For the proprietary adherents the problem was to develop popular sources of support in order to overcome Quaker domination of the assembly. Both parties therefore began thinking more system-atically about the German vote. Neither the Quaker-dominated assembly party nor the Anglican-based proprietary party welcomed the inundation of German immigrants, for Englishmen of both groups regarded them as crude, alien, and too numerous. But neither could afford to leave the politicization of the Germans (who were more interested in farming and family than in politics) to the other side.

The efforts to court the German vote on electoral participation had a dramatic effect. Fewer than 600 persons had voted in the city and county of Philadelphia in 1739; in 1740, the year of the great German mobilization, more than 1,800 persons voted. Although the proprietary party turned out far more voters than at any previous election, the Quakers countered with "about 400 Germans who hardly ever came to elections formerly."[80]

For two years after 1740, the proprietary party courted the electorate and attempted to break the Quaker monopoly on the German vote. The dangers inherent in abandoning the gentlemanly politics that its leaders preferred became frighteningly apparent on election day in 1742, when Philadelphia was shaken by a bloody riot at the polls. Rumors had been circulating that the Quaker party intended to maintain its majority in the assembly not only by garnering the German vote but also by steering unnaturalized German immigrants to the polls. Counterrumors spread that the proprietary party would thwart this attempt by engaging a pack of toughs to frighten away the in-truders. The stories proved to have substance, for when the leaders of the two political factions could not agree on procedures for supervising the election, heated words and curses were exchanged and seventy sailors suddenly appeared at the courthouse, wielding clubs and shout-ing "down with the plain Coats & broad Brims."[81] As the Quaker leaders retreated inside, the sailors filled the air with bricks. German and younger Quakers, momentarily forgetting their pacifist principles, launched a counterattack. "Blood flew plentifully around," the pro-prietary secretary later reported.[82] The Quaker assembly, after con-ducting investigations, concluded that the riot had been engineered by the leaders of the proprietary party. Officially this was denied, but two of the proprietor's chief officials in Philadelphia admitted as much to Thomas Penn.

Unlike the popular disturbances in Boston, the Philadelphia election riot indicated not economic dislocation but rather the lengths to which a minority party would go to defeat its enemies. The proprietary party remained in eclipse for more than a decade after 1742, never offering a full slate of candidates and seldom winning as much as 30 percent of the vote.

In 1747, with French and Spanish privateers operating off the Delaware cape, Benjamin Franklin organized a voluntary military association despite the Quaker-dominated assembly's continued refusal to countenance war appropriations or the formation of a provincial militia. Franklin's extraordinary success in thus influencing public opinion demonstrates how effectively the artisans and shopkeepers of Philadelphia could be recruited by someone outside the established circle of political leaders. Franklin accomplished his goal through his pamphlet *Plain Truth,* published in November 1747. His pitch was to the commonalty, as the title page, signed "A Tradesman," signified. The common folk had always been the heart of civic improvements, he argued, and now must solve for themselves a problem that their leaders had cravenly evaded. Attacking both the Quaker leaders for obstinacy in the face of real danger and the proprietary leaders—"those Great and rich Men, Merchants and others"—for criticizing the Quakers while doing nothing themselves despite their "Wealth and Influence," Franklin called upon the "middling People, the Farmers, Shopkeepers and Tradesmen" to establish their own militia on a volunteer basis.[83] Within days more than a thousand Philadelphians—about one-third of the adult white males—had signed their names to the agreement and begun forming into militia companies.

The Association, as its members called themselves, never engaged the enemy, but they nevertheless conferred upon themselves an enormous collective strength. In Philadelphia, where there was no war-disordered economy, the threat of cannonading by privateers had unified laboring people and given rise to a belief that when difficult work needed to be done, it was the tradesmen and mechanics who could best do it. Boston emerged from King George's War bruised and battered, its population declining, its tax base dwindling, and its streets filled with poverty and resentment against the wealthy. New York and Philadelphia emerged prosperous and expanding, unburdened by heavy taxes or severe poverty and facing the future confidently.

The Seven Years' War
and Its Aftermath

Chapter 5

T HE SEVEN YEARS' WAR, known also as the French and Indian War and the Great War for the Empire, is remembered primarily as the climactic military struggle in which Anglo-American arms finally overcame the hated French and claimed Canada. For the northern seaport towns, however, the war was far more traumatic and paradoxical. The years of bloody fighting on land and at sea lifted the northern commercial centers out of the business depression of 1750–1754, stimulated shipbuilding, meliorated underemployment in Boston, and drove up artisans' and mariners' wages in New York and Philadelphia. Then, after a series of triumphant victories over the French in 1759 and 1760, all three port towns suffered a severe general depression. The war convinced the American colonies of their growing strength and maturity, yet left them depleted of manpower and debt-ridden. It brought an unprecedented infusion of English capital, yet rendered them unusually sensitive to the disadvantages of the British mercantile connection. It promoted the commercialization of life in the port towns, yet exposed in stark detail the social costs of the transition to a capitalistic economy.

Wars have always been engines of social change, and the pattern of wartime boom and postwar bust, usually involving painful political adjustments, is not uncommon. So it is not surprising that the depression that enveloped the seaport towns beginning in 1760 was accompanied by political turmoil. The activation of groups at all levels of society, the elaboration of the apparatus of party politics, the use of shrill rhetoric, and the crystallization of class consciousness had always proceeded most rapidly during periods of economic stress in the port towns and then receded with the return of better days. Each advance in the popularization of politics had swept higher on the beach of traditional ways.

It was not political power itself that the laboring classes yearned for, but an equitable system in which they could pursue their modest goals. Yet their periodic excursions into "radical" politics, in order either to conserve the corporate community or to pry open the doors of opportunity in the new entrepreneurial age, had a cumulative effect. A sense of their own power grew as their trust in those above them diminished and as they acquired experience in making decisions, exercising leadership roles, and refuting those who were supposed to be wiser because they were wealthier. Hence factional politics intensified.

In economic, social, and political terms the Seven Years' War marked a watershed, bringing together all the tendencies of the previous seven decades and setting the maritime centers on a course that led eventually to revolution.

The Resumption of War

The short peace after the Treaty of Aix-la-Chapelle until the outbreak of Anglo-French hostilities in 1748 was really only a time-out from war for regathering strength. France immediately began rebuilding its navy. Meanwhile, American fur traders pushed deep into the Ohio Valley, challenging French interests. But the French had no intention of surrendering the continent to the English, as was apparent from the fort-building program they initiated almost immediately after the peace of 1748.

By 1752 armed hostilities had broken out. The French attacked English trading posts in the Ohio Valley, won the allegiance of several Indian tribes there, and threatened to encircle the American colonists from the west. Internal division crippled colonial attempts to respond to the bold French campaign, as was dismayingly revealed at the Albany Congress of 1754, the first major effort of the colonies to unify for military purposes.

It was decided in the capitals of Europe to force a showdown. In 1754 the ministry in London dispatched General James Braddock, a seasoned veteran, with two regiments and instructed him to recruit two American regiments when he reached the colonies. This united force was to march against the French in the Ohio Valley, restoring to English control areas formerly dominated by Virginia and Pennsylvania traders. Braddock's defeat in 1755, less than twenty miles from Fort Duquesne, by a much smaller French and Indian force was the first of a long string of Anglo-American disasters. But in 1758 the tide turned. Louisbourg, on Cape Breton Island, and Fort Frontenac, at the eastern end of Lake Ontario, fell to Anglo-American assaults. Impressed by the English victories, the Iroquois began to abandon their neutrality. In 1759 Wolfe's dramatic victory at Quebec all but decided the issue. With the fall of Montreal in 1760, French power was irretrievably shattered. Peace was formally established in 1763, when the Treaty of Paris brought an end to almost two centuries of French presence on the continent.

The Seven Years' War brought huge benefits to New York and Philadelphia, smaller ones to Boston. British military operations in North America brought huge war contracts to all the seaports. New York was especially favored because the British strategy against French Canada made it the logical supply base and communications center for the British army.

British troops arrived in the northern ports in numbers that by previous standards were staggering. Two thousand arrived in 1755, 11,000 in 1757, and another 12,000 in 1758. A huge fleet, which in 1758 alone was manned by some 14,000 mariners, also made Boston and New York its new home ports. The ensuing demand for food, alcohol, clothing, boots, and other supplies made fortunes for war contractors and created employment all the way down the line. British expenditures in the northern colonies in 1760 alone were £1,344,309, and spending for the entire war likely topped £5 million. To this must be added another £1.4 million that Parliament granted in subsidies to the colonies for their war effort.[1]

Even merchants who were not major recipients of war contracts did a booming business. With military spending at an all-time high, general prosperity enveloped New York and Philadelphia, creating a strong demand for imports from England; during the war northern consumers purchased English commodities as never before. New York and Philadelphia got most of the military spending, but all the urban centers benefited.

While provisioning contracts made merchant princes of a few well-connected men, privateering enriched others. As in the previous war, New York stood first among the northern ports as a center for the sea marauders. The majority of merchants made more from privateering than from war contracting. In January 1757 thirty New York ships cruised the western Atlantic and ten more were emerging from the shipyards. A year later the governor described "almost a kind of madness to go privateering," a view confirmed by the fact that some 224 privateering ships took to sea before hostilities ceased, about three times the number in King George's War.[2] Not every seaborne soldier of fortune returned a profit to his investors, but 149 prizes were taken in the first two years of the war. One group of seven prizes brought a return of about £100,000 (local currency), and New York's marauders, in capturing 401 prizes, poured more than £2 million into the coffers of the city's investors and prize crews.[3]

Boston and Philadelphia figured much less prominently in this lucrative form of enterprise, although John MacPherson of the Quaker city snared eighteen French vessels on a single voyage in 1758. The fortune he earned made him the greatest parvenu in Philadelphia's history.[4]

By 1759 New York's privateers had so thoroughly cleared the seas of French vessels that they spent their time chasing each other instead of the enemy. The solution to diminishing profits was to divert privateers into illegal trading. Having interdicted most of the French trade to the West Indies, the American merchants now began provisioning the island-bound enemy, which was willing to pay extraordinary prices for foodstuffs rather than starve.

Pennsylvania's wartime governor, William Denny, proved that even the highest appointed officials could be blinded by the vision of war profits. Rather than trading with the enemy, Denny attempted to secure his fortune by selling flags of truce, which enabled the merchant to ship goods to the enemy under the pretext that the vessel was engaged in prisoner exchange. This practice created a fierce demand for French prisoners, who were distributed as broadly as possible among the greatest possible number of ships carrying foodstuffs to the French West Indies. When the supply of prisoners dried up, naturalized Frenchmen in the English ports hired themselves out as surrogate captives. Here was a form of entrepreneurship in which the upper-class official, the middle-class trader, and the lowly French laborer could join hands. Denny began peddling flags of truce in such numbers that by 1759 they were traded speculatively on the New York market.[5]

While merchants gathered in windfall profits from war, artisans, mariners, and laborers in New York and Philadelphia also found their earning power increased. The enormous demand for new ships and the refitting of merchant vessels for naval war brought full employment and sharply higher wages to some twenty crafts associated with ship construction. The frenzied shipyard activity enlarged the Manhattan port's fleet from 157 vessels in 1749 to 477 in 1762 and the combined tonnage from 6,406 to 19,514. This increase of 320 ships in thirteen years meant that New York artisans built more than twenty vessels annually, a hefty increase from previous years. The demand for ship-building craftsmen drove wages up to about double the prewar rate.

For mariners too these were flush times. Dead time between voyages, so prevalent in the trade recession of 1750–1754, was a thing of the past, as the privateering boom put a premium on mariners' labor and drove wages up. So many mariners and landsmen had been attracted to sea banditry that the huge British expeditionary fleet gathered in New York in the spring of 1757 was shorebound because of a shortage of men to hoist the sails. Only the most massive pressing operation ever staged in eighteenth-century America, involving about 3,000 British soldiers who cordoned off the city in the dead of night and plucked clean the taverns and other gathering places of sailors, put the ships to sea. "All kinds of Tradesmen and Negroes" were hauled in, nearly 800 in all, according to printer Hugh Gaine, and about 400 were "retained in the service."[6]

By 1758 privateering had siphoned off so many laboring men that New York's merchants were obliged to offer 5 shillings per day for regular voyages, more than triple the peacetime rate, and the government paid common sailors £5 per month—a master's pay in peacetime—for troop transport service. In Philadelphia mariners' pay doubled between 1754 and 1760, also reaching £5 per month. With such unexampled wages available at sea, who would enlist for military service on land? Desperately trying to attract recruits, New York's assembly kept raising the enlistment bounty, from £1.6 in 1755 to £5 in 1756 to £10 in 1758, and finally in 1759 to £15, the equivalent in peacetime to at least half a year's wages for common laborers.[7] The unscrupulous played both sides of the street. After pocketing their enlistment money for army service, they deserted, headed for the port towns, and signed on the privateers.

For the common tars, however, privateering brought more adventure than profit. They probably garnered on average only about £11 each over the eight years of war, and many suffered injury, imprisonment, or death.[8] The main rewards went to the owner-investors, the officers, and the maritime artisans ashore, who, as a result of the rush to scoop up French riches from an English-dominated sea, received unparalleled wages while enjoying a safe billet.

Prosperity along the waterfront also meant good times for artisans in other sectors of the economy. British soldiers and sailors received wretched pay individually, but collectively they dropped thousands of shillings into the tills of smiling tavernkeepers, barbers, and others in the service trades. By 1757 the British had at least 25,000 army and navy personnel operating in the American theater, and from 1758 to 1760 more than 40,000. Most of them left their meager pay on American shores. Other artisans profited from the business prosperity generated by this massive military spending machine. House construction increased in New York and boomed in Philadelphia, bringing full employment and wages about 25 percent higher than prewar levels for housewrights, bricklayers, stonemasons, glaziers, plasterers, painters, carvers, carters, and ordinary laborers.

While New York and Philadelphia basked in wartime prosperity that extended from lowly laborer to princely merchant, Boston attempted to regain the economic equilibrium that had eluded it for so long. The immediate prewar years had been dismal ones; trade had sunk nearly to the level of forty years before (when the town was only two-thirds as large), housebuilding virtually ceased, and ship construction declined sharply.

War provided an initial mild tonic. But after an expedition against French Canada was mounted from Boston in mid-1755, the staging grounds for military operations shifted southward. Not until 1758, when the assault on Louisbourg was launched, did New England's main seaport get much war business again. Equally dismaying, the prewar loss of shipbuilding to competing maritime centers proved impossible to reverse.

By February 1756, when ship construction was booming in New York, Boston was crying to the legislature for help. The output of the distilleries and sugar bakeries (also mainstays of the town's economy) dropped to less than half the 1746 level. A further blow was struck by the resumption of British impressments, which so disrupted the fishing enterprise that codfish exports fell from 39,756 barrels in 1754 to 22,113 in 1757 and to 16,000 in 1761. With these basic industries crippled and taxes to support the burgeoning poor weighing heavily on those who could find work, many master craftsmen from the middle ranks abandoned the city. The baking business, the selectmen reported, fell by one-third. Tanners had only about 6,000 skins per year to dress from 1754 to 1756, compared with 30,000 per year from 1746 to 1748. Many of the town's fifty glovers, who had produced 1,000 pairs of gloves per year, were "now maintained by Charity in the Alms House."[9] Coopers' work fell by two-thirds. By 1757, according to the selectmen, the unemployed poor were only slightly worse off than a large number of Bostonians "who are . . . in such poor Circumstances that Considering how little business there is to be done in Boston they can scarcely procure from day to day daily Bread for themselves & Families."[10] In the previous war established artisans had had full employment, but rampant currency depreciation had cruelly punished their pocketbooks. In this war the purchasing power of artisans' wages remained stable but work was pitiably hard to find. When Thomas Pownall, the successor to Governor Shirley, arrived in August 1757, he found not the "rich, flourishing, powerful, enterprizing" colony that had been described to him but a colony "ruined and undone."[11]

The war imperiled the economic security not only of those at the bottom of society but also of many in the middle strata, composed of master craftsmen, shopkeepers, and lesser merchants. In the other port towns labor shortages, especially in the maritime sector, sent wage rates up sharply, but in Boston, amid rising food prices, wages remained nearly static. The result was a serious decline of real income for many. In 1757 every seventh adult was receiving poor relief, and annual expenditures for poor relief doubled those of previous years. Because the number of residents able to pay taxes was declining, Boston's poor rates, already by far the highest in North America, more than doubled. The plight of independent artisans and shopkeepers can be surmised from the fact that even sixteen of Boston's wealthiest merchants threatened to relocate in towns with lower tax rates if the legislature would not provide relief. Many middling taxpayers had fallen into arrears by 1757, and the town was obliged to borrow £3,000 from the General Court to pay its schoolteachers, night watchmen, constables, and other municipal employees.

With its local economy badly dislocated and with supply contracts going to New York and Philadelphia, Boston's main contribution to the war proved to be raw manpower. By 1760 nearly every fourth man had been recruited or pressed into wartime service; according to Massachusetts' agent in London, during the entire war "one-third part" of men able to bear arms had "become your Majesty's soldiers."[12] This generous contribution of manpower to military service owed something to the flame of patriotism and antipopery, which burned brighter in the Bay colony than in New York or Pennsylvania, owing to generations of frontier conflict with the French enemy and a heritage of rabid antipapist feeling. But economic necessity was also at work; nowhere else in the northern colonies did so many men lack opportunity and employment. Although neither the bounties nor the pay was half as good as in New York during the first four years of the war, independent craftsmen such as shoemaker Ebenezer MacIntosh, housewright William Curtis, and laborer Obadiah Chandler flocked to the standard.[13]

Philadelphia's mechanics, whether they were masters, journeymen, or apprentices, found steady employment and rising wages. Those who yearned to travel faster roads to fame and fortune could take their chance at privateering, either in their own city or in nearby New York. The city's contribution to the biggest land war in colonial history consisted mostly of a few hundred indentured servants who ran from their masters to join the British colors and a number of recent immigrants who responded to the liberal enlistment bounties that were offered for provincial service.

New York's established artisans found the notion of fighting in the wilderness of Lake Ontario or Lake Champlain even less attractive. War contracts and the rapid growth of shipbuilding ensured excellent wages for almost all craftsmen, and unmarried younger men entertained visions of plundering richly laden French and Spanish ships. At the height of the war New York and Philadelphia contributed no more than 300 and 180 men per year respectively to the troop quotas, and the muster rolls show that a large majority of these were foreign-born— about 90 percent of the New York recruits and 75 percent of the Philadelphians. The muster rolls also show that most were recruited from the lowest ranks of the laboring class, with mariners, laborers, shoemakers, weavers, and tailors predominating.[14]

Not surprisingly, Bostonians also suffered more war casualties than did residents of the other port towns. The 1764 census, taken the year after the peace treaty was signed, listed almost 700 more adult women than men in a town with 2,069 families and 8,100 children. By the early 1760s, as at the end of the previous war, Boston was left with a monumental poverty problem and no solution for employing the large number of husbandless women and fatherless children. Entering the war as a maritime center in difficult straits, the Massachusetts capital suffered as did no other port town, and it was the only northern port not lifted from prewar business depression by the conflict.

Boston's wartime difficulties were capped by one final disaster. Shortly after midnight on March 20, 1760, a fire broke out near the center of town. Boston's ten fire companies fought doggedly against flames and wind, but the blaze raged out of control. The smoke did not clear for four days. "A great part of it now lies in a ruinous heap of ashes," reported one newspaper, "and Boston now looks like a frightful skeleton."[15] Nearly four hundred buildings were in ashes, property worth at least £100,000 sterling was reduced to rubble, and nearly every fifth Boston householder suffered losses, both to the fire and to looters who helped themselves to what remained. Of the 377 victims who received aid, which poured in from churches, private individuals, provincial legislatures, and London merchants, 58 percent were classified as poor. Among widows, who made up almost 30 percent of the sufferers, 82 percent were poor, a final indication that war had left Boston a poor, widowed city in more than one sense.[16]

Postwar Depression

In the aftermath of the North American phase of the Seven Years' War, depression gripped all three northern seaports. In relative terms Boston suffered the least, but that was only because it had known no wartime prosperity. There were a few hopeful signs. The devastating conflagration of March 1760 revived the flagging construction industry. Trade also increased for several years beginning in 1762, but only enough to restore the tonnage entering and clearing the harbor to the levels of the early 1750s, which had been considerably depressed from earlier years. With the end of wartime impressments the fishing industry also regained some of its former vigor.

Offsetting these gains, however, were some severe setbacks to the town's economy. The softest sector was the West Indian trade, always vital to Boston's well-being. Angered by colonial evasions of the Trade Acts during the war, when peace came England sent warships to patrol the northern ports, increased the corps of customs officials, and served notice that it expected the Americans to pay for the maintenance of 10,000 British soldiers who remained on the continent after the Peace of Paris. The new Sugar Act of 1764, governing the duty on foreign molasses, was also strictly enforced. These actions, combined with the severe contraction of British credit after 1762, convulsed Boston's West Indian trade and touched off an epidemic of bankruptcies. By summer the number of vessels employed in that trade had dropped by 80 percent, a heavy blow to all in the maritime crafts and to merchant seamen.[17]

Southward, New York and Philadelphia were stunned by the most serious economic derangement in their histories. The wartime boom had come to a shuddering halt by the end of 1760. War contracts evaporated, and the withdrawal of the British army and navy—18,000 seamen and 22,000 troops in the American theater—meant that English shillings no longer clanked into the tills of tavernkeepers and shopowners. Instead, former indentured servants and British deserters, many of them broken by army service, drifted into the cities in search of employment. As the liberal inflow of specie dried up, credit began to contract and overseas trade languished. The hard money paid to British soldiers and sailors drained back to England. As credit lines were tightened from London, nearly everyone was caught in the contractionary cycle. "Thus the consumers break the shopkeepers," wrote John Dickinson in 1765; "they break the merchants, and the shock must be felt as far as *London*.[18]

4. Plan of Philadelphia in 1762 by Nicholas Scull

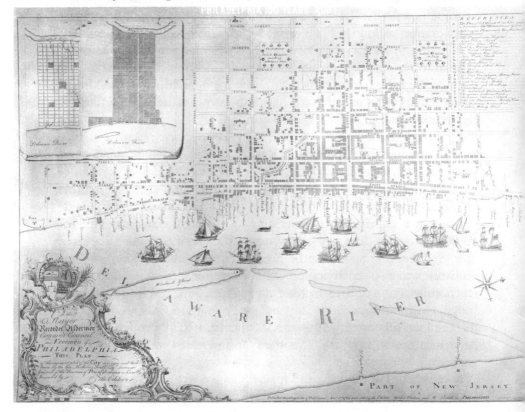

Compounding Philadelphia's problem was the resumption of Irish and German immigration, which had been interrupted during the war. Thousands of poor immigrants arrived to find high prices, few jobs, and reports of spreading conflict between frontier colonists and Native Americans in the frontier areas of new settlement where immigrants generally headed. Many European immigrants who had come to take up farming in western Pennsylvania consequently may have been forced to seek temporary work in the city at a time when the postwar recession was affecting the fortunes of even the best-established families.

Philadelphia's merchants had few resources to combat such business shocks. They had overextended their credit in England in building up large inventories during the war, and now the most precariously situated were forced to declare bankruptcy. Even harder hit were the artisans and laborers. Idle ships meant unemployment for large numbers of merchant seamen and maritime artisans. Not since the 1720s had Philadelphians experienced such a slump, which battered those in the middle ranks as well as those at the bottom. Philadelphia was spared even greater economic misfortune only because the level of house construction remained high.

The postwar downturn also struck New York with a vengeance. In that wartime center of military provisioning, the departure of British troops magnified the boom-and-bust cycle as in no other port. New York got its last contracts as the British fleet fitted out for expeditions against Martinique and Dominica in May 1761. Privateering and illegal trade also dried up as the British fleet drove French ships from the Caribbean and the invigorated British customs service cracked down on American smugglers. "Every thing is tumbling down," cried one of New York's leading merchants early in 1764, "even the Traders themselves."[19] "Trade in this part of the world," lamented a New Yorker in 1765, "is come to so wretched a pass that you would imagine the plague had been here." Another put it bluntly: "The weak must go to the Wall. Frequent Bankruptcies and growing more frequent."[20] House construction also bottomed out after 1763, but sustained shipbuilding mercifully kept that sector of the economy relatively immune from the depression.

In all the seaport towns the greatest hardships imposed by the post-1760 slump fell upon the laboring classes, which included many established craftsmen who occupied positions on the middle rungs of the economic ladder. It was they who had the smallest savings and the thinnest margin between profit and loss. It was also they who lost their modest holdings when they were unable to pay the property taxes. Before 1762 foreclosures in Philadelphia had never totaled more than 50 a year, but they reached 81 in 1763, 90 in 1764, and 111 in 1765.[21]

The plight of the lower and middle classes was compounded by the rising cost of food and firewood and by higher taxes. Wartime demand for food to feed British forces in the Western Hemisphere, followed by crop failure resulting from extended drought, caused a dramatic 29 percent rise in food prices by 1763. In both New York and Philadelphia the cost of living had doubled during the war years. Food prices began to moderate in 1763, but they resumed their upward flight by mid-1765.[22] Country farmers welcomed the higher prices their produce commanded, but for urban artisans and laborers, who spent about half their wages on food, these were distressing times.

Firewood, costing about 9 percent of the household budget, was essential to survival during the winter months. In all the seaport towns wood prices had begun to rise in the 1730s as the deforestation of the urban perimeters sent woodcutters to more distant places, increasing transportation costs. But only during extraordinarily cold winters, such as that of 1740–41, did civic leaders find it necessary to launch public charity drives to provide firewood for the poor. In the winter of 1759–60, however, the price of firewood shot up spectacularly to 3 pounds 10 shillings per cord, an unheard-of price. In the winter of 1760–61, wood prices rose to 40 to 50 shillings per cord in New York.[23] In Philadelphia only a hastily formed Committee to Alleviate the Miseries of the Poor, going door to door to raise contributions and then providing free wood, saved hundreds of families in the town from freezing. When bone-chilling weather returned in 1764–65, the newspapers pleaded for the revival of the committee.[24]

Taxes rose sharply along with food and firewood prices. The Seven Years' War required massive military spending despite parliamentary grants to the colonies of about £1.4 million sterling. For decades Bostonians had had a far heavier tax burden than the propertied citizens in other cities. Now they saw taxes rise to ludicrous heights. In the peacetime years from 1750 to 1754 taxable Bostonians paid an average of about 55 shillings in town and provincial taxes, the highest in history. Town taxes rose only modestly during the war years, but provincial taxes to feed the military machine tripled, shooting up to an average of 88 shillings per person in 1758. The same rate was imposed in 1759 and 1760. For the next five years, with a huge war debt to pay off, the average Bostonian faced an annual tax bill of 89 shillings. But by this time one-half to one-third of the total levies were going uncollected. Bostonians elected their tax collectors partly on the basis of their willingness to collect what they could, given a family's circumstances, and leave the remainder in arrears.

New Yorkers and Philadelphians never felt the tax bite as did Bostonians, but both paid unprecedented taxes to meet the costs of military supplies and salaries. In Pennsylvania the war tax passed in 1756—and continued for the next twenty years—took 1.5 shillings per pound of assessed property from every Philadelphian. This was more than triple the combined provincial, county, and city taxes paid in the prewar years and, when added to spiraling local taxes, exacted from householders about 30 pence per pound of assessed property, compared with the 4.5 pence they had paid from 1718 to 1750 and 7.5 pence from 1751 to 1755.

Gradually the fiscal burden on the laboring classes, especially after the recession beginning in 1760, became intolerable. Unable to extract even the smallest tax from families for whom firewood had to be provided by private or public relief, the assessors began lowering tax levies. But even with these downward adjustments, hundreds of impoverished city dwellers could contribute nothing. Such tax refugees accounted for less than 3 percent of taxables in the period before 1740; in the 1740s and 1750s they rose to about 6.5 percent; with the postwar depression, they totaled nearly 10 percent of the taxable population.

Poverty and Polarization

The severity of the post-1760 depression was most apparent in the rapid growth of a class of truly impoverished persons in the port towns. Pauperism remained most deeply and unshakably rooted in Boston. In 1757 about a thousand people were receiving poor relief. The almshouse was crammed to capacity, especially during the difficult winter months, and officials prevented the problem from becoming even worse only by rigorously applying the warning-out procedure.

In no year before 1753 had as many as 100 people been warned out of Boston. But with the onset of the war, refugees from the frontier began tramping the roads to Boston, and many poor war widows and their children from coastal towns sought a bit of security in the capital city. In every year from 1753 to 1764 the number of those warned out exceeded 100; in two years it rose above 200; and in 1758, when Massachusetts troops suffered heavy casualties at the battles of Ticonderoga and Fort Frontenac, the number reached 326. For the war period as a whole, warnings out totaled about 1,700, almost three times the number for the years from 1745 to 1752. For most of these refugees, jobs were unavailable. Yet they came, hoping against hope that in the colony's largest town things would somehow be better.

Sterling expenditures for the poor, which had never exceeded £730 before 1751, rose rapidly, reaching nearly £2,000 by 1764. In that year Boston began a mass inoculation program to combat an outbreak of smallpox; one-fifth of the 4,977 persons inoculated were described as poor.[25]

The postwar depression also brought suffering to a growing number of New Yorkers. Their households were not widowed to the same extent as Boston's, but hundreds of men had been idled and fell to the care of the town's poor-relief officials. In January 1765 the church-wardens informed the common council that the monies raised for relief of the indigent "have been Long Since Expended" and the "distresses of the Poor" were so great that unless more money was made available immediately, the impoverished "must unavoidably perish" for want of food and firewood.[26] Taking a leaf from Boston's book, wealthy men in the city organized a Society for the Encouragement of Arts, Agri-culture, and Economy, which sponsored a linen manufactory. It em-ployed about three hundred people, but it was only a palliative that could not be sustained.

Philadelphia's poor included not only the unemployed and hard-pressed members of the lower artisanry but also German and Scots-Irish immigrants. The Quaker capital was the best equipped of the port towns to deal with the poor because in the early 1750s, as poverty began to spread, civic leaders had established the Pennsylvania Hospital for the Sick Poor. No project was closer to the heart of Benjamin Franklin, who contended that the care of the sick poor in Philadelphia would not cost one-tenth as much in a hospital as under the old system of out-relief and almshouse care. Moreover, to save the life of an injured or failing mariner or stocking weaver was to ensure that his wife and children would not end up in the almshouse or on the out-pensioner rolls. In addition, such hospitals tended, as an English proponent sug-gested, "to give the poor in general grateful and honorable sentiment and inspire them with proper love and reverence towards their superiors and by consequence promote that harmony and subordination in which the peace and happiness of society consists." Following this line of thought, the managers of the hospital required discharged indigents to sign statements testifying to "the benefit they have received in this hospital to be either published or otherwise disposed of as the managers may think fit."[27]

Beginning in 1752, the hospital played an important role in holding down expenditures for the poor. The number of patients rose steadily and most of those treated were restored to the labor force. That so many of the patients were mariners attests that disease and injury were common among the seagoing part of the lower class. By all accounts the hospital was an uncommon success, benefiting the lower-class laborer and the middle-class taxpayer alike.

By the bitter winter of 1761–62, however, the hospital, almshouse, and modest annual poor tax could no longer support the growing numbers of impoverished Philadelphians. A voluntary Committee to Alleviate the Miseries of the Poor distributed wood, blankets, and stockings to hundreds of destitute laboring families as the rate of those needing assistance rose to about five times the prewar rate.

For four years after the winter of 1761–62 the overseers of the poor struggled to shore up the traditional relief system while urging the government to come to Philadelphia's rescue. Authorities complained in 1763 that "into rooms but ten or eleven Feet square . . . [we] have been obliged to crowd five or six Beds," while other needy persons were billeted in a nearby church.[28] In late 1764, when eleven immigrant ships arrived from Rotterdam and northern Ireland, the distress of the needy again became urgent. Attempts to employ the poor in a hastily erected linen manufactory had no greater success than in New York and Boston, although it employed about two hundred poor women for several winters.

In the harsh winter of 1764–65 emergency measures were reinstituted, private donations solicited, and the poor-tax rate raised from 3 to 5 pence per pound of assessable wealth. The almshouse bulged with about 160 persons, and another 150 received out-relief. Conditions were still not nearly as bad as in Boston, but Philadelphia too now experienced economic derangement and social stress.

The post-1760 depression also struck hard at many in the middle sector. The slippage of many established craftsmen and small shopkeepers was especially important because they were more politically conscious than those below them, who in many cases were recent immigrants, widows, or transients. These middling town dwellers figured importantly in Boston's town meeting, had often sat on New York's common council, and formed the heart of Philadelphia's voluntary militia. A New York artisan, writing in August 1762, spoke movingly of his poverty. He had trimmed every luxury from his household budget, but still "the Expence of living in the most frugal Way has increased so exorbitantly, that I find it beyond my ability to support my Family with my utmost Industry—I am growing every Day more and more behind hand, tho' my Family can scarcely appear with Decency, or have necessaries to subsist." What should he do? he asked his readers. Caught in a wage-price squeeze, he must "starve or be dishonest." His case, he reminded his readers, "is really the Case wih many of the Inhabitants of this City."[29]

The problems of the struggling poor were related to the fact that Americans were becoming less able to control the violent fluctuations in the Atlantic economy. Parliament's drastic overhaul of imperial policy at the close of the war enlarged the American customs bureaucracy, which cracked down hard on colonial smugglers and eliminated profits on the illegal importation of French tea and sugar. The establishment of vice-admiralty courts placed violators of the Navigation Acts beyond the forgiving attitudes of local juries; the Currency Act of 1764, restricting the issue of paper currency in New York and Pennsylvania, put a further damper on trade already shockingly depressed; and the Stamp Act, passed in 1765, laid additional levies on heavily taxed urban dwellers and convinced many that even more fiscal burdens were imminent.

War, it was understood, had required financial sacrifice from everyone in the form of higher taxes. Furthermore, war had spilt much blood, primarily the blood of the lower class. That too was the usual way of things. But to many it was deeply disturbing that eight years of conflict had left in the maritime centers social pyramids that had greatly broadened bases and much-narrowed pinnacles.

This social transformation is statistically measurable in the inventories of estate and tax lists. Most notable is the parallel emergence of the fabulously wealthy and the desperately poor. The growth and commercialization of the port towns had all along provided opportunities for the few to amass wealth, and war accelerated the process by increasing those opportunities. In each city a handful of men in the waning years of the colonial period had estates totaling £50,000 to £100,000 sterling (equivalent to $6 to $12 million in 1985). Wealthy Philadelphians fared better than their Boston counterparts, but in both towns the top 5 percent of taxpayers and decedents with inventoried estates controlled about as much wealth as the other 95 percent combined.

These changes did not go unnoticed by eighteenth-century town dwellers. They could see the urban mansions built during the 1760s, the sharp rise in the number of four-wheeled coaches and carriages imported from London, and the burst of newspaper advertising by those who served the urban rich—wigmakers, silk dyers, retailers of expensive furniture, instructors of music and dancing. In Boston, where fully half the people died with less that £40 personal wealth and one-quarter with £20 or less, John Adams gasped at what he saw when invited to the house of a wealthy merchant. "Went over the House to view the Furniture, which alone cost a thousand Pounds sterling. A seat it is for a noble Man, a Prince. The Turkey Carpets, the painted Hangings, the Marble Tables, the rich Beds with crimson Damask Curtains and Counterpins, the beautiful Chimny Clock, the Spacious Garden, are the most magnificent of any Thing I have ever seen."[30]

This wartime redistribution of wealth, which not only gave the lower classes a smaller share of the community's assets but in the years after 1760 also began to reduce seriously their absolute standard of living, was accompanied by a change in labor relationships and a shift of economic power. One aspect of this was the attempt by some urban artisans, in the boom years of the late 1750s, to free themselves partially from the economic clientage that had traditionally prevailed in the cities. In a free labor market, the artisan moved from job to job, taking his chances of finding employment but commanding higher wages. Usually tied to this practice was the decision to provide his own food rather than eating at his employer's table, thus receiving 1 shilling per day more for providing one's own "diet." As has been pointed out in the English context, "to eat at one's employer's board, to lodge in his barn or above his workshop, was to submit to his supervision."[31] An important part of the transition from the eighteenth-century paternalist labor system to the free labor system of the nineteenth-century factory was to convert these room-and-board benefits into money wages.

This entrepreneurial urge began in the boom era of the Seven Years' War. The carpenters who worked for Isaac Norris, one of Philadelphia's wealthiest merchants and urban developers, had customarily taken their wages on a monthly basis with subsistence provided. Benjamin Morgan agreed in January 1753 to work for 3 pounds 2 shillings 5 pence per month on Norris's diet. He continued to work on these terms through mid-1755. With about twenty-six working days in the month, this figured to about 2.5 shillings per day. If he lost days because of injury or sickness, his pay was not docked. But in 1755, when the construction of the Pennsylvania Hospital for the Sick Poor and of large additions to the statehouse created an unusual demand for artisans in the building trades, Morgan decided to ask for a daily rate at "his own diet," thus sacrificing security of employment but getting 3.5 shillings per day from Norris and 4 shillings for work at the statehouse. William Falk took the same chance in June 1756. Norris agreed "to give him [Falk] after this 3/0 Per Day but not to be obliged to find him work on Rainy days." But the venturesome Falk soon suffered some kind of adversity and was obliged to come to Norris, cap in hand, and ask for a return to the lesser paid but more secure arrangement. "William after writing this Agreement," noted Norris, "changed his Mind and now requests that I advance him Mony to pay his House Rent and agrees to work at 2/6 Per Diem."[32]

The strivings of Benjamin Morgan and William Falk offer a small but crucial fragment of evidence as to how the laboring class was struggling in the second half of the eighteenth century to cut loose from the moorings of an older system. But many learned to their pain that greater freedom involved greater risks—and risks that employers gradually handed willingly over to them. In the postwar slump, many who labored with their hands tried to scurry back to the security of long-term contracts. Meanwhile, those who commanded the labor of voters learned a lesson they would not forget. When times were bad, there was no advantage in making yearly contracts, including the provision of diet, either with artisans on a relatively short-term basis or with indentured servants and slaves on a long-term basis. Contractual labor meant mouths to feed and persons to pay through thick and thin. Converted to wage laborers, these persons could be paid at a higher rate in good times and simply released when business grew slack. Where they would go or how they would subsist became somebody else's problem.

Standing in contrast to these important harbingers of the breakdown of paternalist labor relations in Philadelphia was the persistence of traditional cultural practices in Boston. The leather apron men were the most remarkable of Boston's inhabitants in perpetuating the highly symbolic and ritualistic culture of the laboring classes. The Pope's Day celebration in Boston provides the best glimpse of their universe. Held every November 5 to commemorate the thwarting of the Catholic conspiracy in England, when Guy Fawkes attempted to blow up the Houses of Parliament in 1605, Pope's Day had become the high point of antipopery in New England. Also called Gunpowder Plot Day, this annual festival had special appeal on both sides of the Atlantic among urban artisans, especially of the lower ranks.[33]

In the 1730s or earlier, Boston's artisans began to commemorate the day with a parade and elaborate dramaturgical performances that mocked popery and the Catholic Stuart pretender. For several years artisans from the North End dominated the elaborate mummery. But South Enders soon began competing with them, parading through the streets with their own stage. What started out as friendly competition soon turned into gang battles. The victorious party won the right to carry the opposition's pageantry to the top of a hill and to burn it at night along with their own stage. As the years passed, artisans from both areas formed paramilitary organizations with elaborate preparation preceding the annual event. Though not so intended, Pope's Day became a school for training lower-class leaders, for organizing men who worked with their hands, and for imparting to the lower element a sense of its collective power.

Boston's Pope's Day also involved the ritual of status reversal so well known throughout Europe. November 5 became the day when youth and the lower class ruled, not only in controlling the streets of the town but also in going from house to house to collect money from the affluent for financing the prodigious feasting and drinking that went on from morning to night. These "forced levies" were handed up during the morning by well-to-do householders as a matter of course, for, as Isaiah Thomas, a young printer's apprentice, recalled some years later, "but few thought it quite safe to refuse."[34] Authorities in Boston made attempts to control the violence and indiscipline of Pope's Day, especially after melées in which fatal injuries were inflicted, but in general they were powerless to change its character.

In this increasingly structured social system, in which the distance between rich and poor was widening, the patrician elite could also attempt to demonstrate its power ritually through elaborate weddings, horseracing, fox hunting, dance societies, and other socially exclusive events and organizations. All these manifestations of elite urban culture blossomed rapidly at mid-century. Just as Pope's Day in Boston demonstrated the power and the distinctive cultural traditions of the laboring classes, these upper-class social events exhibited how extensively the wealthy were emulating the patrician conventions of Georgian England.

Yet the crystallizing upper-class cultural forms largely failed to exact deference from those of mean or middling condition. Behind a mask of obeisance, required by the realities of an economic system in which clientage was still widespread, lay an increasingly stormy visage. In the past an irreverent stance toward authority and high status had surfaced episodically during times of stress. Egalitarian feelings had also grown extensively during the Great Awakening. Now hostility toward men of great wealth intensified and the cultural hegemony of the elite, never firmly established, tottered precariously.

For laboring people it was not so much that the opening of a chasm between rich and poor accentuated class differences. Rather, it was that the new wealth of the urban elite, in some not yet fully comprehensible way, was based on class exploitation. When each man could wrest a decent existence from the environment, virtually nobody challenged the concept of social hierarchy or even the accumulation of substantial wealth. But when hard work and frugal living no longer assured leather apron men the basic necessities of life, they began to fathom a connection between their plight and the simultaneous rise of some of their neighbors to towering wealth. By mid-century, poverty in Boston had bred contempt for the rich in a number of political writers and fed the notion that great wealth and grinding poverty were organically connected. "From your Labour and Industry," proclaimed "Phileleutheros" for the mechanics of Boston in 1751, "arises all that can be called Riches, and by your Hands it must be defended: Gentry, Clergy, Lawyers, and military Officers, do all support their Grandeur by your Sweat, and at your Hazard." Yet heavy taxes, stagnation of trade, decay of the crafts, and wartime service "fall signally upon the middle and inferiour Ranks of Mankind."[35] Now such notions entered the consciousness of the laboring classes in the other port towns. "Some individuals," charged a New Yorker in 1765, "by the Smiles of Providence, or some other Means, are enabled to roll in their four wheel'd Carriages, and can support the expense of good Houses, rich Furniture, and Luxurious Living. But is it equitable that 99, rather 999, should suffer for the Extravagance or Grandeur of one? Especially when it is considered that Men frequently owe their Wealth to the impoverishment of their Neighbors?"[36] This was the language of class consciousness, bred of the leather apron men's ancient feelings of worth, nurtured by periodic adversity, and extended and clarified by the depressing aftermath of the Seven Years' War. Direct political action by unlettered but not inarticulate people would follow hard upon such words.

Wartime Politics

Despite these signs of growing class differences and rising class consciousness, the factional politics of the wartime and early postwar years were not always colored by class awareness. From 1755 to 1760 Boston and New York remained quiet. In Boston, despite serious economic difficulties, the political turmoil that had characterized the 1740s ceased. Elections for selectmen and representatives never drew as many people to the polls as had the marketplace controversy of the 1730s. Candidates for selectmen went unopposed.

Boston's popular politicians had no answers for setting the straitened economy to rights other than advocacy of a plentiful paper currency. Impotent to rectify the lack of a staple crop or Boston's waning position in the international commerce of the Atlantic basin, they could only inveigh against the prerogative group's drive for power or appeal to the past, to a simpler world in which communality had stood above individuality.

In New York wartime politics were also unusually quiescent, but for the opposite reason: flush times almost eliminated divisive issues. When profits beckoned and everyone believed he could be a winner in the wartime sweepstakes, the ground for political contention all but disappeared. Only once in this period did New Yorkers so much as go to the polls for a provincial election. Moreover, they were content to let the mercantile elite dominate politics. In marked contrast to the tumultuous 1730s, when artisans had flocked to purchase freemanship and captured control of the municipal corporation, enfranchisement between 1754 and 1760 fell to its lowest level in the colonial period.

New York's only political turmoil during the war emanated from opposition to British policies: the quartering of British troops in the city; impressment, which caused a minor riot in 1758; and an attempt to redirect to British troops American foodstuffs bound for the French enemy in the Caribbean. New Yorkers sought to avoid the inconveniences of war while reaping profits from it.

Only in Philadelphia did the war years roil the political waters. Only here was disagreement widespread on the advisability of pursuing the war and only here did this issue give a faction that had previously quested for power a golden opportunity to mount a political offensive.

The onset of war in 1755 immediately threw Pennsylvania's politics into confusion, for unlike the previous Anglo-French conflicts this one erupted in the colony's backyard. The French moved to gain control of the Ohio Valley and to capture the allegiance of the powerful Indian tribes there. When Braddock's army was thrashed at the Monongahela in July 1755, all of western Pennsylvania, which had been rapidly filling with German and Ulster immigrants for a generation, was thrown into panic. Quaker pacifism seemed ludicrously inappropriate in such a situation. In a stroke the proprietary party, singularly unsuccessful in its quest for power and resigned after the early 1740s to making its weight felt through its control of appointive offices, saw the situation shifting in its favor. The German vote, so crucial in Pennsylvania, might now desert to the proprietary side, for Quaker foot-dragging in the legislature on war appropriations and on a militia act for mobilizing troops was all it would take, or so the proprietary leaders thought, to end the Quaker-German alliance.

The proprietary leaders overestimated their political appeal, however. Germans had not forgotten the deprecatory remarks made earlier about them. What they wanted was not proprietary control of politics but Quaker action on the war emergency. They got it by organizing marches on Philadelphia in November 1755. Seven hundred strong, they demanded what most legislators had already decided—that a militia must be formed and money appropriated to protect the western frontier. Quakers soon began resigning from the assembly. They decided not to run in 1756, a pragmatic concession to the realities of the situation but by no means an abdication of political power, since they continued to exert a strong antiproprietary influence on non-Quakers who ran in their places. After 1755 the issue was no longer whether Pennsylvania would fight but how the war would be prosecuted.

In the end the proprietary party made only small inroads on the hegemony of the popular party and won only a few skirmishes, while losing the larger battles at the polls. Of greater importance was the transformation of Philadelphians' political consciousness during the war, for therein lay the beginning of a wholesale change that reached its climax in the postwar period.

At the heart of this transformation was the involvement of the broad mass of people in fiery political issues and the adoption of political stratagems that struck hard at the management of politics from above. Political mobilization had occurred a generation before when William Keith had led the popular elements in a campaign to pull the town out of the painful depression of the 1720s. The reinitiation of popular politics in the late 1750s, in contrast, occurred during a period of almost unrivaled economic expansion. In both cases, the common threads were a quest for power by two contending factions and the identification by common people of issues that touched their lives. But whereas the conservative element in the 1720s had regarded it as unthinkable

that men of education and substance should indulge in the popularization of politics, the proprietary leaders of the 1750s swallowed all
such elitist pride and hotly pursued the "rabble" whom they despised.
The artisans of Philadelphia found themselves courted simultaneously
by both the assembly party, in which Benjamin Franklin was assuming
a major leadership role as the Quaker politicians retired, and the proprietary party.

At first this broadening of the politically relevant sector was accomplished through resort to the press. In April 1755 an anti-Quaker
pamphlet by Anglican minister William Smith quickly provoked a vitriolic reply. The paper war spread to the pages of the *Pennsylvania
Journal,* and abusive epithets were hurled back and forth. A Franklin
supporter accused Smith of "inveterate calumny, foul-mouth'd Aspersion, shameless Falsehood, and insatiate Malice" and called this prominent Philadelphian a "Frantick Incendiary, A Minister of the Infernal
Prince of Darkness, the Father of LIES."[37] Once the floodgates of literary
assassination had opened, it proved impossible to close them again.
Inevitably, the professional pamphleteer emerged as a new figure in
politics. David James Dove, an ill-paid Philadelphia schoolteacher, seems
to have been the first of this breed, authoring many of the popular
party's poisoned attacks, including a vicious assault in 1758 on the
Philadelphia Academy and its chief tutor and resident, "Dr. Cant," a
man of "slovenly Dress, an awkward slouching Gait, and a blunt mo-
rose, crabbed, paedagogical Behaviour."[38] Dove was so good at his
work that he was soon in the hire of the side he had initially been
employed to attack.

Mixing action with pamphleteering, Franklin followed up his organization of the Philadelphia militia in December 1755 with his clever
XYZ Dialogue, a fictionalized discussion among three Philadelphians
about the volunteer militia act in which "X," an artisan who favored
the law, had all the best arguments. Having "prepared the public mind,"
Franklin went on to orchestrate a general election of militia officers in
each of the city's ten wards and then staged an elaborate parade through
the city of the thousand men who rallied to his private army.[39] As he
had in 1747, Franklin created the sense that the mechanics of Philadelphia were its strength, that the choosing of militia officers was
everyone's concern, and that the proprietary party was out of touch
with the people.

The militia struggle politicized nearly every element of Philadelphia
society. The proprietary leaders organized an independent militia, re-

cruited five companies of supporters, and counterdemonstrated in the streets. Even Franklin's old organization of leather apron men, the Junto, became so obsessed with politics that its Anglican majority harassed supporters of the popular party into resignation. Religious groups split along political lines, and clergymen became parapolitical leaders.

The Anglican clergyman William Smith penned hard-hitting attacks on the Quaker party in 1756 and 1757, causing the assembly to bring a libel suit against him early in 1758. Jailed in January of that year, during the long trial and subsequent appeals to England Smith carried out his clerical duties and political ambitions from the common jail in Philadelphia. Franklin's great popularity enticed many Anglicans away from the proprietary party, and the fact that he was inveterately opposed by the leading Anglican in the city led eventually to a schism in the church. By 1759 about seventy Philadelphia Anglicans—the "lower sort of people," according to William Smith—split off to follow the revivalist preacher William McClanaghan, a "follower of Whitfield's plan" and a man whose "stentorian voice," "strange extempore rhapsody," and "continual ringing . . . upon the words, Regeneration, instantaneous Conversion, imputed Righteousness, the new Birth, &c." deeply offended the conservative followers of the Church of England.[40]

Once they had determined to foray outside their customary strongholds—the courts, the proprietary offices, and the largely powerless city corporation—and to enter the arena of electoral politics, proprietary leaders were obliged to court the people. They circulated petitions door to door. They charged Franklin with "infusing into the people's ears his Republican, Anarchical Notions" and tarred him as a man "of a Republican disposition and levelling Principles."[41] But they could not win the people's vote. Their haughty condescension was obvious, and the people responded with an unrelieved string of electoral defeats for the proprietary party in Philadelphia between 1754 and 1760.

The Intensification of Factional Politics

The beginning of depression in mid-1760 initiated a momentous new phase of politics in the port towns. The economic slump brought no immediate response from those who sought office, for in truth neither popular nor prerogative leaders possessed a formula for economic recovery. As the postwar recession deepened, British imperial reform further impaired the urban economies, damping trade, tightening credit, and limiting the money supply.

While economic conditions worsened in all the northern port towns, political discontent intensified. In Boston, controversy began in 1760, when Thomas Hutchinson and his conservative merchant and lawyer followers decided to renew attempts to dismantle the town meeting system of government. Known in the popular press as the "Junto," Hutchinson's group was composed of wealthy prerogative men who flocked to Governor Francis Bernard when he arrived as Governor Pownall's successor in August 1760. Most of them belonged to the Anglican church and many were related by blood or marriage. These men of the court party had long rankled at the indignity of attending town meetings, where laboring people outnumbered them. As the gulf between top and bottom grew, they became ever more convinced that the herd of common people was congenitally turbulent, incapable of understanding economic issues, moved too much by passion and too little by reason, and unfit to exercise political power. As Governor Shirley had put it in 1747, town meetings were spoiled by too many "working Artificers, Seafaring Men, and low sort of people," who gave them a "mobbish Spirit."[42]

Poverty had erased a large part of Boston's lower class from the roll of voters in the years after Shirley penned this description, and by the 1750s the town meeting had become a thoroughly unplebeian instrument, sending wealthy merchants to the General Court, electing many conservative selectmen, and generally supporting the policies of the well-liked Governor Pownall. But for the Hutchinson Junto this was not enough. Determined to abolish the town meeting, it mounted a campaign to elect four men to the General Court who would convince the legislature to pass a bill for changing Boston into a closed corporation. On the eve of the election a committee of artisans, working with the "old and true" Caucus of the popular party, urged Boston's laboring people to stand up to the Junto and elect men of their own religious persuasion, who would represent their interests.[43]

With both parties courting the electorate, nearly a thousand voters turned out on May 13, 1760—more than had ever before voted in a provincial election. The result was indecisive. Royall Tyler, a rising light in the popular party, was elected, but two of the popular Caucus's candidates lost their seats to moderates whom the Hutchinsonians supported. Not since the marketplace issue of 1736–37 had the populace been so aroused for an election, and as in those years it was the defense of the traditional modus operandi that energized the popular party.

The period immediately after the 1760 election witnessed James Otis's meteoric rise in Boston politics. Otis had practiced law in Boston since 1750, made an advantageous marriage to the daughter of a wealthy merchant, and obtained patronage appointments within the established system. But when Governor Pownall's successor, Francis Bernard, decided to cast his lot principally with the Hutchinsonians of the court persuasion, both Otis and his father, still a power in the House of Representatives, were eclipsed. Bernard's appointment of Hutchinson to a vacancy on the court in September 1760 enraged the Otises and their supporters, and they began a furious offensive against the Hutchinsonians. The issue was the concentration of power in the hands of those who in the popular party view had proved themselves incapable of serving the public good. The special target was Thomas Hutchinson, who by the end of 1760 simultaneously held the positions of lieutenant governor, chief justice of the Superior Court of Judicature, member of the council, probate judge, and captain of Castle William in Boston harbor.

Connected to the issue of narrowly concentrated power was the Writs of Assistance case. It was in the public airing of this case that reaction to new English regulations began to merge with purely local issues. Customs officials in Boston, under strict orders to crack down on years of evasion by Boston's merchants, asked the Superior Court to renew the general search warrants under which the warehouses of suspected smugglers could be entered. Otis joined Oxenbridge Thacher as chief counsel for sixty-three Boston merchants opposing the writs, and Otis's bitter enemy, Chief Justice Hutchinson, sat on the bench.

The legal issue at stake was whether the general search warrants were still authorized by English law and, if so, whether the Massachusetts Superior Court could act as a court of exchequer in issuing such writs. If the answer was yes, then customs officials could reobtain such warrants, which were valid as long as the reigning monarch lived, and use them during daylight to enter any premises in Boston, regardless of whether there was "probable cause" for suspecting illegal goods.

Nothing was decided in court that day in February 1761; Chief Justice Hutchinson adjourned the proceedings for nine months in order to obtain advice from London. In November, after hearing new arguments, he decreed that the writs were legal and authorized the court to issue them. But by this time the case itself had become secondary, for Otis's February oration before a packed courtroom had made him a popular hero. He had argued that Parliament was invading the fundamental rights of her colonists by passing trade laws that violated the "natural equity" of British subjects.[44] The writs were not the real issue, he exhorted, but rather the laws of Parliament that shackled the American economy, laws that made the writs necessary. His stirring words struck a chord among his listeners, and a short time later they elected him to the legislature.

For three years after the 1761 election Otis and other popular party writers filled the *Gazette* with vitriolic assaults on the Hutchinson clique. Hutchinson and his allies answered in kind in the conservative *Evening Post*. Otis molded the opinion of the lower orders, called the "mob" into action, and orchestrated its actions; in doing so, however, he mirrored as well as molded the views of ordinary citizens, whose minds were well attuned to the dangers posed by aristocratic "reformers." Otis did not need to create a feeling of alienation among the struggling Boston artisans. That feeling was already there. Otis played to it with consummate skill.

In his crusade against Hutchinson, Otis was in fact serving two masters—a large group of Boston merchants who had systematically evaded the trade laws and were battling the writs of assistance, and the laboring classes, which had suffered in Boston for more than a generation. To the merchants Otis could offer concrete results: relief from the writs of assistance or, if that failed, legal defense combined with enough resistance within the House of Representatives to hobble Governor Bernard's administration. To the laboring classes Otis had less to offer, since the popular party had no blueprint for economic reform. For now, the middle and lower ranks would have to be satisfied with searing verbal attacks on those who disdained the humble folk and totted up their profits while the poor suffered.

In 1763 the Hutchinson circle mounted another attack on the town meeting system, over which they had all but lost control since the war years of the 1750s. The *Evening Post* ran a scathing "exposé" of the popular party Caucus, which purportedly was written by a former member and thus took on the flavor of an inside report. Caucus leaders, it was explained, conducted all political affairs behind closed doors and in smoke-filled rooms. Convening several weeks before the town meeting, they "appoint town officers, and settle all affairs that are to be transacted at town meeting." Then, "for form sake," the Caucus leaders "prepared a number of warm disputes . . . to entertain the lower sort; who are in an ecstasy to find the old Roman Patriots still surviving." All townspeople were invited to speak at these open meetings, the writer alleged, but to oppose the decisions already made was to earn the "eternal animosity" of the backroom managers, ending forever any chance of obtaining town office.[45] Democracy, as practiced by the Caucus, was nothing but sham, mocked the *Evening Post* author.

In fact the Caucus did operate much as its critic charged. But the electorate did not view this as a betrayal of participatory town politics, because men from the middle ranks were included in the Caucus and it was what the town officers delivered rather than the Caucus's mode of operation that counted with them. Nor could they be swayed by broadsides that sarcastically accused popular politicians of mixing with the mechanics in order to get their votes.

Following the 1763 attacks on the Caucus, 1,089 people went to the polls for town elections, a number never exceeded even in the tumultuous years of the following decade. They drubbed the candidates favored by the court party. James Otis, the leading anti-Hutchinsonian, garnered the largest number of votes and was installed as moderator of the town meeting, equivalent to the leadership role in the anti-prerogative party.

The bitter popular-prerogative party fight of the early 1760s involved a number of specific issues, including the replacement of William Bollan (a leading member of the governor's circle) as the colony's agent in London; the establishment of an Anglican mission in the shadow of Harvard College, which for Congregationalists represented the growing strength and arrogance of those "strangers," who in olden days had persecuted their ancestors; and the multiple offices held by Hutchinson and his network of relatives. But more fundamentally, the struggle involved two competing conceptions of government and society.

James Otis, Samuel Adams, Royall Tyler, Oxenbridge Thacher, and many other respectable if not wealthy Bostonians espoused a vision of politics that gave credence to laboring-class views and regarded as entirely legitimate the participation of artisans in the political process. This was no new conception of the rightful political order but a very old one. The popular party leaders in the early 1760s merely followed in the footsteps of Oliver Noyes, the two Elisha Cookes, James Allen, and Thomas Cushing. The town meeting, open to almost all property owners and responsive to the propertyless as well, at least in theory, was the foundation of this system. Men of social standing filled the leadership roles and garnered most of the important elective posts. Lesser people filled minor offices and voiced their opinions at the town meetings, where they were numerically dominant. The poorest men, excluded from voting and officeholding, tried informally to make themselves heard by the patrician leadership. This was popular, not radical, politics.

For Thomas Hutchinson and his conservative followers, the popular system spelled chaos. "Reform," for these men, meant what it had since the early years of the century—paring the power of the town meeting, substituting appointive for elective officeholders, restricting the freedom of the press, and breaking down the virulent anti-Anglican prejudice that still suffused the popular party.

From 1761 to 1764 proponents of the popular and prerogative conception of politics engaged in a furious battle of verbal abuse that filled the columns of the *Gazette* and *Evening Post*. Charges of "Racoon," "stinking Skunk," "Pimp," "wild beast," "drunkard," and dozens of other choice titles were traded back and forth. But more important than the invective itself was the deep-seated, class-tinged animosity that the polemical pieces exposed: the Hutchinsonians' suspicion of laboring people and hatred of their leaders; the common people's contempt for and anger toward the wealthy, Anglican prerogative elite.

A few examples indicate the depth of feeling. Thomas Pownall, the popular governor from 1757 to 1760, was satirized for ignoring the protocol of class divisions by executing public business without wearing the customary ruffled shirt and powdered wig, by going aboard ships in Boston harbor to talk with "common people about ship-affairs," and by mingling in the streets with the "dirtiest, most lubberly, mutinous, and despised part of the people."[46] The popular leaders, on the other hand, urged Bostonians to oppose "the Leviathan in power [Hutchinson], or those other overgrown Animals, whose influence and importance is only in exact mathematical proportion to the weight of their purses."[47] The popular Caucus, decried a Hutchinsonian, talked incessantly about the right "for every dabbler in politicks to say and print whatever his shallow understanding, or vicious passions may suggest, against the wisest and best men—a liberty for fools and madmen to spit and throw firebrands at those of the most respectable and most amiable character."[48]

The reciprocal animosity and mistrust that suffused the newspapers and pamphlets of the early 1760s reveals how deeply rooted were the social tensions that flourished as Boston's economy, declining in the previous generation, lay enfeebled at the end of the Seven Years' War. The town was no longer one community, a corporate entity with several pyramidally arranged but interdependent parts. Only in the geographic sense did it remain a community at all; in social terms Boston had become fragmented, unsure of itself, filled with internecine animosities. The court party was "modern" in its economic thinking, ready to take its chances in the free play of the international market economy and to welcome the new capitalist age. But its members looked backward in political terms, attempting to convince a broad electorate that the very men who had accumulated fortunes in an era when most had suffered were alone qualified to govern in the interest of the whole community. Lower- and middle-class Bostonians had heard prerogative men voice these ideas for half a century. They understood that each group promoted its particular interests and that aristocratic politicians who claimed to work for the commonweal could not be trusted. Such men employed the catchwords of the traditional system of politics— "public good," "community," "harmony," and "public virtue"—to cloak their own ambitions for aggrandizing wealth and power. The popular party leaders also employed these terms, and some of them wanted to return to what Samuel Adams would later call revealingly "a Christian Sparta"—a simplified, egalitarian sociey in which people were bound by mutual obligation rather than by the cash nexus. But the popular party, while sometimes looking backward nostalgically in its ideal of economic relationships, accepted a participatory form of politics, which alone, it thought, would guarantee economic justice and keep Boston faithful to its traditions.

In Philadelphia also, internal issues overshadowed the new British regulations as a source of conflict in the early 1760s. As in Boston, the political energy unleashed by internal conflict would be rechanneled into the resistance movement against England. For Philadelphians the most galling problem of this era was the refusal of Thomas Penn to pay taxes on his vast proprietary estates. The Seven Years' War obliged the assembly to impose heavy property taxes, and Penn adamantly proclaimed his proprietary right to exempt himself from such levies. The assembly was stymied. It could not refuse to make military appropriations when war was laying in flames large portions of the colony; but unless it bowed to the proprietor's will, he could veto any appropriations bill.

The Pennsylvania assembly twisted and turned but could not find a solution. By 1757 it decided to send to England the master persuader, Benjamin Franklin. His task was to change Penn's mind or to convince the English government to overrule him. But even Franklin's magic was insufficient. In 1758 he began exploring another strategy—direct assumption of Pennsylvania's government by the king. This plan jibed with the prevalent feeling in England that the four colonies in British North America still under proprietary or charter government were anachronisms. For four years Franklin schemed and dreamed in London in vain. The Privy Council took some of the steam out of the movement for royal government by ruling in 1760 that Thomas Penn could not exempt his Pennsylvania estates from taxation; but they also decreed that every Pennsylvania landholder must pay Penn his quitrents in sterling or in Pennsylvania money at the prevailing sterling exchange rate between Philadelphia and London. This was an advantage that Penn had sought for years, for the Pennsylvania money in which his rents were collected was worth only one-half to two-thirds of its sterling equivalent.

This problem of proprietary taxes and rents lay dormant in the early 1760s because with the war at an end, the government needed no new levies. But in the summer of 1763 Pontiac's uprising in the trans-Allegheny west brought war to Pennsylvania's frontier again. One after another, the British forts in the Ohio Valley fell to this pan-Indian offensive, and by June 1763 the Pennsylvania frontier lay under heavy attack.

Once again the assembly had to face the issue of troops and taxes. It voted small supply bills in order to put 700 provincial soldiers in the field, drawing not upon a general land tax but on liquor taxes, slave import duties, and other miscellaneous sources. The frontiersmen were far from satisfied. The troops performed abominably and the angry farmers became convinced that they would have to descend on Philadelphia with clubs and pitchforks to get their point across. Come they did, calling themselves the "Paxton Boys," and on their way they murdered two bands of peaceful, Christianized Indians who lived about a hundred miles west of Philadelphia. Franklin called the Paxton Boys "White Savages" for their mass killing of innocent persons, but most Philadelphians displayed more concern for their own skins than for those of Indians.[49] Backs to the wall, the assemblymen prepared a bill for issuing £50,000 in paper money and raising 1,000 troops, but at the same time they caved in to the principle that the paper money issued to pay the troops could not be used to pay proprietary quitrents.

The Paxton Boys reached the outskirts of Philadelphia several days later, on Febrary 5, 1764, but by then Franklin had again quickly organized a voluntary association of citizen soldiers for the city's defense.

The dénouement of the Paxton affair was not civil war in Pennsylvania but intensified denominationalism and a renewal of the movement to obtain royal government. The Paxton Boys got the legislative action they wanted and returned to the frontier, Pontiac's rebellion was squelched by British troops, Franklin's personal army disbanded in Philadelphia, and the need for additional paper money disappeared. But the air had been dreadfully poisoned, first by the refusal of the resident governor, Thomas Penn's nephew, to sign the military revenue bill unless it contained a clause that would assess the proprietor's most valuable lands, such as vacant lots in Philadelphia, at the same rate as the poorest lands in the colony; and second, by the Quaker-Presbyterian enmity that broke out over the march of the Paxton farmers on Philadelphia.

Thomas Penn readily conceded the first issue, once he heard that his nephew, misled by the proprietary attorney general in the colony, had insisted on such an inequitable provision. Nevertheless, the squabble greatly increased sentiment for royal government. The second issue brought Quakers and Presbyterians to each other's throats because the Paxton Boys were known to be mostly Scots-Irish Presbyterians. Quaker and Presbyterian pamphleteers unloosed an unprecedented barrage of philippics against each other. Quaker pamphleteers portrayed the descent of the Paxton Boys on Philadelphia as part of a global conspiracy, "the latest installment in a perpetual Presbyterian holy war against the mild and beneficent government of the Kings of England."[50] Presbyterian writers attacked the Quakers for being "soft" on Indians and for holding on to civil power when pacifist principles made its exercise during wartime hopelessly ineffectual.

Proprietary policies and the Paxton Boys débacle completely overshadowed the issue of trade regulation in the winter of 1763–64. Equally important, the bitter Quaker-Presbyterian split began to divide the laboring classes. By March 1764 the animus toward proprietor Thomas Penn was so great that Franklin was able to revive the flagging campaign to obtain royal government and thrust it into the center of public concern, an unwise move at a time when royal authority was widely feared, suspected, and even despised.

The renewed campaign for royal government politicized Philadelphia to an extraordinary degree. Franklin orchestrated the blitz against proprietary government, working tirelessly in the assembly and calling for the gathering of signatures on a petition to the crown to assume the colony's government. The ensuing petition war between proprietary and antiproprietary factions was accompanied by pamphleteering, speechmaking, and public assemblies for open-air meetings on an unparalleled scale.

For the proprietary party, the attack on proprietary government was more a blessing than a curse. Having failed to become a force in electoral politics thus far, it now had an issue with which to appeal to the public. Franklin and the assembly party were in fact making the political mistake of their lives, advocating royal government when most people believed that royal government, up and down the coast, had laid siege to traditional rights. The papers were filled with reports of the stamp duties about to be imposed without the colonies' consent; of a currency act that would abolish Pennsylvania's paper money, embraced since the 1720s as a boon to the colony's prosperity; of the vice-admiralty courts, which would try violators of the Navigation Acts before a distant judge rather than before local juries; and of the British men-of-war that patrolled the lower Delaware Bay, searching every ship standing out from Philadelphia for illegal goods. Under these circumstances, the people proved hard to convince. The proprietary party had by far the more popular appeal: keep provincial government out of royal hands.

The long-range outcome of the fierce politicking over royal versus proprietary government was that Thomas Penn retained his proprietary power until the outbreak of revolution. The short-range result was that Franklin was defeated in the assembly election of October 1764, the only defeat he ever suffered at the polls. More significantly, the campaign involved an extraordinary advance of the people at large to a position of importance. The Franklin forces began the process with mass meetings and door-to-door solicitation of signatures in April and May 1764. The proprietary party replied with counterpetitions. Every white adult male in Philadelphia found himself being courted by the leaders of the two political factions. His religion, class, or ideological position mattered not so long as he would sign. Never in Pennsylvania's history had the few needed the many so much.

As the battle thickened, pamphleteers reached new pinnacles of abuse and scurrility. Franklin was reviled as an intellectual charlatan who begged and bought honorary degrees in England, a corrupt politician,

and a lecherous old man. His friends responded by labeling an opposition pamphleteer "a Reptile" who "like a Toad, by the pestilential
Fumes of his virulent Slabber," attempted "to blast the fame of a
PATRIOT." William Smith, coordinator of the opposition, was advertised to be a "consumate Sycophant," an "indefatigable" liar, and an
impudent knave with a heart "bloated with *infernal Malice*" and a head
full of "*flatulent Preachments*."[51] As for the Presbyterians, a Franklinite
pamphleteer renamed them "Piss-Brute-tarians (a bigotted, cruel and
revengeful sect)."[52]

The more scabrous the literature became the more widely it was
distributed, often gratis, to all who would accept it. Before the campaign was over, more than thirty-five broadsides and pamphlets, not
to mention scores of newspaper fusillades, filled the streets. Chief Justice William Allen, a man who had risen from sugar boiler to wealthy
merchant, found himself called "Old Drip-pan," an adulterer who had
slept with his Negro slaves for twenty years, and "a tricking Judge,
and Presbyterian Jew." The pamphleteer David Dove stood accused
of sodomy, misogyny, miscegenation, concupiscence, and the almost
unheard-of flaw of teratology. William Smith was charged with spreading venereal disease to his female slaves, and Franklin too was charged
with sexual irregularities.[53]

Beneath the mudslinging lay the tension created by a combination
of events: the economic depression of the early 1760s, the bitter disputes with proprietor Thomas Penn, the renewal of Indian attacks
along the colony's frontier, the anger and anxiety created by the Paxton
marchers, and the threat imposed by the restrictive new British policies.
Never in the city's history had so many adversities torn simultaneously
at the fabric of society. Never had answers to such intricate problems
been so hard to find, and, in the absence of clear-cut solutions, the
pervasive uneasiness was translated into party feuding and personal
invective.

Religious leaders were inevitably drawn into the fray. Foremost
among them were the Presbyterian ministers Gilbert Tennent, Francis
Alison, and John Ewing. Neither they nor their religious brethren were
fond of proprietary government, but given the bitter Quaker attacks
on Presbyterians and their conviction that the move for royal government was designed in part to perpetuate Quaker supremacy in the
colony, these antiproprietary sentiments evaporated. Presbyterians put
aside their internal divisions and began to organize as a pressure group.
The first committees of correspondence in the revolutionary era were

formed not in Boston by radical opponents of English policy but by Pennsylvania Presbyterians, who by May 1764 had created a colony-wide network in order to fight Franklin's campaign for royal government.

German religious leaders were also sucked into the political maelstrom. There had always been considerable tension between the German church groups—Lutherans and German Reformed—and the German sectarians—Moravians, Schwenkfelders, and other pietist groups. For many decades Quakers had enjoyed the support of most Germans, regardless of their religious leanings. But since the 1740s the more hierarchical, conservative church groups had very slowly been drawn toward the strongly Anglican proprietary party. The Anglicans now worked hard to convert them to the anti–royal government position. By the fall of 1764 Carl Wrangel and Henry Muhlenberg, the Lutheran church leaders in Philadelphia, and Christopher Sauer, Jr., and Heinrich Miller, the German printers, were in the fold. All of them wrote, translated, or printed anti-Quaker pamphlets for distribution in German neighborhoods and helped to garner German signatures on petitions opposing royal government.

The disastrous campaign for royal government splintered not only the Germans of Philadelphia but also the city's non-German laboring men. Those gathering signatures for the royal government petitions in the spring of 1764 fared poorly. The proprietary party proved at least as successful in recruiting plebeian support.

When the petition war merged into the annual assembly elections of October 1, the damage sustained by the assembly party became apparent. Heartened by their successful appeal to the laboring classes, and particularly to Germans and Presbyterians, the proprietary leaders petitioned Thomas Penn for the appointment of German justices of the peace to the county courts and astutely arranged to place one Scots-Irish and two German candidates on the eight-man Philadelphia proprietary ticket. They also disbursed money liberally for the naturalization fees of recently arrived Germans, who thereby acquired voting privileges. Presbyterian and Anglican clergymen also sought to influence voters from the pulpit. Beleaguered Quakers and Franklinites, accustomed to the solid support of laboring people, could only privately deplore the "unwearied Endeavours [of the proprietary leaders] to prejudice the minds of the lower class of people."[54]

Inflammatory rhetoric, a flood of polemical literature, the churches' unabashed participation in politics, the mobilization of social layers previously quiescent and unwelcome in political affairs—all combined to produce an election in which almost everybody's integrity was questioned and every public figure's use of power was attacked. Both sides presented themselves as true representatives of "the people." The effects were dramatic: a record number of Philadelphians, nearly 1,500, including the infirm and aged who were carried to the courthouse in litters and chairs, turned out for the election. A bit of postelection doggerel caught the spirit of the contest:

> A Pleasant sight tis to Behold
> The beggars hal'd from Hedges
> The Deaf, the Blind, the Young the Old:
> T'Secure their priveledges
> They're bundled up steps, each sort Goes
> A Very Pretty Farce Sir:
> Some without Stockings, some no Shoes
> Nor Breeches to their A——e Sir.[55]

When the returns were counted, both Franklin and his political protégé Galloway had lost in the city to men on the proprietary slate, and four of their ticket, all incumbents, had lost seats from Philadelphia County. Franklin had been defeated by defecting Germans and Presbyterians. How deeply the laboring ranks had been split is evident from the city vote: Franklin and his running mate garnered 707 and 669 votes respectively; their proprietary opponents received 815 and 786. The master politician, who had so often in the past swung the public behind his programs for reform, had badly miscalculated sentiment among his own leather apron men.

Issues of local political control, broached when postwar recession and onerous new British policies had shaken the seaport economies, brought popular politics to a new pitch in the early 1760s. The prerogative party in Boston was almost entirely Anglican and highly aristocratic and therefore could make virtually no inroads on the city's strongly Congregational artisans and shopkeepers. In Philadelphia, in contrast, the laboring ranks were composed of roughly equal numbers of Scots-Irish Presbyterians, Lutheran and Reformed Germans, and English Quakers, whose unity dissolved in the face of issues with no specific economic content—issues such as the Paxton Boys' march or the move to dismantle the proprietary government. Taking advantage of these rifts, the Anglicans were able to draw to their side, at least temporarily, a major part of the laboring classes. In New York artisans and shopkeepers were also divided in the election of 1761, when Anglicans and Dutch Reformed voters were opposed by Presbyterians in a continuation of a long-standing religious split. But neither party was attempting to alter the ground rules of politics as in the other two cities, so New York was relatively unscathed by divisive issues as the imperial crisis loomed.

Despite the unique features of political life in each port town, there were aspects and effects of turmoil in the early 1760s that the cities shared. In each the elite was divided, their attempts to activate and obtain the support of the lower classes were unusually strenuous, the presses turned out polemical literature as never before, the clergy became deeply involved in politics, and electoral participation reached new heights. The full significance of these developments would not become apparent until local conflicts began to intersect with imperial issues. This convergence occurred with dramatic swiftness in the shocking events that took place in the summer and fall of 1765.

The Stamp Act

ONLY THE ECONOMIC buffeting suffered by the seaport towns after 1760 and the buildup of antagonisms on local issues can fully explain the extraordinary response to the Stamp Act. Likewise, only the social circumstances and previous political experience of each city can explain the striking contrast between Philadelphia's reaction to the Stamp Act and those of Boston and New York.

The Stamp Act crisis in the cities also provides a key to the course of revolutionary politics in the years that followed. The extraordinary disturbances in the northern cities show dramatically how discontent over England's tightening of the screws on her American colonies merged with resentment over local events. In 1765 the first signals of the dual revolution appeared. The defiance of authority and destruction of property by people from the lower social ranks redefined the dynamics of urban politics and initiated a ten-year internal struggle for political control among the various social elements protesting English rule. The mass disorders surrounding the Stamp Act revealed to many in the urban patriciate the ghastly logic of four generations of political development in the American commercial centers and convinced them that the enemy within was as dangerous as the enemy without.

Crowd Action in Boston

The Boston press had been filled for months with reports of the impending stamp duties. Parliament's intention in passing the Stamp Act was to make the Americans share the cost of keeping 10,000 British regulars in North America as guardians of the frontiers and to remind the ill-disciplined colonial subjects that they were still beholden to the mother country. No amount of colonial lobbying had altered Parliament's decision to put the Stamp Act in force on November 1, 1765.

In an impoverished town whose tax burden was already by far the greatest in the British empire, the additional stamps, required on every newspaper, pamphlet, almanac, legal document, liquor license, college diploma, and pack of playing cards, were highly unpopular.

At dawn on August 14, Bostonians awoke to find a rag-clad effigy of stamp distributor Andrew Oliver hanging from a huge elm tree at the crossing of Essex and Orange streets in the South End. Dangling beside it was an effigy representing two men close to the king who were thought to have played the largest role in fashioning the detested new imperial policies—the earl of Bute, the king's trusted adviser, and George Grenville, first lord of the Treasury.

When Sheriff Stephen Greenleaf attempted to cut down the effigies at the order of Chief Justice Hutchinson, he was surrounded by an animated crowd. All day the town buzzed with rumors. Every farmer bringing produce into town was detained by the crowd until he had got his goods 'stamped." At the end of working hours, a mass of working men began to form for a mock funeral. Their leader was Ebenezer MacIntosh, a twenty-eight-year-old shoemaker who knew poverty at first hand. His mother had died when he was fourteen and his father, for years a part of the tramping poor of eastern Massachusetts, had been warned out of Boston two years later, in 1753, although he had served as a soldier at Castle William in the 1730s and 1740s.

With MacIntosh acting as leader, the crowd cut down Oliver's effigy as dark came on and headed toward the South End wharves, where Oliver had built a brick office in July, rumored to be the place from which stamps would be distributed. It took less than thirty minutes to level the building. The timbers were "stamped" in derision of the Stamp Act and carried to Oliver's luxurious house at the foot of Fort Hill. At nightfall they were used to start a bonfire atop the hill. Oliver's brother-in-law Thomas Hutchinson tried to reason with the people, by now in high spirits and completely unopposed, but his appearance only maddened the crowd, which began to destroy Oliver's stable and his coach and chaise. Finally the mob tore into Oliver's house, breaking windows and looking glasses, demolishing the elegant furniture, emptying the contents of the splendidly stocked wine cellar, and tearing up the gardens. Oliver promptly asked to be relieved of his commission as stamp distributor.

Twelve days later it was Thomas Hutchinson's turn. The crowd warmed up by attacking the luxurious houses of William Story, deputy register of the Vice-Admiralty Court, and Benjamin Hallowell, comptroller of customs. Then they moved across town to Hutchinson's mansion. Catching the chief justice and his family at the dinner table, the crowd smashed in the doors with axes, sent the family packing, and then systematically reduced the furniture to splinters, stripped the walls bare, chopped through inner partitions until the house was a hollow shell, destroyed the formal gardens in the rear of the mansion, drank the wine cellar dry, stole £900 sterling in coin, and carried off objects of value. Led by MacIntosh, the crowd worked with almost military precision to raze the building. "The Mob was so general," wrote the governor, "and so supported that all civil Power ceased in an Instant, and I had not the least authority to oppose or quiet the Mob."[1] The next day, tears in his eyes and bereft of his judicial robes, Hutchinson appeared in his courtroom, an anguished man who had been savagely discredited in the town he believed he had dutifully served for thirty years.

In pillaging the Boston mansions of Oliver and Hutchinson, and in storming the houses of William Story and Benjamin Hallowell, the crowd was demonstrating against the Stamp Act and the tightening of trade restrictions. But it was also expressing its anger at far more than parliamentary policy. Stamp distributors were intimidated and handled roughly in many other towns, but nowhere did the crowd destroy property on such a grand scale and with such exacting thoroughness.

The Boston disturbances demonstrate the fragile and shifting relationship among different elements in the popular party. James Otis commanded the columns of the *Boston Gazette* and Samuel Adams directed the Caucus. But who controlled the streets? The effigies of Oliver and others were prepared under the direction of some members of the Caucus who had formed themselves into the "Loyal Nine"— including Benjamin Edes, printer of the radical *Gazette;* John Avery and Thomas Chase, distillers; John Smith and Stephen Cleverly, braziers; and Thomas Crafts, a painter. These were established tradesmen who had long suffered from Boston's sunken economy. However, the marches themselves and most of the carefully planned dirty work on the houses of the wealthy had been left to the lower artisans, laborers, and mariners, while the more "respectable" members of the alliance melted into the night. The crowd, led by a poor shoemaker, demonstrated its deep hostility to elitist oppressors such as Hutchinson, who had given his opinion in the last war that a £5 bounty offered to the poor for enlisting was too generous.

Besides intimidating British officialdom and its colonial collaborators, which is probably all that its leaders intended, the crowd gave vent to years of resentment at the accumulation of wealth and power by the prerogative faction. Behind every swing of the ax and every hurled stone lay the fury of a Bostonian who had read or heard the repeated reference to impoverished people as "rabble" and to the Caucus as a "herd of fools, tools, and sycophants," and who had suffered economic hardship while others fattened their purses.[2] These activists had heard it said over and over that "Luxury and extravagance are . . . destructive of those virtues which are necessary for the preservation of liberty and the happiness of the people." They had burned inwardly at the assertion that poverty was the best inducement for industry and frugality and that "the common people of this town and country live too well."[3] Now, in August 1765, they had some scores to settle. They had lost faith that opportunity or equitable relations any longer prevailed in their town. If they could not change this situation, they could at least administer their own kind of rough justice to those who judged them so harshly.

The political consciousness of the crowd and its use of the Stamp Act protests as an opportunity for an attack on wealth itself were remarked upon again and again in the aftermath of the August forays. The mob that had worked "with a rage scarce to be exemplified by the most savage people," wrote the governor, targeted fifteen additional houses in what was becoming "a War of Plunder, of general levelling and taking away the Distinction of rich and poor."[4] On September 10, two weeks after the destruction of Hutchinson's house, a Boston merchant wrote that "the rich men in the town" were seized with apprehension and "were moveing their cash & valuable furniture, &c" to the homes of poorer friends who were above the resentment of the lower class. Another merchant confirmed that the "infernal Mob" was threatening "many of the most respectable Inhabitants with destruction to their Houses, Furnitur &c."[5]

Many of the Caucus leaders deplored the sacking of property on the night of August 26 while upholding the actions of August 14 as a legitimate defense of the people's rights. Violence in limited doses was all they were ready to prescribe. Intimidation of obnoxious officials, not class warfare, was what they wanted. The town meeting hurriedly expressed its "utter detestation" of the recent violence.[6] But this was as far as the middle-class Caucus members and Whig merchants were prepared to go. Every effort by Hutchinson and the governor to indict the mob leaders, who could easily have been identified, was frustrated. No one stepped forward to claim the £300 reward offered for information leading to the conviction of the riot leaders.

Seen in the context of three generations of social and economic change in Boston, the Stamp Act riots provide the most illuminating example of how the molten metal of group consciousness and feeling was smithied out in the course of defying authority and restoring the "moral economy." Members of the Boston "mob" needed no upper-class leaders to tell them that economic stagnation had been strangling their opportunities and otherwise affecting their lives. They had indeed acted in "a rage," as so many of the accounts expressed it, and their rage was directly linked to the conditions of their lives and to the connection they perceived between their plight and the exercise of power by the prerogative elite. The rituals of public humiliation carried out on the nights of August 14 and 26 marked the culmination of an era of mounting protest against oligarchic wealth and power. At the same time they were attacks on the symbols of wealth and ostentatious displays of wealth rather than frontal assaults on the economic and social order. In addition, the crowd actions demonstrated the fragility of the union between protesting city dwellers who occupied places in the lower strata of the laboring community and their more bourgeois partners, who in the uninhibited attacks on property saw their control melting away. It was Ebenezer MacIntosh who controlled the crowd, not Samuel Adams, James Otis, or any of the Loyal Nine.

This rapid emergence of MacIntosh was obvious to everyone in Boston. By the time Pope's Day arrived, less than ten weeks after the destruction of Hutchinson's house, the press was calling him "Commander of the South [End]" and was giving him coverage for effecting a "treaty" with his North End counterpart whereby a peaceful and united Pope's Day parade would replace the traditional bone-breaking brawl. It was no wonder that the elite began to refer to MacIntosh as "a Masaniello."[7] Like the Neapolitan rebel of 1647, he had come from nowhere to take command of a force so powerful that it appeared nobody could stop it.

By mid-December MacIntosh's power had become even more apparent. Several weeks before, Andrew Oliver's commission as stamp distributor had arrived from England, and although Oliver had previously promised that he would give up his commission, Bostonians wanted an immediate and unequivocal renunciation. They also wanted his public humiliation. In the end, MacIntosh marched him across town in pelting rain to the Liberty Tree in the South End, where the crowd watched Oliver eat humble pie as he sardonically declared that he would "always think myself very happy when it shall be in my power to serve this people."[8] The drenched observers cheered and returned to their places of work. Having forced Oliver's resignation, the alliance of protesting merchants, shopkeepers, artisans, laborers, and mariners convinced the customs officers to open their doors for business, allowing the portbound fleet to embark, in defiance of an act of Parliament, with unstamped clearance papers.

Popular Resistance in New York

In New York and Philadelphia the growing resentment toward wealth and luxurious living, the rejection of an elitist conception of politics, the articulation of laboring-class interests, and the struggle for power within the emerging patriot movement also gained momentum in 1765. As in Boston, the extraordinary new vigor of urban laboring people in defining and pursuing their goals raised the specter of a radicalized form of politics and a radically changed society in the minds of many middle- and upper-class city dwellers. Many of the initial leaders of the resistance movement against England would later abandon it out of their fear of social disorder.

In New York, where the postwar depression wreaked havoc among the hundreds of shipbuilders and mariners who had been essential to the town's impressive maritime advance during the war, resistance to the Stamp Act began later than in Boston but followed a similar pattern. By late August sentiment among the lower ranks, especially maritime workers, had coalesced sufficiently to convince stamp distributor James McEvers, a wealthy merchant, to resign his post, fearing that "my House would have been Pillag'd, my Person Abused and His Majestys Revenue Impair'd."[9] A month later, when the English ship carrying the stamps for New York arrived, several thousand New Yorkers swarmed to the shoreline to prevent them from being landed. On October 24, after a military regiment brought the stamps ashore in the dead of night and took them to Fort George, handwritten placards appeared throughout the town warning that "the first Man that either distributes or makes use of Stampt Paper let him take Care of his House, Person, and Effects. We dare. VOX POPULI."[10]

November 1 was the date when the Stamp Act went into force. Thereafter no ship could leave a colonial harbor without customs clear-

5. *Plan of New York in 1767 by Bernard Ratzer*

ance documents to which the hated stamps had been properly affixed. As the fateful day approached, tension mounted. On October 31 the town's merchants met at Burns's City Tavern and agreed not to import any English goods while the Stamp Act was in effect. Simultaneously artisans, mariners, and laborers met on the common and displayed their collective strength by marching down Broadway to Fort George and back in the most impressive show of lower-class power since the days of Jacob Leisler. Badly split in the election of 1761, they were now showing strong signs of solidarity. The response of seventy-seven-year-old Governor Cadwallader Colden was an order to strengthen the fortifications at Fort George in preparation for a showdown with the mob.

If action was what Colden craved, he did not have long to wait. On the night of October 31 the crowd assembled and soon was roaring through the streets, threatening the homes of those suspected of sympathizing with British policy. "Some thousands of windows Broke," wrote one British officer who watched the scene. But this was only a warm-up for the next night. On November 1 a huge crowd assembled and agreed to deliver a strident message to the governor, calling him "the Chief Murderer of their Rights and Privileges" and warning that "you'll die a Martyr to your own Villainy, and be Hang'd like Porteis, upon a Signpost, as a Memento to all wicked Governors, and that every Man, that assists you, Shall be, surely, put to Death."[11]

At nightfall the street theater began. Some two thousand New Yorkers marched by candlelight to Fort George, where they strung up effigies of the devil and Governor Colden. After figuratively hanging the governor, the crowd cut down the effigy, carried it to his mansion, liberated his prize chariot, and with "the grossest ribaldry" paraded the effigy around the town in the coach.[12] The high point of the celebration came when the shouting crowd hurled the governor's coach and two sleighs into a bonfire and hoisted Colden's effigy atop the flaming heap.

Warming to their task, the people then surged through the streets to the house of Major Thomas James, commander of the sixtieth Regiment of royal artillery at Fort George. Hated for his outspoken defense of the Stamp Act and his promise that "the stamps would be crammed down New Yorkers' throats," James now felt the power of the crowd, which gutted his house and destroyed its furnishings.[13] Not until four in the morning did the throng retire.

Four days later the crowd regathered, this time to demand the surrender of the stamps that were housed at Fort George. Several thousand people marched to the walls of the fort, taunting the guards to fire and hurling insults liberally interspersed with bricks, stones, and garbage. The troops held their fire, and Colden, withdrawing from the brink, agreed to surrender the stamps to the city officials. A few days later, with five thousand people lining the streets, the stamps were hauled in carts to the city hall and handed over to the mayor and aldermen.

In New York no Masaniello arose from the anonymous masses to lead the crowd as in Boston. Leadership was more fragmented, resting mostly in the hands of a group of popular tradesmen and privateering captains who had risen from obscurity to small-trader status during the Seven Years' War. They included several ship carpenters, instrumentmaker John Lamb, upholsterer Marinus Willett, ship captains Isaac Sears and Alexander McDougall, and schoolteacher Hugh Hughes. Styling themselves the "Sons of Liberty," they maneuvered for control of men in the lower ranks. Also contending for the allegiance of the laboring people were Whig merchants and lawyers William Smith, Jr., John Morin Scott, and William Livingston, the anti-DeLancey triumvirate that had worked hard in the elections of 1761 to gain the artisans' support. After the "General Terror of November 1–4" the lawyers, closely tied to the city's Whig merchants, secured the backing of McDougall and then "went around to every part of the town," attempting to enlist the support of other sea captains and their lower-class followers.[14] They knew they could not do so without the support of those below them, but they were also coming to fear the awful power of the assembled artisans and their maritime compatriots.

The tension between upper-class Whigs and laboring-class radicals increased throughout the remainder of 1765. Even though the stamp distributor resigned his post, the law went into effect on November 1. Thereafter any ship leaving port without stamped documents defied the king and Parliament. The alternatives for the American seaport dwellers were to maintain an embargo until British policy changed or to ship in defiance of the law. New Yorkers met on November 26 to decide on instructions to the city's representatives to the assembly, which was debating the issue. Such an open-air referendum was itself a radical innovation in New York, for it invited all the people to debate publicly and to reach a decision on a momentous issue in a town meeting format that had been known previously only in Boston. The outcome, however, was less than radical, for the Livingston Whigs, preferring passive resistance through embargo to active defiance of English law, gained control of the popular meeting and pushed through their embargo resolution.

Thwarted at this meeting, the radicals found other ways to gain their objective. They exerted pressure on the customs officials, who opened the port and cleared ships without stamped papers. "This step," wrote the latter, "we thought more adviseable as we understood the Mob (which are daily increasing and gathering strength, from the arrival of Seamen, and none going out, and who are the people that are most dangerous on these occasions, as their whole dependance for a subsistence is upon Trade) were soon to have a meeting."[15] As in Boston, the lower ranks were feeling their power and beginning to take independent action.

In two significant ways, however, the New York radicals differed from their Boston counterparts. First, New York had prospered during the Seven Years' War whereas Boston had languished, and leaders such as Lamb, Sears, and McDougall, who were sons of artisans, had risen into the middle class whereas men such as Ebenezer MacIntosh had not. Thus the voices raised against the wealthy were more muted in New York than in the capital of Massachusetts. Second, in Boston the radicals were wont to invoke the old Puritan ideals of community and to deplore the pursuit of private interest. New Yorkers, legatees of a far more utilitarian, less religiously oriented culture and part of an urban society in which entrepreneurship had been legitimated by the successes of the Seven Years' War, looked self-interest in the eye and made no apologies for it. "*Self Interest* is the grand Principle of all Human Actions," declared John Holt's radical *New-York Gazette;* "it is unreasonable and vain to expect Service from a Man who must act contrary to his own Interests to perform it . . . The publick Happiness is then in the most perfect State, when each Individual acts the most agreeably to his own Interest."[16] Here was an argument that could be aptly employed in the resistance to oppressive English policies. As "Freeman" observed, both the colonies and the mother country had interests that were legitimate to pursue, and if "the benefit of one must necessarily be in the same degree hurtful to the others, then these two Interests can never unite in the same government; their connection should be broken off, the jarring interest should be removed, or new modelled into Harmony & confidence with the Rest."[17] Thus "the radicals reduced reason to a mere calculation of personal interest," a formulation that would have drawn immediate howls from the likes of Samuel Adams or James Otis in Boston.[18]

Political Alignments in Philadelphia

Philadelphia's reaction to the Stamp Act contrasted starkly with those of Boston and New York. Stamps were no less hated in Pennsylvania's capital, but the city remained singularly free of the ritual processions, effigy burnings, and property destruction that characterized the other port towns. Philadelphia's stamp distributor was John Hughes, a baker turned merchant, one of Franklin's oldest friends, a brother of New York radical Hugh Hughes, and, until 1765, a stalwart of the popular assembly party.

By September 1765, Hughes was one of the least popular men in Philadelphia and the proprietary party was charging that his patron, Franklin, had actually helped write the Stamp Act in London. On the evening of September 16, when news arrived that George Grenville, one of the authors of the Stamp Act, had resigned as chief minister, a celebrating crowd assembled at the London Coffee House, owned by Presbyterian William Bradford, printer of the *Pennsylvania Journal* and a member of the newly formed Philadelphia Sons of Liberty. Toasts to Grenville's ill health turned to cries that the houses of Franklin, Galloway, Hughes, and others involved in supporting the Stamp Act "should be level'd with the Street."[19] It appeared that the angry crowd might emulate their Boston brethren until Joseph Galloway marshaled about eight hundred men, whom he had organized into an Association for the Preservation of the Peace. The Association was really a private army of Franklin's artisan supporters, and on cue they took their places in front of the threatened houses.

Now artisan faced artisan. The anti–Stamp Act crowd, according to Hughes, was made up of "the lower class," whipped up by "Presbyterians and proprietary Emissaries" led by Chief Justice William Allen's son; the Franklin-Galloway stalwarts were made up of two groups of ship carpenters, the White Oaks and the Hearts of Oak, as well as many other "hones(t) good tradesmen," as Franklin's wife described them.[20] These mechanics had no love for the Stamp Act, but they had stood with Franklin for years. They hoped the rumors about his complicity in the Stamp Act were simply part of the proprietary mudslinging campaign; in the meantime they intended to defend the property and families of Franklin and his friends.

In Boston master artisans and petty entrepreneurs had organized powerfully in the Sons of Liberty, and lower artisans and laborers of the South and North Ends had submerged their rivalry and united behind a poor shoemaker. In Philadelphia, the royal government issue had deeply divided the working people, permitting upper-class leaders to retain control of both parts of the laboring populations. Face to face with Franklin's artisan friends, the anti–Stamp Act crowd could only burn "a Figure that they call'd a Stamp-man" and then melt away into the night.[21]

Two weeks later Philadelphians went to the polls for an election even more tumultuous than the one in 1764. For months Galloway and other assembly leaders had been working to reverse the defeats of the previous year. To recapture the allegiance of the Germans, they paid naturalization fees, settled tavern bills, courted German leaders, and added a German merchant to the assembly party slate. The unpopular Hughes was purged from the ticket and one proprietary winner from 1764 was induced to switch to the assembly party. The proprietary party struggled to maintain its edge. Its leaders convinced Governor John Penn to appoint dozens of Presbyterian justices of the peace and to issue charters of incorporation to German churches, a reversal of a long-maintained proprietary policy. The leaders also worked hard on the Scots-Irish and German working men. The city's presses again worked overtime to turn out campaign literature.

The polls remained open for three days as nearly 2,000 voters, or about 80 percent of the eligible males, cast ballots. When the votes were counted, the assembly party rejoiced to find that they had recouped most of their losses from the previous year. The deep division of laboring men was stunningly recorded in the vote for the city's two burgesses. Thomas Willing, a middle-of-the-road merchant, ran on both tickets, but the other place was hotly contested by James Pemberton, a venerable Quaker brought out of retirement by the Franklin-Galloway party, and George Bryan, the Presbyterian merchant who had defeated Franklin in 1764. Pemberton and Bryan each polled 902 votes, forcing a runoff election won by Pemberton later in October. No other port had such an electoral turnout during the revolutionary era, and never again would laboring-class voters be so divided.

On two occasions after the election, the anti–Stamp Act crowd tried to force Hughes to resign as stamp distributor. Both times the artisan supporters of the Franklin party formed a cordon around Hughes's house, but they extracted from him, as the price of protection, a promise not to execute the Stamp Act "until the King's further pleasure was known, or until the act should be put into execution in the neighbouring provinces."[22]

The issue of royal government in Pennsylvania was so emotional that it diverted attention from the more fundamental issues of economic stagnation and British imperial policies, distorted the ideological positions of the proprietary and assembly parties, and divided those who in terms of economic interest had a natural affinity for each other. The assembly party, known for many decades for its defense of popular rights, continued misguidedly to seek royal government, which alone could shear the hated Thomas Penn of his proprietorship. Accordingly the popular party attempted to mute opposition to the Stamp Act. No less did the proprietary party reverse its traditional role. It wooed the Presbyterian Scots-Irish and the Lutheran and Reformed Germans by opposing the Stamp Act. This was so uncharacteristic a role that even the more liberal proprietary party members squirmed. But, after all, how often did their old enemy Franklin blunder so monumentally?

Unnatural alliances can last only so long and politicians cannot act out of character forever. Once the quest for royal government was recognized as a phantom goal, Philadelphia's occupational and religious groups began to realign. Even during the Stamp Act protests, a reknitting of the laboring classes began. By early November, lower-class pressure forced Philadelphia's merchants to stop importing English goods until the Stamp Act was repealed. One of Philadelphia's wealthiest merchants believed his house would be gutted if he conformed to the Stamp Act, and another anticipated "a deluge of blood" if merchants evaded the boycott of imported goods.[23]

Outgoing trade along coastal routes and to the Caribbean was a different matter. To shut it off would idle a large part of the maritime laboring force and the tradesmen connected to it. Therefore, as in the other ports, popular pressure was strong to clear outgoing ships without stamped papers. As in New York, the clamor of the seamen, along with pressure from some merchants, soon compelled port officials to issue such clearances.

By the summer of 1766 the alliance of proprietary Anglicans and their Presbyterian supporters had cracked wide open. Presbyterians became convinced that the Anglicans were set upon establishing an American bishopric that would make life difficult for all dissenting groups; Anglicans became increasingly uncomfortable opposing policies devised in England; the disappearance of the royal government issue detached the Germans and Scots-Irish from their confederation with the proprietary party; and Quakers began to split between those who favored a conciliatory approach to the Anglo-American tension and those who counseled active opposition. Out of the kaleidoscopic shifting of groups a wholly new force was about to make its appearance in city politics—a Presbyterian-led, artisan-based radical Whig party that would more closely resemble the popular parties in Boston and New York.

The Aftereffects of the Stamp Act

In December 1765 all the northern seaports reopened for trade. Their doughty citizens could rejoice at having successfully resisted English authority, even though formal repeal of the Stamp Act did not come until the following year. But among the upper-class merchants and lawyers who had attempted to lead the resistance movement, the taste of victory was soured by the knowledge that in several instances the protest movement had slipped beyond their control. In working to counteract what they saw as a punitive British imperial policy, the Whig leadership of the port towns had welcomed the *vox populi* and the assembled force of the crowds. In fact they could not do without them. But once the genie was out of the bottle, how could it be imprisoned again?

The "mob," of course, has been feared throughout history by both upper-class holders of power and intellectuals on the assumption that the masses are irrational, are stirred into violent paroxysms by irresponsible rabble-rousers, and are indiscriminate in selecting their targets. Once unloosed, the mob is capable of almost anything. Hence eighteenth-century writers, including many Whigs, referred to the assembled commonalty over and over again as "the unthinking multitude," the "hellish crew," the "impassioned dregs of society," and the like. William Douglass was convinced that the Land Bank leaders in Boston in 1740 had succeeded in "debauching" the minds of unthinking people, "instilling into them some pernicious Principles, destructive of all Society, and good Government," particularly "that *common Consent,* or the Humour of the Multitude, ought to be the *Ratio Ultima* in every Thing."[24] Peter Oliver, brother of the Boston stamp distributor, believed that the crowd in his city, like all mobs, was a "perfect

Machine, wound up by any Hand who might first take the Winch."[25]

The seaport crowds of 1765 can best be understood, however, as large groups of disaffected citizens, drawn heavily but not entirely from the laboring ranks, who worked in purposeful and coordinated ways to protest British policies and express opposition to local oligarchies. Leadership of the crowds varied from port to port. In Boston, where poverty was endemic and where the Pope's Day tradition and recurrent street demonstrations since the late 1730s had taught the laboring classes the basic lessons of organization and protest, the crowd leaders emerged from the lower social ranks and were tenuously tied to those above them. In New York, where poverty had arrived only in the wake of the Seven Years' War and there was no recent history of crowd protests, the Stamp Act demonstrators were led by men somewhat higher up the social ladder—ship captains, master craftsmen, and even lawyers. In Philadelphia, where prosperity had also inhibited the development of class consciousness before 1760 and where local political issues divided artisans and shopkeepers, upper-class representatives such as Joseph Galloway and James Allen led the people.

Despite these differences, in all three towns the struggle for political control was in a highly fluid state. Thomas Hutchinson believed that in Boston a tight chain of command linked the upper, middle, and lower ranks. It began, he said, with members of the Merchants Committee; descended to the master craftsmen, who were organized through the Loyal Nine, several branches of the Caucus, and the fire companies; and finally tapped the laborers, mariners, servants, and even slaves. Hutchinson was half right, correctly identifying the social layering in Boston and describing how Whig merchant leaders wished their political system to operate. But he overestimated the ability of the merchants and lawyers to control the crowd because he underestimated the self-energizing capabilities of common people. "The Boston Mob," wrote one observer, "raised first by the Instigation of Many of the Principal Inhabitants, Allured by Plunder, rose shortly after of their own Accord."[26]

In New York it was much the same. General Thomas Gage believed that "people of Property" had raised "the lower Class to prevent the Execution of the [Stamp] Law." The inferior people would not have stirred, Gage asserted, except that "very great Pains were taken to rouse them," especially the sailors, who "are entirely at the Command of the Merchants who employ them."[27] Gage exaggerated the power of the merchants but soon altered his vision of the lower class as so much water to be pumped from a well by the propertied elite. After five days of tumult in New York, the "people of property," he wrote, "having no more influence over them [the crowd], began to be filled with terrors for their own Safety."[28]

Both prerogative men and Whig leaders underestimated the self-activating capacity of the crowd. But by the end of 1765, a year of extraordinary significance in the social history of the port towns, the scales had been lifted from upper-class eyes. The momentous question at the end of that year, as the resistance movement against England began to lay bare signs of great internal stress, was this: If the "mob" controlled the streets, who would control the "mob"? The Whig leaders "began to be terrified at the Spirit they had raised," warned Gage, "to perceive that popular Fury was not to be guided, and each Individual feared he might be the next Victim to their Rapacity."[29] That, it was clear to men accustomed to political power and the obeisance of those beneath them, must not happen.

The Onset of Revolution

T HE YEAR 1765 had been the most explosive in the history of the seaport towns. Urban dwellers deeply resented and violently opposed new British policies. Local political factionalism produced bitter campaigns at the polls. Obscure men assumed leadership roles among the mass of ordinary people, upper-class Whiggish leaders maneuvered to maintain control of popular politics, and prerogative men shuddered at the outburst of leveling sentiments. The reopening of the northern ports at the end of the year revived commerce, and news that the Stamp Act had been repealed in May 1766 gave hope that the dispute with the mother country might be laid to rest. But optimism was short-lived, for the English crown swiftly signaled that it had no intention of permitting the Americans to go their own way. Parliament passed new legislation in 1767 designed to bring the colonies to heel. The Townshend Acts levied duties on paper, lead, painters' colors, and tea. They also sent a board of determined customs commissioners to the colonies to enforce trade restrictions and suspended New York's assembly until that body adhered to the Quartering Act of 1765 by providing properly for British troops who had been garrisoned in the colony since the end of the Seven Years' War. From this moment on, the colonies and the parent country proceeded toward revolution.

The colonists did not become revolutionaries lightly. They engaged in a full decade of debate and internal struggle before deciding to break the chains of dependence and to fight for separation. In this evolving revolutionary impulse in the northern ports, ideological principles and economic interests were intimately conjoined. Everyone, with the possible exception of a handful of ascetic recluses, has economic interests; and everyone, including the least educated members of the community, has an ideology. Ebenezer MacIntosh, the debt-ridden street commander of the Boston crowd in 1765, knew how to measure the price of bread and the cost of imported English cloth against the wages he could earn at the cobbler's bench, just as Thomas Hutchinson, the wealthy merchant and government official, understood how the sterling exchange rate affected his margin of profit.

Like so many of New England's laboring poor, MacIntosh was fervently antipapist and only slightly less anti-Anglican. He was also convinced that affluence and self-indulgence had corrupted Boston's elite. He baptized his firstborn son Pascale Paoli MacIntosh, and in this commemoration of the humble Corsican patriot can be seen the cast of his values. Hutchinson named no children after English aristocrats but embraced his own ideology no less warmly. Traditional English rights, including religious freedom, balanced government, limits on executive authority, and an electorate of substantial propertyholders, formed the foundation of his thought. With lesser men keeping to their places and deferring to the judgments of their betters, social order would be maintained.

Many others have explored in fine detail the step-by-step alienation from England and the final call to arms. The concern here is the internal struggle for a new social order that accompanied the severing of ties with England and was centered in events in the three port towns.

The crucial decade after 1765 produced the most violent economic fluctuations and the most difficult circumstances that people of all ranks in the port towns had ever known. Two silent streams of unplanned change—the effect of English policies on local economies and the cumulative effect of long-range changes that were largely unrelated to decisions hammered out in London—exerted a major influence on urban dwellers' reactions to the policies of the English government after 1765.

Economic Change and New Commercial Policies

Among the alterations in the northern seaport towns in the last decade of the colonial era, none was more noticeable than sheer physical expansion. Philadelphia spurted ahead spectacularly—from about 18,000 in 1765 to nearly 25,000 a decade later. New York had reached 22,000 by 1771 and perhaps a few thousand more by the time of the Revolution. Only Boston failed to share in the rapid urban development, but it did end thirty years of demographic stagnation by adding perhaps a thousand persons to its population, thus returning to the size it had been in the early 1740s.

One immediate advantage of population growth was the spurring of the building trades. Work for construction artisans was sporadic at best in Boston; in the decade after 1765 the number of houses increased by only about twenty per year. But in New York and Philadelphia construction boomed. The Manhattan port added about a thousand houses from 1765 to 1776 and Philadelphia more than twice that number. In 1774 roof beams were raised for more houses in Pennsylvania's capital than in Boston during the entire prerevolutionary decade. Expansion of this magnitude also created a need for more churches and public buildings. While Boston's craftsmen erected only one major public building in the final decade of the colonial period, their counterparts in Philadelphia were building the "New College" for the emerging University of Pennsylvania, Carpenters Hall, new churches for the Anglicans, Lutherans, and Presbyterians, and the two largest structures erected in colonial America, the Bettering House and the Walnut Street Prison.

The success of these Philadelphia construction tradesmen relative to their Boston cousins is systematically recorded in their inventories of estate. Among seventeen construction artisans whose estates were inventoried in Boston from 1766 to 1775 the median personal wealth left at death was £60 sterling; in Philadelphia, among nineteen artisans, it was £198.

While Boston's construction artisans scrambled for work in the 1760s and 1770s, the fortunes of shipbuilding craftsmen brightened slightly from the dismal days of the 1750s. Philadelphia, however, surpassed its New England rival in ship construction by the eve of the Revolution. Meanwhile, ship construction in New York fell badly.

Boston's problems were also compounded by the loss of much of its fishing industry to outlying ports and by the reduced amount of tonnage, relative to New York and Philadelphia, entering and clearing its harbor. By the 1760s New York had gained on Boston, and Philadelphia had surpassed it.

Despite its eclipse as North America's premier entrepôt, Boston staged a commercial recovery in the late 1760s and early 1770s. Tonnage clearing the harbor rose almost 40 percent in the last decade of the colonial period from the previous fifteen years, and this trend must have brought regular employment to most of the town's large maritime labor force. Yet Boston could not halt its decline relative to Philadelphia and New York, for the latter two ports, especially Philadelphia, were the shipping points for prospering agricultural hinterlands that expanded rapidly after the Peace of Paris. Boston remained the commercial center for a relatively unproductive interior whose excess population, unable to extract a living from the thin New England soils, drifted off to the forests and rocky coastline of New Hampshire and Maine. By the end of the colonial period the people of Massachusetts could not even feed themselves. From 1768 to 1772 the Bay colony was a large net importer of bread and flour, wheat, corn, beef, and pork. About 14 percent of its basic foodstuff requirements had to be purchased from other colonies.

New York and Philadelphia, on the other hand, were becoming the breadbaskets not only for colonies to the north but also for England and southern Europe, where crippling droughts created an unprecedented demand for grains from the Middle Atlantic region from 1764 onward. New York was able to export almost 30 percent of its own food requirements from 1768 to 1772, and Pennsylvania more than half.

For merchants and large shopkeepers, the most troubling problem of the prerevolutionary decade was the growing domination of the American commercial process by English decision makers and English capital. To be sure, the colonial economy had always been the servant of the metropolitan master; that was what it meant to be a colony, to be an exporter of foodstuffs and raw products and an importer of finished goods. Nobody expected or even desired economic sovereignty. But as the colonial economies matured, restrictions on local development began to grate. In the wake of the Seven Years' War, when those restrictions multiplied rapidly, the situation seemed less and less tolerable.

Among the developments that northern merchants found worrisome was British merchants' increasing tendency to sell directly to shopkeepers or to organize auctions for selling English goods directly to the public. These "vendue sales," which had customarily been reserved for the disposal of damaged goods, became an ever larger part of commercial life in the northern ports. But cutting out the colonial middleman, this method of dumping goods on the American market struck directly at the interests of the seaboard merchant and shopkeeper. Vendue sales, complained one Philadelphian in 1772 "have gone near to deprive many an honest Family of a Living."[1] The Tea Act, passed by Parliament the following year, aroused bitter opposition because it represented further intervention in the American marketing process. The act offered urban consumers a lower price by allowing the East

India Company to sell its product directly to the American public through its agents in the colonies. The angry reaction of most northern merchants stemmed not only from the fact that many of them had trafficked profitably in smuggled Dutch tea, which was now to be undersold, but also from the fact that they viewed the Tea Act as an invidious plan to wrest control of the internal workings of the American economy from the hands of its own people.

A second commercial difficulty was British policymakers' increasingly heavy restriction of the colonial currency system. The Currency Act of 1764 strictly limited the authority of Pennsylvania and New York to issue paper currency. In the northern port towns, especially New York and Philadelphia, the hard money drain was a fact of life, for shipping gold and silver to the mother country was the only way to make up for an excess of imports over exports. Locally issued paper money provided the circulating medium of local trade. When it was disallowed, internal trade withered, hurting merchant and artisan alike and obliging traders to concoct ingenious schemes for issuing fiat money that might gain legislative approval and escape royal notice.

Another aspect of the monetary problem was the erratic flow of British credit after the Seven Years' War. Eyeing the dynamic growth of the colonial population, English and Scottish merchants at first vastly increased credit sales to American importers in order to spur the consumption of British goods. American merchants willingly increased their orders and passed their indebtedness on to retailers and consumers as book credit, where it became, in effect, a part of the colonial supply of money. Accepting credit in order to expand was not in itself a disadvantageous policy, but it made borrowers far more vulnerable to cyclical swings in the British credit structure. Hence, during the English financial crisis of 1762 and 1772, when sharp business contractions obliged British lenders to call in their colonial debts, many seaboard merchants were unable to meet the demands of their overseas creditors and went bankrupt.

The credit crisis of 1772 was especially severe. The bankruptcy rate doubled and panic swept both sides of the Atlantic, causing a "marked deterioration" of "debtor-creditor relations between the thirteen colonies and the mother country."[2] The scramble for liquidity was greatest among the southern planters, whose level of indebtedness was the highest in the colonies. But the northern commercial centers were also hard hit. Many merchants found themselves pinched. Haled into court for settlement of accounts and committed to debtors' prison when they could not pay, they began to lose faith in the violently cyclical behavior of the Anglo-American commercial system.

In their quarrel with England the merchants were also concerned about constitutional and natural rights. In fact they made no distinction between England's onerous new economic regulation and its encroachment on the political rights of American subjects. They saw a coordinated attack on their "lives, liberties, and property," as they so frequently phrased it. Their economic interests and ideological principles were so closely interwoven as to be virtually inseparable.

Economic life after 1765 was not always determined in the same ways for the laboring classes as for merchants and shopkeepers, although there was often coincidence of interests. The sudden contraction of a merchant's credit brought demands upon artisans to settle accounts. If work had been slow, a laboring man in debt could find himself in court or even in debtors' prison, where his earning power was brought to a dead halt. But vendue sales, hated by many merchants, ensured the availability of cheaper imported goods. Trade doldrums hurt merchants, artisans, and mariners, but they also tended to drive land values and house rents down, thus easing budgetary pressures on laboring people who rented rooms or houses.

The economic volatility of the late colonial period accentuated the uncertainty of the preindustrial craftsman's work rhythms. When the postwar commercial depression bottomed out early in 1765, hopes revived for better times. But within a year substantial unemployment was reported in all the port towns. The Philadelphia grand jury lamented early in 1766 that many of "the labouring People, and others in low circumstances . . . who are willing to work, cannot obtain sufficient Employment to support themselves and their Families."[3] Reports of unemployment continued in 1767 and 1768, and by the end of 1768 forced sales of property reached an all-time high. The nadir came in 1769, when New York property values declined by one-half or more and the city's prison bulged with insolvent debtors. Unemployment was still widespread in early 1770, when the employment of moonlighting British troops at cut-rate wages brought a storm of protest from the artisan class. In the same year a friend of Governor Hutchinson found many of Boston's laboring people "almost starving for want of Employment" and believed that in their desperation they would soon be "going to plunder the Rich and then cutting their throats."[4]

Commercial revival came later in 1770. But in 1772 the contraction of British credit was felt from the top to the bottom of the social scale. Shops failed, unemployment spread again, and the jails filled to overflowing with formerly respectable citizens who could not pay their debts.

Another sign of economic difficulties was the rapid abandonment of bound labor in favor of free labor during the last two decades of the colonial era. In uncertain times, those who still possessed the resources to command the labor of others learned that they were better off hiring labor when they needed it while remaining free of the obligation to maintain unremunerative workers during dull periods.

The importation of slaves dropped sharply at the end of the Seven Years' War in all three northern towns. By 1768 importations had virtually ceased in Philadelphia and Boston, and the town meeting in the latter city was instructing its representatives to advocate total abolition of the slave trade. In Philadelphia the number of slaves fell by almost half from 1767 to 1775, and the proportion of unfree laboring males dropped from about 60 to 35 percent. In New York, where slaves had constituted about 20 percent of the population in the 1730s and 1740s, they made up only 14 percent by 1771. In Boston the number of slaves dropped from 1,544 in 1752 to 811 in 1765 and probably fell below 500 by the outbreak of the war. Immigrating indentured servants entered the city at a trickle. On the eve of the Revolution bound laborers made up no more than 15 percent of those who worked with their hands.

While employers phased out bound labor, artisans also helped to usher in a new labor system. As times grew hard, their resentment of slave-labor competition increased. It is no coincidence that the strongest attacks on slavery in the prerevolutionary decade, excluding those by Quakers, who had made abolition a central part of their reformist zeal since the 1950s, were those by artisan spokesmen such as James Otis and Nathaniel Appleton in Boston and Benjamin Rush and Thomas Paine in Philadelphia. Self-interest also motivated those slave owners who freed their aged or infirm slaves who could no longer work, thus saving the shilling per day that it cost to feed them. This forced freedom became extensive enough in New York that in 1773 the legislature passed a law imposing a £20 fine on the last owner of a freedman beggar—a measure taken more to keep the relief rolls down than to guarantee humane treatment for worn-out slaves. Paternalistic relations between employer and worker, either black or white, were giving way to a system in which cooler calculations of supply and demand governed the labor market and wage rates were determined not by custom but by market conditions.

Boycotts of British goods also affected the availability of work in the port towns. Three times—in 1765–66, 1767–70, and 1774–75—the three northern ports attempted to collaborate in pledging not to consume or import British goods until their grievances were redressed. This tri-city cooperation was never perfected, but all the ports, for greater or lesser periods, curbed imports from England. These boycotts hampered a number of artisans who relied on imported materials such as glass, glue, and certain metals but gave prospects for fuller employment to a far larger number of craftsmen whose domestic handicrafts were stimulated when English goods were banned. The "buy American" campaigns, which were initially designed to force repeal of odious English legislation, thus moved far beyond their original purpose. They became remedies for unemployment, raised embryonic visions of economic nationalism, and spread the idea that artisans, through forging political pressure groups, could influence public policy in ways that increased their earning power.

During these years, as the dispute with England became more acrimonious, prices made their final cyclical swing. In Philadelphia food costs began to drop in 1765 and reached a low point in 1769. Then they began a climactic five-year climb that increased the cost of food by nearly 25 percent from 1769 to 1774. The managers of Philadelphia's Bettering House complained in 1775 that they were paying twice as much for food items as they had in previous years. New York prices followed a similar trend: a modest decline in the mid-1760s, followed by another punishing upswing early in the 1770s.

To make matters worse, the period of highest prices nearly coincided with the second major commercial downturn, which began in 1772 after the sudden contraction of British credit reverberated all along the seaboard. As in the deep slump from 1760 to 1764, the recession came just when food costs for laboring families were rising sharply. There was no general *crise de subsistance,* but the situation was serious enough for the Philadelphia overseers of the poor to distribute thousands of loaves of bread.

The cost of other items in the household budget—firewood, rent, and clothing—remained fairly stable during the ten years before the Revolution, and after 1767 New York's share of debt from the Seven Years' War was retired. But in Massachusetts and Pennsylvania the huge war debt had to be retired by land taxes scheduled into the 1770s, and local taxes continued to increase to keep up with climbing poor-relief expenses.

As in the depression of the early 1760s, wage rates often failed to keep pace with price hikes and in fact fell among the least skilled laborers. Philadelphia's mariners, whose wages during the Seven Years' War had risen to an all-time high of £4 and even £5 per month, saw their pay drop to traditional levels of £3 to £3.5 per month by 1763. Henceforth, the high level of immigration, which ensured a plentiful supply of seagoing men, kept wages at this level. Boston's mariners toiled for similar wages, and New York's mariners, who had commanded 6 shillings a day in 1759, also returned to the traditional £2 to £3 per month, a 50 percent decrease from the wartime heyday. Laborers fared no better. The wartime boom had lifted their daily wage to 4 shillings and occasionally a bit higher. But amid rising unemployment, wages fell in the mid-1760s. By 1769 laborers averaged barely 3 shillings per day in Philadelphia; in the early 1770s they earned even less. With new immigrants arriving almost weekly and many idle hands available, employers had no difficulty finding workers at these rates. The earning power of Philadelphia's dock workers, chimney sweeps, watchmen, woodcutters, well diggers, street scavengers, porters, and the like fell a full 30 percent between the height of the Seven Years' War and the outbreak of the Revolution.

In the face of severe budgetary pressures it is not surprising that seaport dwellers embarked on the most intense organizing in their history. Those who were able to organize and present a united front were best able to obtain higher wages. Philadelphia's ship captains, for example, who were closely tied to merchant shipowners, were able to protect the £7 (local currency) per month wage they had achieved during the Seven Years' War throughout the remainder of the colonial period. Operating from strength, they organized the Society for the Relief of Poor and Distressed Masters of Ships in 1765. Presumably a "friendly society" with charitable and fraternal purposes, the society, like its New England predecessor, the Marine Society of Boston, seems to have played an important role in maintaining the £7 per month wage.

Carpenters were also able to organize effectively. Philadelphia's master carpenters had been organized since the 1720s, but in the difficult 1760s its journeymen carpenters, who most frequently hired out to master craftsmen, established their own company and attempted to set rates that would allow them a decent living. New York's carpenters organized in 1767 and Boston's some time before 1750. Philadelphia's ship carpenters were also organized effectively, and the political unity they displayed in 1765 in protecting the houses of Franklin and Hughes was probably matched by comparable solidarity on economic questions. In the years just before the Revolution, organized artisans were able to obtain a measure of wage security.

Men who worked in the least skilled occupations—mariners, laborers, cordwainers, tailors, and coopers—had far less success than those higher in the occupational hierarchy. This trend inexorably drove a wedge in the laboring classes, separating struggling lower artisans, who suffered greatly in the 1760s and 1770s, from upper artisans, who were able to maintain a degree of economic security and in some cases even to forge ahead.

Growing Poverty and Whig Remedies

In studying the momentous events that carried Americans into the Revolution, historians have understandably concentrated on the dramatic events of the decade after the Stamp Act riots: New York's resistance to the Quartering Act of 1765, the Townshend Acts of 1767 and the nonimportation movement that followed them, the occupation of Boston by British troops in 1768, the Boston Massacre of 1770, the Tea Act of 1773 and the subsequent Tea Party, the Intolerable Acts of 1774, the convening of the Continental Congress late in that year, and, finally, the outbreak of armed hostility at Lexington and Concord in the spring of 1775. These were the central events in the unfolding drama. But giving them impetus were social processes that themselves provided the origins of the American Revolution.

One important social change was the impoverishment of large segments of the urban populations. By and large, those who reluctantly went to the almshouses or gratefully accepted out-relief from overseers of the poor were not actively involved in the radical movement. Many of them, including widows, children, the sick and elderly, were politically inert. The active segment was composed of the wage-earning laborers and mariners in the lower echelon and of the artisans, small shopkeepers, and struggling professionals who joined the Sons of Liberty, threw tea into Boston harbor, and enforced the nonimportation agreements. The impoverishment of the lower quarter or third of society was important to these middling men, however, because the spread of poverty in the lowest laboring ranks, not simply among the aged and infirm, signaled sickness in the body economic as surely as corruption betokened putridness in the body politic.

Local leaders had to face economic malaise at the same time that they had to confront English threats to American liberties. Hence, while Samuel Adams was dispensing impassioned rhetoric about British tyranny and the erosion of the rights of freeborn English subjects in Boston, overseers of the poor Samuel Whitwell and Samuel Abbot were dispensing out-relief to 15 percent of the householders in their wards and sending others to the workhouse or almshouse. New Yorkers learned about the Tea Act in 1773 at the same time that their newspapers were reporting a wave of thefts and shop burglaries and were noting that 425 souls were jostling for space in the overcrowded almshouse while hundreds of others lived on out-relief. In other words, in urban locales the entire discussion of American constitutional rights was carried out in the context of nagging poverty at the bottom of society and the crumbling of economic security in the middle. These factors gave rise to intense concern about the future and created a crisis in class relations.

While attempting to maintain control over the growing resistance to English policies, urban Whig leaders searched for solutions to local economic problems. In Philadelphia, for example, a group of merchants erected a linen manufactory in 1764 and employed several hundred poor women there. But the project died within two years because the manufactory could not produce quality sailcloth, linen, and ticking as cheaply as English imports available in the shops.

Two years later a group of Quaker merchants proposed a striking new plan for administering relief. The taxpayers, they argued, were now supporting a record 220 paupers in the overcrowded almshouse. The merchants proposed to incorporate a group of private citizens who, in return for raising a substantial sum for constructing a large new almshouse, would be given control over the management of the poor. The Bettering House, as it came to be called, would consist of an almshouse for the aged and disabled and a workhouse for the able-bodied poor. Into the workhouse would go all out-pensioners who had formerly received direct cash payments from the overseers of the poor. Gathered together, they could be clothed and fed inexpensively. More important, they could contribute to their own maintenance. The assembly, grateful that Philadelphians were proposing to solve their own problem, gladly consented.

The Bettering House that rose on Spruce Street was more than a monument to the philanthropic impulses of Philadelphia's Quakers; it was also a response to the swelling ranks of immigrant and itinerant poor who were seeking work in the city, the increasing cost of relief, and the spreading notion that poor rates were rising because more and more people were content to live the life of the idler, the profligate, or the street beggar rather than pursue an honest trade. The Bettering House was in fact a cross between Boston's workhouse, whose book of rules the Quaker managers purchased, and the Boston linen manufactory of the 1750s. Quaker leaders adopted a plan strikingly similar to the one that had proved a failure three hundred miles to the north.

The hand of Benjamin Franklin is highly visible in the organization of the Bettering House. Appointed to the assembly committee for reorganizing the poor law in 1763 and to another for erecting a workhouse in 1764, Franklin was no doubt carefully listened to, for he had an unmatched reputation as an architect of problem-solving urban institutions. He expressed the core of his thought in a letter written shortly after his return to England in 1765. Angered by the London poor's mobbing of grain wagons to prevent wheat exports at a time when bread was scarce, Franklin publicly advised that "the more public provisions were made for the poor, the less they provided for themselves, and of course became poorer. And, on the contrary, the less was done for them, the more they did for themselves, and became richer."[5] Repeal the poor laws by which the indigent were supported, he advised, and the poor would go back to work.

Philadelphia did not adopt Franklin's drastic proposal to eliminate poor relief, but the decision to turn over to the Quaker merchants the management of the poor-relief system, with the Bettering House as its centerpiece, embodied the philosophy behind his proposals. Even the name of the institution indicated the growing tendency to regard the poor as flawed members of society who needed to be reformed rather than relieved. The old familial system now gave way to nonfamilial institutions, reflecting the emergence of the new social order.

Controlling the disbursement of all funds gathered under the poor-tax laws, the Bettering House managers worked to end the payment of out-pensions after the Bettering House opened in the fall of 1767. Despite considerable resistance to this policy, they ultimately succeeded in channeling all but about 15 percent of relief moneys into the institutional relief of people compelled to quit their abodes.

The decision to end out-relief embroiled the managers in a heated dispute with the overseers of the poor. Drawn mostly from the ranks of established artisans and usually not members of the Society of Friends, the overseers were far closer to the needy in their neighborhoods. They understood the resentment of the non-Quaker poor who were being herded into a Quaker-dominated institution for their moral betterment. The fact that the Quakers had few poor of their own, since they were the best established economic group in the city and cared for their own indigent in a small Quaker almshouse, may have made the new policy all the more obnoxious. The overseers of the poor had been stripped of their power to distribute out-relief and were being pressured to send to the Bettering House persons who might make it through the winter with small sums of money and some firewood. They objected to carting the infirm and aged to the Bettering House, decried the "Cruelty" of "breaking up many Familys" by sending members behind closed doors, and pointed out that because of the compulsory segregation of men and women there many husbands and wives were being miserably committed "to Live in a Separate State."[6]

Sharply criticized, the Quaker managers started issuing annual reports containing statistics on inmate production. Those who read the fine print, however, would have noticed that it was proving impossible to work the poor at a profit. The managers spent more each year to procure materials for manufacture and to pay supervisory salaries than they received from selling the products of the inmates' labor.

By 1775, after half a dozen years of controversy, all parties—the Quaker managers, the overseers of the poor, the taxpayers, and the poor themselves—were thoroughly disillusioned. Robert Honyman, an English doctor, was surprised when a number of women "begged me to try to get them out" of a reportedly model institution.[7] The overseers of the poor engaged in a kind of sabotage by refusing to press their straitened neighbors for poor-tax payments, and tax collections fell further and further behind. The rising price of provisions, coinciding with only slight increases in the income derived from poor taxes, reduced what the managers had to work with. As for the reform of dissolute persons, the Quaker philanthropists simply gave up. The poor entered the Bettering House, then ran away, and were returned "mostly as sick, naked, and burthensome as at first, and proceed this way with Impunity, as often as they please." Work could be extracted from few of them, and so, the managers confessed, they "are entirely dead Weight."[8]

The attempts to deal with the poor revealed the limitations of Whig ideology as applied to internal social problems. Whig political theory, especially in Philadelphia, had evolved in an environment of widespread opportunity for almost two generations before the end of the Seven Years' War. Hard work and frugality had led to material success, not only for merchants, professionals, and extraordinary lower-class sons such as Benjamin Franklin, but also for scores of artisans. Hence when poverty began to spread, the best-established part of the community, whose ideas had been formed in a different economic milieu, subscribed fully to Franklin's notion that "the best way of doing good to the poor is not making them easy *in* poverty, but leading or driving them *out* of it."[9]

The response of the poor indicates how deeply shaken was the concentration of cultural authority in the upper class in this troubled era. The poor—and many lower-echelon artisans—staunchly resisted the ideology reflected in the Bettering House solution to poverty, even though it had the support of a wide range of city leaders. Those who had known better days "declared in a Solemn manner that they would rather perish through want" than go to the Bettering House.[10] They scraped by as best they could, aided by friends, churches, and charitable societies. Those who could not escape confinement did as little labor as possible within the walls.

The failure of the poor to play the role assigned to them reveals much about the deep fissures that were appearing in northern urban society. In New York, rather than acting the part of grateful supplicants, the poor looked to the affluent as an exploiting class that owed them relief, not because charity required it but because justice demanded it. It was the poor, one of their spokesmen wrote in 1769, "who, by their Industry heretofore, have contributed so much to make our Circumstances easy: It is to the meaner Class of Mankind, the industrious Poor, that so many of us are indebted for those goodly Dwellings we inhabit, for that comfortable Substance we enjoy, while others are languishing under the disagreeable Sensations of Penury and Want."[11] Other writers pointed to the class injustice represented by the astounding increase in expensive carriages in New York—from five to seventy in the four years after the Peace of Paris —while at the same time laboring people were selling their household goods to pay rents to rich landlords.[12]

In all the northern seaports poverty and unemployment also inspired new attempts to do what had proved impossible in Boston in the 1750s: erect large buildings, fill them with spinning wheels and looms, recruit cheap labor, and manufacture cloth at a profit. The nonimportation movements, it was believed, would raise the demand for domestic cloth through a combination of patriotic sentiment and a shortage of English-produced material. The hope of providing employment for the poor converged neatly with the desires to lower poor taxes and to pressure England into repealing repugnant policies.

During the first nonimportation movement, which accompanied the Stamp Act protests, merchants in New York and Philadelphia set up cloth manufactories and recruited several hundred poor women to work in them. Both factories collapsed, however, when the resumption of English imports in 1766 flooded urban markets with better-quality goods and consumers made their preferences known.

All three port towns tried cloth manufacturing again during the second nonimportation movement, in 1767–1770. New York's manufactory employed more than three hundred poor people by early 1768. In Philadelphia the managers of the new Bettering House purchased "sundry Looms, Wheels, Sleigh Geers, Shuttles &c" from the defunct linen manufactory and set their captive labor force to work without any wages.[13]

Boston moved more slowly. A committee appointed in October 1767 to study the situation returned in January 1768 with a plan for using the old Manufactory House for the production of sailcloth. It obtained the town's permission to proceed but did not get the £3,000 interest-free loan it requested, and the scheme died. In March 1769 the town meeting again considered ways of employing the poor. This time a committee proposed to teach large numbers of women and children to spin. The new plan differed from its predecessors in several regards. First, no suggestion was made that the women and children should actually work in the manufactory; the presumption is strong that they were to remain in their homes, spinning yarn as household routines allowed. Second, the man who stepped forward to manage the project was William Molineux, one of the most important radical leaders in Boston. Molineux had come to Boston in the 1740s and developed a substantial business as a hardware merchant. He suffered badly in the post-1760 depression. Never before involved in politics, he now entered the public arena and rose rapidly in radical Whig circles. Whenever confrontations were staged with the governor or with Tory merchants who refused to comply with the nonimportation agreements, Molineux was at the head of the crowd. Whereas the shoemaker MacIntosh had named his son Pascale Paoli after the Corsican revolutionary, the new director of Boston's legion of poor spinners was himself known as "Paoli" Molineux.

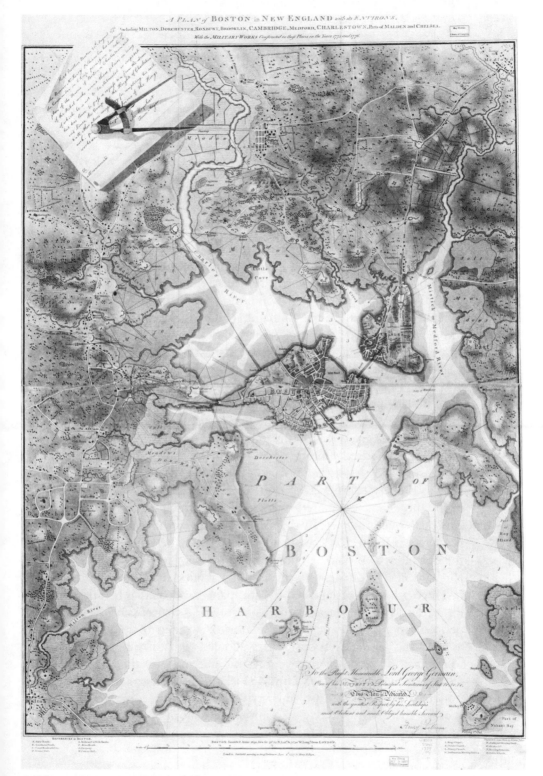

6. Plan of Boston in 1777 by Henry Pelham

Even Molineux's direction of the cloth manufactory did not enjoy complete success. Neither he nor anyone else could solve Boston's poverty problem or substantially lower the costs of poor relief. But because he made no attempt to coerce Boston's poor women into factory work and enjoyed great popularity among the lower classes he did better than his predecessors. Molineux could never by force of personality accustom Bostonians to repetitive, confining, year-round labor, nor could he solve the problems of the erratic supply of raw materials and lack of technologically skilled personnel needed to turn out cloth of fine quality. But he adjusted to these realities, suspending operations during the winter, obtaining the services of English-trained "manufacturers" for dying and finishing the cloth, and letting women and children work in their homes rather than attempting to impose an industrial discipline on them. His relative success also owes much to the Whig campaign to turn spinning into a patriotic activity and a symbol of defiance against England. Under radical Whig leadership the manufacture of cloth took on a political character and became a part of the self-denying zeal and reaffirmation of community by which well-to-do radical Whigs hoped to bind the lower classes to their leadership.

In Philadelphia the attempt to manufacture cloth finally succeeded in the year before the Revolution. The movement for domestic manufacturing had received a healthy impetus from the last nonimportation movement as radical protests against England careered to a climax in 1774 and 1775. Also, the pool of impoverished and unemployed persons in the city had never been greater. Both factors were important in the success of the United Company of Philadelphia for Promoting American Manufactures. By themselves, however, they probably would not have guaranteed success, and certainly not the kind that enabled the company to provide employment for nearly five hundred persons and to declare a dividend two years after its first meeting.

Three other factors allowed the company to succeed as had none of its predecessors in the port towns through a quarter-century of experimentation. First, the company allowed women to spin at home, as time and familial responsibilities allowed, and to bring their yarn to the factory for payment. Second, this system enabled the company to avoid heavy capital expenditures for a large building to accommodate hundreds of spinners. Instead, it rented a house for a mere £40 per year for the looms and dyeing equipment. This allowed the company to begin operations quickly and to put its money into equipment rather than buildings. Third, the company was organized and operated by a group of middling men, many of them artisans, who came from mixed religious and ethnic backgrounds, had close ties to the poor in their neighborhoods, and were deeply involved in radical politics. The president of the company was Daniel Roberdeau, an important radical leader and shortly to be elected commander of the Pennsylvania militia. James Cannon, a radical schoolteacher and principal author of the radical Constitution of 1776, was secretary. The twelve-man Board of Managers included five members of the radical Committee of 100, elected five months after the company organized to enforce nonimportation. While production figures plummeted at the Bettering House, run by wealthy Quaker merchants, they soared at the United Company of Philadelphia, run by popular leaders with close ties to the laboring people and an ability to convince them that spinning and weaving contributed to the defense of liberty against a selfish and despotic crown.

The Ideological Spectrum

How urban dwellers perceived and experienced economic change after 1765 varied markedly according to their position in society. Thomas Hutchinson, who had riches aplenty but little peace of mind as he tried to govern Massachusetts from 1770 to 1774, blithely concluded that north of Maryland "you scarce see a man destitute of a competency to make him easy."[14] Many others, equally oblivious to growing penury in their midst, shared the perpetual optimism that comes easily to those in comfortable circumstances—they saw nothing amiss in America and wished only for the troublemaking radicals to sink into oblivion. At the other end of the spectrum were pitiable persons such as John McCleary, who scratched out pathetic requests for assistance to the overseer of the poor in his North End ward: "I hope you will be so kind as to Lett Me have a Little wood for I have not had one Stick to burn since I wrote you before and I am almost perished with the Cold," or "the Room that I lye in is all over Run with water." [15]

Between these two extremes stood the majority of merchant seamen, laborers, artisans, shopkeepers, professionals, and merchants of the port towns. For the most favorably positioned of them, onerous new trade regulations, restrictions on the issuing of paper currency, violent expansion and contraction of credit, heavy taxes, and strict customs enforcement were causes of anxiety. Trade continued, sometimes at very high levels, and artisan production continued, though unevenly. But the burdens of the mercantilist connection with England and the prospects for an independent economic order that the boycotts of the era aroused among urban artificers, along with the disturbing sight of poverty and unemployment among the lowest ranks, nurtured a profound uneasiness among many concerning the course of economic change and the future of their world. It was hard to ignore the fact that in all the cities the largest buildings erected after 1765—cloth manufactories, almshouses, and prisons—were constructed to contain the impoverished, a growing criminal element spawned by poverty, and a noncriminal middle-class group whose only offense against society was an inability to weather the economic storms of the period. This was not the world of their fathers.

Despite a general relationship between the circumstances of urban people's everyday lives and their susceptibility to particular ideas, there was no strict correspondence between occupation or wealth and ideological outlook. The two broadly prevailing ideologies themselves overlapped at some points and those subscribing to them were by no means unified on all issues.

The reigning ideology of eighteenth-century America was Whig. One group, which can be loosely designated conservative Whigs, included a large part of the urban gentry, especially import-export merchants, important officeholders, many lawyers and clergymen, and a sprinkling of lesser men who by temperament or family ties were connected to this generally affluent group. By and large these prosperous men adhered to the canons of Whig political theory, including balanced government, the vital role of a legislature elected by propertyholders, and equal justice before the law. In the port towns many were Anglicans from families whose wealth stretched back several generations, and they often had close connections in England, both to large mercantile houses and to important men in government. They openly espoused international trade and capitalist relations and in this limited sense were "modernizers." In their social philosophy, however, they were profoundly conservative. Hierarchy and order imposed from above were the central tenets of their social credo. They believed deeply that the "multitude, who have not a sufficient stock of reason and knowledge to guide them," should defer to their betters. They were rationalists who subscribed to many Enlightenment ideas, and they took pride in their roles as leaders of their communities.

The conservative Whigs included the placeholders and wealthy merchants around Thomas Hutchinson in Boston, the members of the Anglican-based, mercantile-led proprietary faction in Philadelphia, and the merchants and lawyers of the DeLancey party in New York. Their central goals after 1765 were to keep resistance to English policies within orderly bonds and, in the face of the Stamp Act demonstrators' affronts to authority and social order, to preserve their power in the capitals as leaders and officeholders of the court party. Many of them would become loyalists; others would maintain a precarious neutrality during the war. Still others would swallow their distrust of a radicalized polity and emerge during and after the war as leaders of a movement to reverse what they regarded as the dangerous excesses of the revolutionary era.

A second group of Whigs, who may be labeled liberals, was composed of some wealthy import-export merchants and many more local traders, ship captains, unpedigreed lawyers, non-Anglican clergymen, small manufacturers, and craftsmen, especially those in the more remunerative trades. Economic growth had meant opportunity for most of them, and so long as the doors of opportunity were open, which most frequently meant access to capital and labor, they opted to participate in a social system that was by now only faintly disguising the pursuit of self-interest with traditional rhetoric about serving the public good. Many of them owned property, commanded the labor of slaves and indentured servants, and competed avidly in a world of credit, investment, and speculation. These were the men who led the opposition to England's closer regulation of American economic life, including limitations on their right to issue paper money, attempts to eliminate American middlemen from certain sectors of international marketing, and interference with smuggling, which they viewed as a means of opening channels of free trade in the face of monopolistic regulation.

In their political philosophy the liberal Whigs were far more open than the conservative Whigs to participatory public affairs. In Boston they celebrated the town meeting as an instrument for guarding the people's liberties, whereas the conservatives condemned it as an exercise in mobocracy. In New York they almost always controlled the common council and other elected municipal offices. In Philadelphia they levied and collected the taxes, supervised poor relief, and spearheaded civic improvement projects. They were strongly Lockean in their belief that liberty was essentially the condition of being secure in one's property, which they held in modest to substantial amounts, and they had little desire to share political power with the unpropertied by extending the franchise or, in New York and Philadelphia, by instituting a town meeting system of local government. Because they were themselves products of intergenerational mobility, they did not shrink from the ideal of social fluidity as did the conservative Whigs; but they distrusted the growing mass of propertyless and impoverished city dwellers below them and sometimes suspected that such people lacked the cardinal qualities of industry and frugality that accounted for their own success. If social stability, acceptance of capitalistic economic relations, and political stewardship were the identifying tenets of the conservative Whigs, then equality of opportunity, enthusiasm for the market economy, and political liberty were those of the liberal Whigs. Their central goal after 1765 was to lead the movement to resist British policy, employing those below them as necessary to create mass protest without losing control of the popular assembly parties that they dominated.

The other widely popular ideology in the cities was Evangelicalism. Though overlapping with Whig ideology at many points, especially in its advocacy of balanced government, electoral institutions, and freedom of speech and the press, the Evangelicals expressed themselves in a different language of public discourse and had a different vision of the direction in which society ought to change. Like the Whigs, they were divided internally into two major groups. One of these, which may be called radicals, was composed of the lower elements in the urban social hierarchy—laborers, merchant seamen, and artisans in the least remunerative trades such as shoemakers, tailors, coopers, ship caulkers, and stocking weavers. Most slaves and indentured servants were also in this group ideologically. To all these people capitalist enterprise was of small concern, for they owned little property. They were socially (though not geographically) immobile, had limited aspirations, and clung to traditional ideas of a moral economy in which the fair wage and just price rather than free competition and the laws of supply and demand ruled. Family, pride in workmanship, religion, and community counted for more than capital accumulation. "Proud of [our] rank, we aspired no higher," they asserted.[16]

In Boston the radical Evangelicals (along with many of the liberal Whigs) worked to sabotage the public markets, stopped the exportation of grain when food was in short supply, defended themselves against impressment and attempts to coerce their labor in workhouses, and attacked the mansions of the wealthy during the Stamp Act disturbances. Their leaders were sometimes drawn from their own ranks, such as shoemakers Ebenezer MacIntosh in Boston and Samuel Simpson in Philadelphia, and sometimes from the middle stratum, with men such as Thomas Young, Alexander McDougall, and James Cannon, who themselves had risen out of poverty, retained bone-deep egalitarian notions, and still identified with the lowest ranks. Much of their consciousness harked back to the levelers of mid-seventeenth-century England. They found their folk heroes in men such as Cornet George Joyce, an obscure tailor in Cromwell's army who in 1647 had captured Charles I, urged his death, and, according to folklore, stood at the executioner's side when the ax fell.

A great social and economic distance separated these dispossessed and struggling residents of the port towns from the conservative Whigs, who saw them as rabble whose profligacy consigned them forever to self-imposed poverty. In turn, the poor and unfree saw the mercantile elite as oppressors and believed that the laboring poor were "a vital part of God's great plan for the redemption of the world." Most of them would have agreed with Adam Smith, the great codifier of the rising philosophy of self-interest, that "Civil Authority, so far as it is instituted for the security of property, is in reality instituted for the defense of the rich against the poor, or of those who have some property against those who have none at all."[17] Less distance separated them from the liberal Whigs, with whom they sometimes joined forces.

The other major group of Evangelicals was made up of social reformers, mostly clergymen, with a sprinkling of middle-class doctors, lawyers, tradesmen, and teachers. Unified primarily by a highly moralistic temperament, they shared with Whigs a commitment to political liberty and protection of property but simultaneously decried the Whig commercial spirit, which they believed was corrupting American society. They wanted to reverse the course of historical development, particularly to halt the growth of capitalistic activity, and to return society to its ascetic beginnings, when civic virtue, spartan living, and a disdain for worldly things had prevailed. For them the Revolution was the millennium.

It seems clear that this impulse to reverse the course of commercial development was much stronger in Boston than in New York and Philadelphia. One reason was the greater hold of the seventeenth-century past on New England. The Puritan ethic, with its suspicion of wealth and grudging tolerance of mercantile activity, persisted in Boston. Looking backward to ancestral virtue and communal attachment, some of the descendants of the Puritan founders saw the Revolution as an opportunity to restore dedication to the "Corporate Christian values that stressed denial more than opportunity and social order more than mobility."[18]

In revolutionary situations those who speak for moral regeneration, root-and-branch reform, self-sacrifice, service to the common cause, and the possibility of perfecting society have a built-in advantage. To engage in revolution is to wipe the slate clean. Upon the fresh surface anything may be written, and those who speak for a *novus ordo saeculorum*—a new civil polity—are hard to resist. The social and political ideology of these spokesmen provided the major rationale for resisting English invasion of the liberties of Englishmen in America and a substantial impetus for the reformation of American society. Though resisting the Evangelical bias against the growth of commercial capitalism, many Whigs were tinged by the moral strictures of the reformers.

The reformers believed in classical republicanism or civic humanism, the principal elements of which were the sacrifice of individual interests to the pursuit of the common good (a characteristic so central that it became encapsulated in the word "virtue"); balanced government, which provided stability while guarding against corruption by any element of society; and the maintenance of a general equality in society, which would prevent concentration of political power and the oligarchy or despotism that inevitably followed. Republicanism was not a detailed plan of government; it was, more fundamentally, an attitude toward government, toward society, and toward the character of the people.

The clash between the Whig and Evangelical casts of mind is visible in the strong resistance to several elements of republicanism by broad segments of the urban populace. One point of tension was the republican notion that virtue, "the passion for pursuing the public good," was incompatible with the pursuit of private interest.[19] Especially in the cities, though to some extent throughout the colonies, Americans had cleaved to the competing notion that the public good in a market society was best served by each individual's pursuing his own self-interest. This eventually became known as the ideology of economic liberalism, an elaborate defense of which was published in 1776 by Adam Smith.

A second element of republicanism that never gained acceptance among most urban people was the notion that commerce corrupts. American republicanism remained ambivalent on the subject. Many of its agrarian exponents vilified the cities, scourged trade, and heaped abuse on the urban Whig gentility for their ostentation and affluence.

But even farmers were tied into an Atlantic commercial network, so in the end most of the reformers succumbed to the doctrine of free trade.

The third element of republicanism that many in the cities could not easily digest was the emphasis on social equality. The republican writers saw an organic connection between economic and political power. They regarded general economic equality as absolutely essential to political freedom. The concentration of wealth led ineluctably to oligarchy. Republicanism could flourish only in a society of independent, roughly equal citizens. The chances of achieving this polity were greatest in simple, agricultural societies in which land was widely held and agrarian laws prevented the concentration of property. Advocates of such a society came to be known as the "country party."

For many Whigs in the cities, merchants foremost among them, the idea that a republican society must be based on general equality of condition was unacceptable. Given the course of colonial development, such equality could be accomplished only by a massive redistribution of property, and protection of property was one of the main incentives for resisting England. So equality and freedom, the latter defined as being secure in one's property, stood opposed to each other. Many of the Evangelicals, who wrote and published their pamphlets in the cities, minimized the issue of equality and concentrated instead on moral corruption and the need to reinstill a concern for the general welfare. John Adams was one of those who had read republican theory carefully enough to understand the connection between economic inequality and political corruption. In his manuscript of *Dissertation on the Feudal and Canon Law,* one of the most powerful republican statements of the 1760s, Adams wrote: "Property monopolized or in the Possession of a few is a Curse to Mankind. We should preserve not an Absolute Equality—this is unnecessary, but preserve all from extreme Poverty, and all others from extravagant Riches."[20] However, caught between Whig and Evangelical modes of thinking, and engaged as he was with wealthy Whig merchants in the early stages of resistance, Adams thought better of the statement and deleted it from his text. He never again called for smoothing out inequities in wealth. Most of the reformers chose not to speak about structural inequalities, but concentrated on defects in the colonial character as it had evolved over past generations. Morality became the badge of the reformers, and the radicals were left to bear the standards of equality.

It is the presence of these different ideologies—sometimes overlapping, often antagonistic, none appearing in pure form, and all of them changing during these tumultuous years—that makes the urban experience after 1765 so difficult to comprehend. It is also what made the resistance movement and the social upheaval in the cities so difficult to control. Samuel Adams might inveigh that "Luxury & Extravagance are in my opinion totally destructive of those Virtues which are necessary for the Preservation of the Liberty and Happiness of the People."[21] Yet Adams, though himself devoid of capitalistic urges, was trying to lead a radical movement from New England's largest commercial center and had to work with John Hancock, who lived high on the hill and stocked his cellar with the best Madeira wines. Hancock's purse and prestige were vital to the success of the Massachusetts patriot movement, and he was not risking his life and fortune for a return to arcadian simplicity. Similarly, Benjamin Rush in Philadelphia believed that revolution would usher in the millennial Second Coming and achieve the purification of American society, but Rush had to march in step with John Dickinson, an urbane lawyer with a country estate, a retinue of slaves, and a fondness for the aristocratic life-style.

Thus different groups in the port towns began walking the road to revolution with different social ideals. Even within groups that had the same attitudes toward economic activity, such as the merchants and higher artisans, acrid divisions would arise as the Revolution drew nearer. What remains is to examine how these groups—especially merchants, manufacturers and master craftsmen, and the lower levels of the laboring classes—struggled after 1765 to maintain or acquire political power in order to implement their vision of the future. Why was the urban gentry so successful in maintaining its hold on the levers of power in Boston, somewhat less so in New York, and utterly unsuccessful in Philadelphia?

Resurgence of the Gentry in Boston

In Boston, where the Stamp Act disturbances had been most intense and the merchant-lawyer gentry had blanched as an impoverished shoemaker veteran of the Seven Years' War gained control of the streets, the Whig leadership reasserted itself after 1765. "Captain-General" MacIntosh disappeared as a crowd leader and shortly after the Boston Massacre in 1770 was languishing in debtors' jail.

The eclipse of MacIntosh did not bring peace to Boston's streets. The arrival of the new Board of Custom Commissioners, which made its headquarters in Boston in 1767, the imposition of the hated Town-shend duties in the same year, and the arrival of British troops to occupy the recalcitrant town in 1768 all kept the Massachusetts capital in a state of turmoil. Nor did crowd activity or organized violence against crown officials end. The battering of customs official Benjamin Hallowell after his seizure of John Hancock's ship *Liberty* in 1768, the confrontation with British troops on the icy night of March 5, 1770, and the Tea Party in 1773 are only the most spectacular of a series of incidents that made Boston by far the most turbulent northern seaport in the climactic years before the Revolution.

As the Whig leaders regained their influence with laboring people, they carefully drew a line between controlled violence directed at ob-noxious crown officials and their supporters and mass violence that sprang from internal social grievances. James Otis, moderator of the town meeting in 1767, tried to smooth over interclass hostility by asserting that "let our burthens be ever so heavy, or our grievances ever so great, no possible circumstances, tho' ever so oppressive, could be supposed sufficient to justify private tumults and disorders."[22] The *Boston Gazette,* the most influential paper among the laboring people, called repeatedly for "No Mobs or Tumults," and early in 1768 Samuel Adams, now emerging as the principal radical leader, assumed the name "Populus" and wrote that the people should remain quiet and follow the *Gazette*'s advice—"NO MOBS—NO CONFUSIONS—NO TUMULTS."[23] When effigies of Customs Commissioner Charles Paxton and Inspector General John Williams were discovered hanging from the Liberty Tree in the South End in March 1768, three members of the Loyal Nine cut them down before a crowd could assemble. Shortly after that an angry crowd, smashing windows and burning the property of customs officials in retaliation for the seizure of the *Liberty*, were dispersed by radical leaders who rushed to the scene crying "To your Tents O Israel."[24]

After 1766 Samuel Adams, who came closer than any other Amer-ican to becoming a professional politician, emerged as the leader of the Whig resistance. Operating through the North End Caucus, the Masonic lodge, the fire companies, and the taverns, he was shortly known in England as one of the most dangerous men in the colonies. Although Adams spoke the language of the old Puritans, stressing the need for moral reform, an end to luxury and extravagance, and a return to the rustic simplicity of bygone days, his utopian vision did not prevent him from working effectively with Boston's Whig merchants, who sought the end of the tough new policy of trade regulation. From 1766 to 1770 Adams served on town meeting committees with the most politically active merchants, including John Hancock, who financed many of the patriotic celebrations and feasts that kept politics on everyone's mind and helped to build interclass bridges during these years.

Passage of the Townshend duties in 1767 put the revived Whig leadership to the test. Nonconsumption of British goods was the first response and helped to unify Boston's social ranks. Adams reveled in nonconsumption as a means of drawing every member of the community into a political fellowship, a latter-day Puritan community covenant whose common goal was repeal of the Townshend Acts. At the same time, eschewing imported British finery would "mow down luxury and high living in New England."[25] Adams had always been offended by mercantile affluence in Boston and liked to compare the ostentatious shows of wealth by Boston's rich with the humble rusticity of the Bay colony's founders. Boston's merchants could afford to endure these barbs, for in nonconsumption they saw their best chance of reversing British policy. For Boston's mechanics the economic boycott also had advantages because it provided the biggest boon to home manufacturing in the town's history.

The effectiveness of economic boycott depended on stopping all goods at the water's edge, and many merchants in Boston who were engaged in international trade and closely attached to the governor's interests had no intention of being bound by a community compact that had no force in law. Exhortation and insult could do only so much to change the minds of these high-placed men, who included many of the colony's largest importers. In the end persuasion of a more physical kind proved necessary. Street brigades were used to terrify uncooperative importers and to disrupt the work of the reinforced customs corps, which was increasingly effective in stopping the smuggling of Dutch tea, French molasses, and other contraband goods that had built the fortunes of many Whig merchants and provided employment for hundreds of artisans in the town. Whig leaders in 1768 began resorting to crowd action to "rescue" goods seized by customs officials and to intimidate them from doing their work when illegal goods were about to be landed. But Whig leaders continued to promote the distinction between violence directed at external enemies—or their local agents—and violence inspired by demands for internal reform.

During the years of nonimportation, from 1768 to 1770, Whig

leaders found two men who proved particularly effective in directing street crowds. The first was William Molineux, a small trader who was passionate for the Whig cause. Given to both rhetorical and physical violence, and down-to-earth enough to mingle easily with lesser artisans and waterfront roughnecks, Molineux was firmly connected to the merchant leadership that still controlled the town meeting and worked hand in hand with the best-established artisans and petty entrepreneurs who composed the Sons of Liberty. It was he who led nearly every mass action from 1768 to 1771.

The second important street leader and intermediary between the Whig leaders and the laboring classes of Boston during these years was Thomas Young, a doctor who had come in 1766 from Albany, New York. His hostility toward men of wealth and power, expressed earlier in his attacks on grasping landlords and speculators in New York, and his iconoclastic religious views made him an unlikely lieutenant of the merchant Whigs of Boston. He sat repeatedly on committees of the Sons of Liberty, the town meeting, and the North End Caucus, led crowds to enforce nonimportation, and participated in the Tea Party. Like Molineux, he also played a crucial role in halting undesired violence.

Young was far more radical than Boston's Whig leadership. Shortly after his arrival he was writing in the papers that an "increase of property," which made its owners "haughty and imperious" and "cruel and oppressive," was the great danger in government. "People of the lower ranks" must share political power in order to restrict the grip of the rich and powerful, and the town should have a building commodious enough to hold "all that chose to attend" the debates of the legislature. He referred to the common people as "those worthy members of society," the people who would "form the revolution of the other ranks of citizens."[26]

With MacIntosh no longer at the center of mass politics, men such as Young and Molineux were vitally important to Whig leaders because they were popular among the artisans and laborers. The relationship was doubtless tenuous at times—both between these middle-class intermediaries and the lower ranks and between the merchant leadership and the intermediaries. On several occasions laboring Bostonians acted on their own, as in the waterfront brawls in 1769 and 1770 between ropewalk workers and moonlighting British soldiers. But through their street captains the Whig leaders regained, even if precariously, their direction of affairs in the town.

In 1770 the repeal of all the Townshend duties except the one on tea drove a wedge deep into the interclass Whig coalition in Boston. News of the impending repeal had reached the colony in December 1769, bringing many merchants to the verge of breaking ranks. Some of them had seen enough violence; others were eager to get black ink back on their ledgers. January 1, 1770, had been specified as the deadline of the original agreement, and immediately afterward a number of merchants began selling goods that had been stored in warehouses for months. Whig leaders responded by organizing the populace, male and female, franchised and unfranchised, free and bound, into a group styled "The Body of the People," a name heavily laden with covenant connotations, to descend on the merchants' meetings at Faneuil Hall. Four times in January 1770 the leaders around Samuel Adams called meetings of "The Body." Anti-British leaders, the conservative *Boston Chronicle* reported, went "trotting from house to house, to engage the master workmen to suffer their journeymen and apprentices to attend."[27] From twelve hundred to two thousand people responded.

The rift that appeared between merchants and mechanics is not hard to understand: most of the former had much to gain by resuming importation and most of the latter had much to lose. In the summer of 1770, when New York and Philadelphia merchants also resumed importing, conflict in Boston came to a head. By fall the interclass coalition verged on collapse. Moderate merchants had become convinced that mercantile interest had nothing further to gain from nonimportation.

The broad division in Whig ranks continued to grow, and the Tea Act in 1773 widened it further. As before, economic sanctions were viewed as the most effective response to an obnoxious act. Seeking the broadest possible base, the radical leadership convened "The Body," defined as the entire community of concerned individuals. As many as five thousand turned out to determine an appropriate response to threats upon their liberties. The Committee of Correspondence, formed late in 1772 to promote unified intercolony action, adopted nonimportation as its formal response to the latest British outrage but took clandestine action of a less peaceful sort, organizing the destruction of £9,000 worth of tea.

Governor Hutchinson believed that although men of wealth were present, the huge crowds that gathered to decide what Boston should do with the tea consignees "consisted principally of the lower Ranks of the People"; "even Journeymen Tradesmen," he sputtered, "were brought to increase the Number and the Rabble were not excluded."[28] The merchants tried desperately to head off a crisis with England by subscribing money to pay for the destroyed tea. At the same time they opposed the growing movement for nonimportation. England's response to the Tea Party was to pass the Coercive Acts, which closed Boston harbor until payment was made for the tea; virtually to end representative government in Massachusetts and its capital; and to put Boston under the military rule of General Thomas Gage. Samuel Adams and his cohorts, organizing resistance through the Boston Committee of Correspondence, countered with "The Solemn League and Covenant," a community compact for boycotting all English goods.

The Solemn League and Covenant was beamed at the ordinary people and explicitly denigrated the merchants, who were all but excluded from the meaning of community. "This effectual plan," wrote the Committee of Correspondence, "has been originated and been thus carried through by the two venerable orders of men styled Mechanicks and Husbandmen, the strength of every community." No longer trust-

7. *View of Boston in 1774 by Paul Revere*

ing "mercantile Avarice," members of the committee carried the compact around the town, asking both men and women to sign it.[29]

Most merchants now concluded that they must repulse those who
were moving the populace along a suicidal course. They came in force
to a town meeting in June 1774, intending to censure and abolish the
Committee of Correspondence. The debate carried over to the next
day, when the radical committee finally gained an overwhelming vote
of confidence. The merchants trooped out, disheartened and bitter.
One hundred thirty-seven of them promptly signed petitions protesting
that the Solemn League would cripple Boston's trade. They were now
irreparably divided from most of Boston's laboring people. Some merchants such as Hancock and John Rowe attempted to maintain a middle
position, opposing nonimportation and eschewing the radical resistance leadership yet not going over publicly to the Hutchinson circle.
But Boston was now under military rule and the die was cast.

What is most remarkable about the turbulent years after 1765 is
that laboring people in Boston, though defiant of the British and more
active in the streets than people in other port towns, were conspicuously
inactive as a separate group and made virtually no demands for an
enlargement of their role in the political process. The electorate continued to fill the important town offices with merchants, doctors, and
lawyers. The same was true of the special committees appointed by
the town meeting to recommend how the town should respond to
such emergencies as the Massacre, the Tea Act, and the Port Act. The
Committee of Correspondence and all the other ad hoc committees
were routinely filled with professional men such as James Otis, Joseph
Warren, Benjamin Church, and Thomas Young and the most anti-
British merchants such as William Molineux, Nathaniel Appleton, Oliver
Wendell, Caleb Davis, and Robert Pierpont.

Second, the artisans never organized a Mechanics Committee as in
the other cities to push their own demands for internal reforms and
made no demands for democratizing politics. The single change in the
political modus operandi came in 1766 when the House of Representatives agreed to erect a public gallery at the instigation of the voters
of Cambridge. This proposal passed because Whig politicians, seeking
to broaden their support, decided to turn the House of Representatives
into a "School of Political Learning," as Thomas Young put it.[30]

Third, the lower artisans and laborers seem to have made no demands in Boston for a broadening of the suffrage, which was narrower
at the beginning of the 1760s than in either New York or Philadelphia.

Finally, artisans' voices were conspicuously absent from Boston news-papers and broadsides, whereas in both New York and Philadelphia after 1767 dozens of partisan pleas were specifically addressed to or signed by "A Tradesman," "A Mechanic," "A Carpenter," or others who spoke for the laboring segment of urban society. In Boston radical Whig appeals emanated from "Publius," "Americanus," "Publicola," and other spokesmen of the corporate whole.

There are several reasons why challenges to the gentry's control in Boston receded after 1765. Of great importance was the presence of the British army, which served to focus the attention of all Bostonians on the external crisis with England and thus to mute interclass hostility. No less important in the submersion of social tension between ranks was the ability of the radical resistance leaders to employ the struggle against the English as a means of reaffirming the ancient Puritan con-cept of corporate communalism. By insisting that Boston must fight as a community against British oppression and traitorous townsmen who knuckled under to British perversions of constitutional rights, Samuel Adams and other leaders were able to convince laboring people that they were essential to the struggle for freedom, even if they could not vote. By a de facto inclusion of everyone in the political community, the radical leadership preempted demands for a broadened suffrage, for artisan officeholders, or for separate mechanics' organizations. This process began in 1767 when the nonconsumption pact was drawn up not by merchants, as in the case of the economic boycott of 1765, but by the town meeting, which then circulated the agreement among all the townspeople for signing.

In 1769, when Boston merchants began to break ranks on non-importation, the resistance leaders began calling into action "The Body of the People," which included everyone, regardless of age, sex, rank, or voting status. Especially in policing the nonimportation agreement in 1768 and 1769, the people at large assumed the functions of civil government, ferreting out violators, fastening on them the opprobrium of the community, and coercing them to mend their ways. The hum-blest laborers on Boston's wharves, even adolescents and slaves, became part of the political community when they daubed the houses of im-porters with "Hillsborough paint," a peculiar recipe of body wastes, or pummeled zealous royal panjandrums who searched for smuggled goods. In this spirit, when some conservatives challenged the presence of unfranchised mechanics at an important town meeting in 1770, they were shouted down by men who argued that "if they had no Property

they had Liberty, and their posterity might have property."³¹ By the
early 1770s the Boston town meeting itself was frequently convened
as "The Body of the People."

A high degree of religious uniformity in Whig ranks and the ability
of leaders such as Samuel Adams to turn the resistance movement into
a kind of religious crusade also muted class discord and diverted attention from internal restructuring. In 1774 the notion of an interclass
crusade, in which politics, religion, and morality were inseparable, was
summed up in "The Solemn League and Covenant." Every Bostonian
knew that this was the name of the alliance of Scottish and English
Puritans who had labored twelve decades before to reform the Anglican
church and had finally rebelled against Charles I. Now all latter-day
Puritans—women as well as men—must reform a corrupt England by
denying themselves imported goods, an act not only of economic coer-
cion but also of self-denial and purification. Later in 1774 the Quebec
Act, which established the Catholic religion and French law in the
conquered Canadian territories, further heightened Boston Protestants'
sense of the need to unite to resist the English government.

It was not only their receptivity to corporate ideology, the religious
cast of the resistance movement, and the role they were given in "The
Body of the People" that led Boston's laboring people to acquiesce in
leadership from above in the decade after 1765. They were also well
served by the economic policies of their leaders. Nonimportation was
not uniformly beneficial to artisans and laborers, but it benefited a very
substantial number. For those who were hurt the resistance leaders did
what they could through make-work projects, primarily in textile production and in out-relief. When the Boston Port Act closed the harbor
completely in mid-1774, laboring people were reduced to desperate
straits; but by that time everyone was suffering and the Whig leaders
could at least serve the laboring classes by directing the collection and
distribution of poor-relief funds that were flowing in from other colonies.

Thus the forging of class consciousness and demands for a new
social order, which burst forth in 1765 and might have been expected
to crystallize in the most turbulent and disordered decade in Boston's
history, were halted in their tracks. Many merchants became loyalists
or tried to maintain a neutral position. A larger number, including
most of the lesser merchants and inland traders, held their ground and
learned that the mechanics and merchant seamen would accept their
leadership if, in the name of the corporate community, their needs and

their political particiption were considered, even if not legitimized in law.

Struggle for Power in New York

In New York the last decade before revolution witnessed the rapid growth of the techniques of popular politics, but Whig merchants and lawyers, both liberal and conservative, clung to political control until 1775. Of the three northern ports New York had by far the most liberal franchise and hence the largest number of laboring men participating in electoral politics, and more artisans there were elected to important municipal offices than in any other city. Yet they could not unite after 1765. The artisans did develop group consciousness, they gave vent to strong class feelings, and they deeply distrusted the men who occupied the leadership positions. But they were unable to use this collective identity to dislodge the city's wealthiest merchants until the shot heard around the world sent many of the latter into loyalist retirement.

In their participation in the formal political arena New York's laboring men were far in advance of their Boston and Philadelphia counterparts during these years. At least two-thirds of free adult males could vote, compared with less than half in Boston and Philadelphia, for freemanship in New York was not tied to property ownership but was available upon payment of a modest fee if one was of age and satisfied the residency requirement. Craftsmen were also elected to important city offices in substantial numbers. From 1761 to 1771, 61 percent of the constables, collectors, and assessors elected were artisans, compared with about 20 percent of the second-level officials in Boston and 46 percent in Philadelphia. Even more striking, 30 percent of the common councilmen chosen in New York from 1761 to 1775 were mechanics, whereas in Boston less than 10 percent of the selectmen and moderators were chosen from artisan ranks. It is also clear from the political broadsides and pamphlets in the elections of 1768 and 1769 that appeals for the votes of artisans and laborers were essential for winning office.

The exercise of political power outside formal political institutions also grew enormously in New York during the prerevolutionary decade. Mass meetings, at which everyone had a voice, and house-to-house canvassing became common. Thousands attended open-air gatherings on the issues of nonimportation in 1768, the quartering of British troops in 1769, the abandonment of nonimportation in 1770, its reinstitution in 1773, and the Intolerable Acts in 1774. In 1770, opposing factions decided to resolve the importation question by going door to door, conducting what was perhaps the first public opinion poll in American history. The will of the people was being determined quite apart from whether individuals were franchised or not.

Artisan participation, however, did not necessarily bring artisan power, as laboring men learned in 1770, when most New York merchants privately agreed to abandon nonimportation after Parliament rescinded all the Townshend duties except the one on tea. Artisans regarded the merchants' actions as a betrayal of a community compact and concluded that only by forming associations of their own and developing an independent voice could they hope to achieve their patriotic goals and defend their own economic interests.

Since the merchants had shattered the united front, the mechanics determined to act autonomously. A broadside issued on May 2, 1770, dripped with sarcasm at the defecting merchants. They had initially agreed to nonimportation, it was charged, in order "to collect in their debts, to vend their moth-eaten fragments, and to clear at least fifteen percent." Mechanics, in their view, were only "two legged pack horses . . . created solely to contribute to the ease and affluence of a few importers," and "a kind of beast of burden, who . . . may be seen in a state but should not be heard." After resuming importation, the merchants, it was recommended, should bend their efforts toward erecting a new manufactory where mechanics and their families, who were "inured to the severest bodily labour," would be compelled to work. When they expired, merchants could skin them and take their hides to the company tanyards. Another manufactory could be erected at the taxpayers' expense "for dressing, currying, and tanning the said hides" of laboring people and the profits could then be handed over to the merchants.[32] Productive labor, in this Swiftian satire, was now pitted against capitalist investment.

Despite growing class consciousness and alienation from the merchant gentry, New York's laboring men could not unite in these years. The artisan vote was deeply split in both 1768 and 1769 between the conservative DeLancey and moderate Livingston parties. The house-by-house canvass in 1770 produced 1,180 signatures for resuming importation and only 350 for maintaining the boycott, although the Sons of Liberty claimed that bribes or misunderstanding produced most of the signatures for resuming trade.

As in the other ports, artisans generally favored nonimportation because it gave them a protected market. Those who benefited especially were artificers in the metal crafts and textile production; furniture-, coach-, and instrumentmakers; and shoemakers, saddlers, hatters, and glovers—those who produced for the gentry, who had previously purchased these items from England. Those whom nonimportation could not help, and often hurt, were building craftsmen, the ship construction trades, petty retailers, and some woodworkers such as coopers and turners. They were hurt in a general economic decline that, at least according to the importing merchants, was the inevitable result of economic boycott. Mariners, who were numerous and extremely active in resistance activities, were not affected much by nonimportation, because the volume of tonnage in and out of New York did not decline during periods of nonimportation but was merely rechanneled elsewhere or continued to England in items such as furs and grain, which were not included in the nonintercourse sanctions.

Personal loyalty had another, more important dimension, which may be labeled economic clientage. Many master artisans owned their own houses and shops, worked independently to fill customers' orders, and thus were at least partially insulated from economic pressure from above. Far more numerous were those beholden to merchants, lawyers, and urban landholders who controlled their rents, job opportunities, credit, and even personal affairs. Seventy percent of the mechanics who voted in the 1768 and 1769 elections or obtained voting rights in 1770 could not qualify to vote as freeholders—owners of £40 of real property. Most of these were tenants whose rent and house tenure were at risk as they stepped to the polling place. For many others, such as mariners and ship construction workers, jobs were at stake because merchants controlled the investment capital necessary for maritime construction and their ship masters could give or withhold berths as they pleased. Even though the system of dependent labor was weakening, an extensive network of economic clientage remained.

Economic dependency also existed in the other port towns, but in New York it translated into political loyalty to an unusual degree because only there was voice balloting, called viva voce voting, used instead of the secret ballot. Each shipwright, shoemaker, baker, and laborer had to step forward and publicly announce his preference before the assembled gentry. This voting method canceled out all the supposedly greater political power that the more lenient franchise requirements and the tradition of artisan officeholding seemed to confer.

In 1769 New York's popular leaders and their laboring-class sup-

porters launched an all-out effort to substitute a system of secret balloting such as Boston and Philadelphia had used for decades. The
previous year Oliver DeLancey and his wealthy cohorts had "posted
themselves at the approaches to the City's election green" and "coaxed
and bullied each voter as he strode to the poll" to announce his choice.[33]
The campaign for secret balloting, led by the liberal Whigs, reached
its height in late 1769 and early 1770. Newspaper and broadside writers
argued that if this "antidote to Corruption" was passed by the assembly
"no Man of Opulence will be able to procure a Seat . . . by an undue
influence upon the Fears of the Electors."[34] But after rallies and coun-
terrallies, petitions and counterpetitions, the voice vote remained entrenched. New York's representatives, all wealthy merchants of the
DeLancey faction, paid little heed to the broad demand for reform,
voting unanimously against the balloting bill in the assembly in January
1770. Even so, the vote ended in a twelve-twelve tie, but went down
to defeat on the speaker's negative vote.

The power of viva voce voting to intimidate voters from the lower
ranks, especially in times of economic hardship, when artisans and
laborers needed credit and employment, explains much about the failure of laboring New Yorkers to unite. It casts in a new light the
merchants' house-by-house poll of their tenant-tradesmen in 1770,
whose results showed a two-thirds majority in favor of resuming full
commercial ties with England. Leaders of the lower ranks attempted
to instill courage in ordinary people by calling a meeting for resisting
the petition, but the knocks on the door could not go unanswered.
Despite its democratic appearance, the house-to-house canvass was
simply another form of political arm-twisting.

After the détente in British-American relations in 1771 and 1772
the radical resistance leaders of New York, who had experienced such
difficulties in unifying laboring men, made their final push. When news
of the Tea Act reached the city, Alexander McDougall and others
distributed fifteen hundred copies of a broadside entitled *Association of
the Sons of Liberty*, which condemned those who accepted consignments
of East India Company tea as traitors and declared a boycott of their
businesses. Two thousand New Yorkers stood in the rain at a mass
rally in December 1773 to approve a total ban on tea. But tea leaves
proved not to be the issue that could unite laboring men either for
opposition to British policies or for the promotion of internal reforms.
Even though New Yorkers staged their own tea party, destroying a
small shipment that Captain James Chambers attempted to smuggle

into the city in April 1774, the radicals could not maintain their momentum. In fact the tea episode so frightened conservative New Yorkers that they began an all-out effort to reassert their authority. One writer, a sworn foe "to *Cobblers and Tailors* so long as they take upon their everlasting and immeasurable shoulders the power of directing the loyal and sensible inhabitants of the city," declared the determination of propertied men to halt popular action. More and more the question became who would control the extralegal committees that were called into being by mass meetings of the people. "After the destruction of Captain Chamber's tea and some other violent proceedings of the pretended patriots," wrote Governor Colden, "the principal inhabitants began to be apprehensive and resolved to attend the meetings of the inhabitants when called together by hand bills."[35]

Another test of the locus of political power came when New Yorkers had to decide how to respond to the closing of the port of Boston in May 1774. Separate meetings were called by the importing merchants and by small traders and artisans. For several days the two groups contested the appointment of a committee to stay in touch with the Boston Committee of Correspondence and to hammer out a policy for New Yorkers. Indicative of their growing class consciousness, the artisans now formed a Mechanics Committee, which soon superseded the Sons of Liberty and nominated a slate of twenty-five persons to correspond with Boston's resistance leaders and to enforce any new economic boycott. The Merchants Committee responded with a slate of fifty-one, which included some of the Sons of Liberty as a concession but was predominantly conservative. As an impasse with England approached, the voters were asked to decide which slate should be presented for popular endorsement. The young aristocrat Gouverneur Morris reported "a great concourse of the inhabitants" on May 19 to contend "about the future forms of our government, whether it should be founded upon Aristocratic or democratic principles." Looking down on the crowd from a balcony, Morris described the scene: "on my right hand were ranged all the people of property, with some few dependents, and on the other all the tradesmen."[36]

The meeting produced a victory for the conservative merchants, whose Committee of 51 was chosen. "You may rest assured," wrote one jubilant patrician, "no non-im[portation], nor non-exportation will be agreed upon . . . The power over our crowd is no longer in the hands of Sears, Lamb, or such unimportant persons . . . Their power . . . expired instantly upon the election of the . . . Fifty-one."[37]

Although New York's conservative merchants squelched the commercial boycott and stifled the movement for internal reform, they had not reckoned with the possibility that their hard-won ground would be cut from under them by the First Continental Congress, which met in Philadelphia in the fall of 1774. New York's four delegates represented the sentiments of the victorious conservatives, but they could not prevent the formation of a Continental Association that pledged all the colonies to adhere to a step-by-step cessation of commercial relations with Great Britain. This gave a tremendous boost to the mechanics of New York, and they used it to secure nearly half of the places on the Committee of 60 that was selected at the end of the year to enforce the association. By the following April, when fighting broke out at Lexington and Concord, public order was crumbling in New York, and the DeLanceyites, who had controlled the extralegal committees, were resigning their places and establishing their credit with the loyalist element around the governor. They had held on tenaciously to the very end.

Interclass relations in New York were significantly different from those in Boston, although in both cities British soldiers became the target of much of the resentment that the poor and unemployed might otherwise have channeled into efforts to restructure society. It was the vote of James DeLancey for the Quartering Act in 1769 that drove radical resistance leaders Sears and Lamb to reunite with McDougall and the moderate Livingston-led party. Their followers doggedly defended the Liberty Pole against royal soldiers in the fall of 1766 and fought them intermittently thereafter. Two bloody fights between troops and populace on Golden Hill and in Nassau Street in 1770 served as equivalents to the fracases that led to the Boston Massacre in the same year. Unemployment and high food prices were the issues for those in the lowest levels of the economy, but impressment by the British navy and moonlighting by British soldiers provided the most immediate focuses for their discontent.

A second reason for the absence of a strong artisan bloc in politics, despite growing class hostility, was the lack of a secret ballot, which restricted collective action. When laboring men were forced by canvasses or public polls to declare themselves, some gave their support to those with economic power over them. Rather than displaying political deference or internalizing the values of their superiors, laboring New Yorkers were responding to a pervasive use of economic leverage from above.

Another factor affecting the coalescence of artisans and laborers in New York was religious tension, particularly between Presbyterians and Anglicans. Religious ties were strong among many people and cannot be ignored; but too much can also be made of them. Shoemakers and bakers, whose religious affiliations varied, voted decisively for the Livingston party in 1768 and 1769, and cartmen unified behind the DeLanceyites in 1774 to endorse the Committee of 51. These are clues that the political preferences of laboring men were determined less by religion than by considerations of economic survival. Yet the large degree of religious homogeneity that promoted interclass unity among Whigs in Boston did not exist in New York.

The power of New York's gentry also owed something to the sheer strength of conservative merchants and professionals to resist pressure from below. More merchants in Boston joined the forces of resistance than in New York, and the most flexible retained their power by convincing laboring people that their cause was one. A greater proportion of New York's merchants were diehard conservatives and wished to concede nothing to reformers. Animated "by fear of a civil war" and by anxiety that "the levelling spirit of New England should propagate itself into New York," the elite spoke not the language of covenant but the language of an embattled class.[38] When the time came for a final decision, they joined the loyalist cause in numbers unmatched in any other port town, leaving a partial vacuum into which artisan radicals could step.

Once war became a certainty and conservatives began abandoning New York, the city teemed with cries for social reform. When Whig leaders proposed the drafting of a constitution, the Mechanics Committee demanded popular ratification of any document produced and a provision for "an uncontrolled power to alter the constitution in the same manner that it shall have been received."[39] Throughout the first half of 1776 the city's newspapers were filled with articles proposing annual assembly elections, rotation of offices, secret balloting, universal adult male suffrage, equal apportionment, popular election of local officials, and the abolition of slavery and of imprisonment for debt. In the last months before the Revolution the city seethed with artisan voices and artisan action, as the wealthy fled in anticipation of military occupation by the army of the Continental Congress and patriotic committees of inspection disarmed the Tories.

Liberal Whig leaders such as John Jay, Philip Schuyler, James Duane, and Robert Livingston had eagerly sought the support of the lower ranks in their opposition to English policies; but on internal issues they resisted pressure from below and countenanced far less extensive reform than their social inferiors. In repulsing most of the demands of lower-class radicals, New York's liberal Whigs were greatly aided by the arrival of Washington's continental troops in the spring of 1776.

Radical Triumph in Philadelphia

Philadelphia artisans had participated least in political affairs before 1765, and during the Stamp Act crisis they were so deeply split that one group of mechanics had opposed another group. Yet laboring men in Philadelphia coalesced so well after 1770 that this was the place where artisans most effectively infiltrated the extralegal committee structure and took the most radical steps to reform society internally.

Before 1770 artisans seldom held office in Philadelphia, except occasionally as an overseer of the poor, street commissioner, or tax collector. But artisan voices were rising in answer to economic insecurity. Writing in the *Pennsylvania Chronicle* in 1767, "Tom Trudge" expressed his objection to the annual road tax that went primarily to pave the roads and remove the refuse in parts of the city where the well-to-do were concentrated. The poor, like himself, "sup on a cup of skim milk and have a parcel of half-naked children about our doors"; but rarely did they see the city dung carts come to their "penurious" alleyways. Why should they pay "for cleaning the yards of the opulent merchants and gentry"?[40]

Philadelphia's artisans exerted themselves as a separate political entity for the first time in the spring of 1768 in attempting, like their counterparts in Boston and New York, to spur foot-dragging merchants to adopt a nonimportation policy. Not until March 1769, a year after Boston and New York had adopted nonimportation, did this popular pressure succeed, and by then the artisans' disillusionment with the merchants was widespread. The merchants attempted to break free of the nonimportation agreement early in 1770, imperiously informing the mechanics that they had "no Right to give their sentiments respecting an importation" and calling them "a Rabble."[41]

It took nothing more to convince the artisans that they must work independently for their objectives and even assume responsibility for setting and enforcing the community's goals. They called a public meeting of their fellows in May 1770 and formed their own Mechanics Committee, four years before a similar all-craft organization was established in New York. They managed to delay the abandonment of nonimportation and showed how far deference toward the merchants had crumbled by promising in June that importing merchants "will be dealt with by the Mechanicks Committee."[42]

By the fall of 1770 merchants were importing again and artisans were on the move. For the first time in many decades an artisan ran for sheriff. Artisans soon began to fill positions as tax assessors and collectors, wardens and street commissioners, and insisted on their right to participate equally with merchants and gentlemen in the nomination of assemblymen and other important officeholders. Addressing his "Brethern the Tradesmen, Mechanics, &c," an artisan who called himself "Brother Chip" gave notice that laboring men would no longer tamely endorse men nominated by the elite, who were always from the upper class.[43]

The assembly election in 1770 was a turning point in Philadelphia politics. Brother Chip's strident call, published in the *Pennsylvania Gazette,* marked the beginning of a new political party, strongly Presbyterian and laboring class in composition, strongly radical in its opposition to British policies, and bent on restructuring society internally. Organizing a new ticket, which included tailor Joseph Parker, the first tradesman to run for the assembly since the 1680s, the emerging radical party won at the polls. "Many Threats, Reflections, Sarcasms, and Burlesques" were hurled against the artisans, according to one Philadelphia merchant, but this kind of abuse did little to deter them; secret balloting kept them largely immune from the economic influence of those they offended.[44]

Inspirited by success in electing their own kind to important offices, Philadelphia's artisans began pressing the legislature in 1772 for economic programs that would benefit them. They opposed excise taxes on liquor because they fell with greatest weight on "the middling and poorer Class of the inhabitants." Similarly, they declared that a Leather Act that drove up the price of skins "oppresses the Poor, by Shoes being considerably advanced in Price."[45] At a meeting in October 1772 artisans issued a call for weekly publication of the full assembly debates and roll calls on important issues—a demand indicative of their distrust of patrician legislators and of their determination to vote only for those who responded to their needs. They also challenged "the absurd and Tyrannical custom of shutting the Assembly doors during debate" and demanded the erection of public galleries there.[46] The artisans won legislative approval on all points. It was enough to leave some genteel

Philadelphians muttering, "It is Time the Tradesmen were checked—they take too much upon them—they ought not to intermeddle in State Affairs—they will become too powerful."⁴⁷

The power of the port towns' most unified and aggressive artisan community showed itself dramatically in Philadelphia's response to the closing of Boston harbor in 1774. As in New York, conservative merchants and lawyers realized that they must assert themselves, both to head off another nonimportation movement and to prevent the extra-legal committee system, to which more and more civil authority was falling, from slipping into the hands of the radicals. Some of Philadelphia's popular leaders, such as Charles Thomson, joined with the more conservative merchants to construct a fusion ticket of nineteen candidates, composed primarily of well-to-do merchants, to act as a Committee of Correspondence for coordinating strategies of resistance with other cities. But the artisans called their own meeting, assembled twelve hundred strong at the statehouse on June 9, 1774, and forced their way into what they called the "Merchants Committee." Faced with this kind of artisan power, the Whig leaders made broad concessions. They dropped two merchant committeemen obnoxious to the artisans and added four Germans, including a baker and a tanner, and six other tradesmen put forward by the Mechanics Committee. About one-third of the resulting Committee of 43, which assumed direction of the city's response to the Boston Port Act, were artisans and small manufacturers—a far cry from New York's Committee of 51, which was composed entirely of merchants and lawyers.

The contrast among the northern ports was equally evident in the elections of enforcement committees after the Continental Congress scheduled a full-scale boycott of English trade in October 1774. Even the fact that the meeting was held in Carpenters Hall rather than in the statehouse was a symbolic victory for artisan radicals, and they accounted for thirteen of the twenty-four inspectors chosen to supervise the election of a sixty-six-person Committee of Inspection. Recognizing their growing strength, the mechanics put forward a radical ticket that excluded every leading conservative from the previous Committee of 43 and gave places to artisans, shopkeepers, and minor merchants from the city's various religious groups and neighborhoods. A conservative merchant slate went down to defeat. Both of the tradesmen's main demands—one reflecting external concerns, one internal—had been fulfilled: that Pennsylvania commit itself unequivocally to an economic boycott and that they participate fully in the extralegal government by committee.

The New York and Boston committees elected in November 1774 to enforce the Continental Association also represented a victory for the radical Whig resistance to the latest British policy, but the composition of the committees reveals the differences in the dynamics of internal social relations. In New York the conservatives still had enough power to oblige the radicals to accept a fusion ticket rather than present the electors with a clear choice of slates, as in Philadelphia. Moreover, the slate of sixty included twelve merchants who would later become loyalists. In Boston the Committee of 63 had no conservative merchants because the Whig leadership had no need to concede anything to a group that had been isolated from the majority of Boston's patriots for several years. Ten artisans, well-situated men such as silversmith Paul Revere, sailmaker Norman Greenough, and blacksmith Richard Boylston, were also represented on the committee. But only in Philadelphia had artisans operating as a self-conscious group been able to grasp the levers of political action.

The implications of this maturing of artisan consciousness became evident in the final year before the Revolution. A new surge of radicalism, led by Thomas Young, James Cannon, Thomas Paine, and Timothy Matlack and centered in the thirty-one companies of the Philadelphia militia that had been organized in the spring of 1775, produced demands for the most radical reforms yet suggested in the colonies. The themes of curbing the individual accumulation of wealth, opening up opportunity, divorcing the franchise from property ownership, and driving the mercantile elite from power became explicit in a flood of polemical literature. "Our great merchants . . . [are] making immense fortunes at the expense of the people," charged a "Tradesman" in April 1775. Sounding the tocsin on economic inequality, which English and European republican writers had stressed but genteel American Whigs saw fit to ignore, Tradesman argued that the merchants "will soon have the whole wealth of the province in their hands, and then the people will be nearly in the condition that the East-India Company reduced the poor natives of Bengal to." Men of this kind must be stopped in "their present prospect of making enormous estates at our expense." Once their "golden harvests" were ended, "all ranks and conditions would come in for their just share of the wealth."[48] Tradesman and others envisioned an independence that included greater economic equality.

By the fall of 1775 the Philadelphia militia had become a school of political education, much in the manner of Cromwell's New Model Army. Organizing their own Committee of Correspondence, the privates began exerting pressure on the assembly to take a more assertive stand on independence. They also made three radical demands for internal change: first, that militiamen be given the right to elect their officers, rather than only their junior officers, as the assembly had specified in the militia law; second, that the franchise be conferred on all militiamen, regardless of age and economic condition; and third, that the assembly impose a heavy financial penalty, proportionate to the size of his estate, on every man who refused militia service, and use this money to support the families of poor militiamen.

The greater ability of Philadelphia's laboring classes to organize and to assert their collective strength was best exemplified in the move to broaden the franchise to include the propertyless and the poor. Coming at a time when a decreasing number of the laboring class held property, this break with the past was of enormous significance. It swept away the traditional view that propertyholding was proof of political competence. In New York and Boston, where the franchise was broad but where economic derangements had impoverished many former propertyholders and hence disqualified them from voting, there was no move to follow Philadelphia's example. The liberal Whig gentry, especially in Boston, were able to maintain control of the political process and to prevent any move toward separating political rights from property ownership.

Why did group consciousness and class power proceed furthest in the city where laboring people had been most deeply divided and least politically active only eleven years before independence? One factor was the absence of the British army, which in Boston and New York had acted as a lightning rod for artisan discontent, especially in times of scarce employment, and had promoted interclass unity by serving as a visible common enemy. Philadelphia never saw more than a token military force.

A second factor was the ability of radical leaders, such as the small merchant Charles Thomson, schoolteacher James Cannon, itinerant physician and organizer Thomas Young, physician Benjamin Rush, apothecary Christopher Marshall, hardware retailer Timothy Matlack, and instrumentmaker David Rittenhouse, to overcome religious factionalism in what had always been a religiously heterogeneous town. In Boston religious homogeneity and the adroit promotion of political action by "The Body of the People" curbed the growth of class identity. In New York Anglican-Presbyterian enmity, though not a major factor, could never be completely overcome by radical leaders such as Sears,

McDougall, and Lamb. But in Philadelphia the radicals came from every religious persuasion and consciously worked to promote inter-denominationalism by including representatives of each ethnic and religious group on the radical committee slates. Out of the shambles of the old assembly party of Galloway and Franklin rose a new popular party. Though often labeled "Presbyterian" by Quakers and Anglicans, who sought thus to discredit it, the new party enjoyed support from laboring men in all congregations except the Quakers. By 1776 it could be said that class identity rather than religious affiliation or an older association with either the proprietary or assembly party was the determining factor in people's political choices.

Two other, closely related, factors promoting greater pressure for internal reform in Philadelphia than in either Boston or New York were the quality and ideology of radical leadership. By the eve of the Revolution, Philadelphia was the home not only of radical native sons such as Matlack, Marshall, and Rittenhouse but also of talented polemicists and organizers such as James Cannon, who had arrived from Edinburgh in 1765; Thomas Paine, who emigrated from England in 1774; and Thomas Young, who came from Boston by way of Newport the following year. In 1767 William Goddard had arrived from New York and begun what soon became the most trenchant vehicle of artisan views in the colonies, the *Pennsylvania Chronicle*. What is more, Philadelphia's radical leaders voiced very different goals from Boston's Samuel Adams. His was to return to the austere Christian commonwealth of the forefathers; theirs was to create a world in which the channels upward were clear, political and economic power was widely shared, and social justice did not give way to the contractual law of a society organized around market relations. Some of Philadelphia's leaders, including Rush and Paine, would later change their views, but in 1775 and 1776 they were at the core of an interdenominational, egalitarian circle that had close ties to the lowest echelons of Philadelphia society.

Finally, the success of Philadelphia's laboring classes was also related to the partial vacuum of political leadership created by the Quakers' withdrawal from positions of power. Violence in politics and the specter of war with England drove many Quakers, who had dominated the assembly party for years, into retirement and sapped conservative Whiggism of much of its strength. One symptom of this retreat was the weakness of the conservative press in Philadelphia, in contrast to the situation in New York, where *Rivington's Gazetteer* continued well into the war years its offensive against radical attempts to transform politics. This galloping anemia afflicting conservatism was also related to the anxiety evoked by the rising strength of the laboring classes. In no other city did the propertied upper class face such vigorous articulation of the radical point of view or such pressure by artisans and those below them against traditional institutions. Conservative strength ebbed fastest where it was challenged directly by those who had developed their own consciousness and organizational base.

The growth and commercial development of the northern seaport towns brought about the restructuring of social groups, the redistribution of wealth, the alteration of labor relations, the emergence of states of consciousness that cut horizontally through society, and the political mobilization of the lower ranks of laboring people. Many in the cities haltingly recognized that the ligaments of the traditional corporate society had been torn in ways that struck at their opportunities, wellbeing, and sense of a prevailing equity. From this centurylong process there emerged no perfect crystallization of classes or class consciousness. But both master craftsmen and small retailers in the middle ranks and the artisans, merchant seamen, and laborers below them learned to define their interests and to identify the self-interested behavior in those they had been taught to believe acted for the good of the whole. They began with the issues that most closely affected their daily existence and throughout their struggle developed a consciousness of their separate roles and of their conflicting interests with others in their communities.

On a wide ensemble of issues—including not only political rights but also wages and prices, charity, taxes, market and labor relations, and evangelical religion—the urban lower orders formulated distinctly different points of view from those held by the people above them. There was no unifying ideology among those who worked with their hands or among those who did not, and on several important issues interclass agreement prevailed. Nevertheless, all classes of urban dwellers saw their world changing. As the Revolution approached, these changes led to the rise of a radical consciousness among many and to an interplay between calls for internal reform and insurgency against external forces that adversely affected the lives of city people. Challenges to the concentration of economic, political, and cultural authority ultimately shattered the old system of social relations.

Although no social revolution occurred in America in the 1770s, the American Revolution could not have unfolded when or as it did without the self-conscious action of urban laboring people from the bottom and middle strata who became convinced that they must either create power where none had existed before or watch their position deteriorate, in both absolute and relative terms. Thus the history of the Revolution is in part the history of popular collective action and challenges to the gentry's claim that their rule was legitimized by custom, law, and divine will. Ordinary people, sometimes violently, took over the power and the procedures of the constituted authorities. As wealth became increasingly concentrated, plebeian urban dwellers forced their way into the political arena, not so much through the formal mechanisms of electoral politics as through street demonstrations, mass meetings, extralegal committees that assumed governmental powers, the intimidation of their enemies, and, in some cases, spirited defenses of traditional norms. This reordering of political power required a mental breakthrough, for it challenged a model of social relations, established by the elite, that asserted the superior wisdom and public-mindedness of the educated and wealthy and prescribed deference as the customary and proper role of "inferior" people.

This shattering of the habit of obedience, advanced by the Great Awakening, proceeded far more rapidly in Boston in the second third of the century than in the other port towns. Yet it relapsed there after 1765 as traditional leaders, aided by the British military presence reasserted themselves and as ordinary people closed ranks in a reaffirmation of the spirit of covenant. In New York and Philadelphia the political leadership of the elite was challenged only sporadically until the end of the Seven Years' War, when economic derangements and internal factionalism set the stage for the rise of laboring men to political power. But in all the cities those who labored with their hands, especially those who found it most difficult to weather the changes that had overcome their society, formed a picture of the social arrangements by which they lived. That picture was political in its composition and increasingly vivid in its portrayal of the port towns as places where men struggled against each other rather than working harmoniously for the mutual good of the whole society.

Abbreviations

Notes

Index

Abbreviations

BTR	*Reports of the Record Commissioners of the City of Boston*, William H. Whitemore et al., ed. 39 vols. (Boston, 1876–1908)
CSM Pub.	*Publications of the Colonial Society of Massachusetts*
CSP Colonial	*Calendar of State Papers, Colonial Series, America and West Indies*, ed. W. Noel Sainsbury, J. W. Fortescue, et al., 44 vols. (London, 1860–1969)
HSP	Historical Society of Pennsylvania
MHS	Massachusetts Historical Society
MHS Coll.	*Collections of the Massachusetts Historical Society*
MHS Proc.	*Proceedings of the Massachusetts Historical Society*
NYCD	*Documents Relative to the Colonial History of the State of New York*, ed. Edmund B. O'Callaghan and Berthold Fernow, 15 vols. (Albany, 1853–87)
NYHS	New-York Historical Society
NYHS Coll.	*Collections of the New York Historical Society*
Pa. Votes	*Votes and Proceedings of the House of Representatives of the Province of Pennsylvania*, ed. Gertrude MacKinney, *Pennsylvania Archives*, 8th ser., 8 vols. (Harrisburg, 1931–35)
PBF	*The Papers of Benjamin Franklin*, ed. Leonard Labaree et al., 24 vols. to date (New Haven, 1959-)
PMHB	*Pennsylvania Magazine of History and Biography*
WMQ	*William and Mary Quarterly*, 3d ser.

Notes

Preface to the Abridged Edition

1. *A Letter from Sir Richard Cox, Bart. To Thomas Prior, Esq.; Shewing from Experience a sure Method to establish the Linnen-Manufacture* (Boston, 1750), p. 10.

2. E. P. Thompson, "Eighteenth-Century English Society: Class Struggle without Class?" *Social History,* 3 (1978), 149.

3. Raymond Williams, "Base and Superstructure in Marxist Cultural Theory," *New Left Review,* no. 82 (1973), 5–6.

1. The Web of Seaport Life

1. All existing estimates of population in the northern towns are flawed in some particulars; the most accurate are in W. S. Rossiter, ed., *A Century of Population Growth from the First Census of the United States to the Twelfth* (Washington, D.C., 1909), pp. 11, 78. For my own population estimates for the period 1690–1776 see *The Urban Crucible: Social Change, Political Consciousness, and the Origins of the American Revolution* (Cambridge, Mass., 1979), appendix, fig. 1. All subsequent references to *The Urban Crucible* are to the original edition.

2. "Diary of James Allen, Esq., of Philadelphia," *PMHB,* 9 (1885), 185.

3. William Gouge, *Of Domesticall Duties* (London, 1622), cited in John Demos, *A Little Commonwealth: Family Life in Plymouth Colony* (New York, 1970), following p. xvi.

4. "A Modell of Christian Charity" (1630), *MHS Coll.,* 3d ser. VII (Boston, 1838), 33.

5. Quoted in Marcus W. Jernegan, *The American Colonies, 1492–1750: A Study of Their Political, Economic, and Social Development* (New York, 1929), pp. 179–180.

6. Of 304 Boston estates inventoried in 1685–1699, 35 (11.5 percent) contained slaves. Lorenzo J. Greene estimates 400 slaves in 1708; *The Negro in Colonial New England* (New York, 1942), p. 84. Unless specified otherwise, all estimates of Boston's and Philadelphia's slave populations are based on inventories of estates

at death, Office of the Recorder of Wills and Suffolk County Probate Records, Suffolk County Courthouse, Boston; and Office of the Recorder of Wills, City Hall Annex, Philadelphia. Slave ownership in the two cities is summarized in *The Urban Crucible,* appendix, table 9.

7. The 1698 census is reprinted in Evarts B. Greene and Virginia D. Harrington, *American Population before the Federal Census of 1790* (New York, 1932), p. 92; the 1703 census is in *The Documentary History of the State of New York,* ed. Edmund B. O'Callaghan, 4 vols. (Albany, 1849–51), I, 395–405.

8. Gary B. Nash, "Slaves and Slaveowners in Colonial Philadelphia," *WMQ,* 30 (1973), 224–226.

9. Abbot Emerson Smith, *Colonists in Bondage: White Servitude and Convict Labor in America, 1607–1776* (Chapel Hill, N.C., 1947). Two studies of indentured servitude in Pennsylvania are Cheesman A. Herrick, *White Servitude in Pennsylvania: Indentured and Redemption Labor in Colony and Commonwealth* (Philadelphia, 1926); and Karl Frederick Geiser, *Redemptioners and Indentured Servants in . . . Pennsylvania* (New Haven, 1901).

10. *BTR;* Robert Francis Seybolt, *The Public Schoolmasters of Colonial Boston* (Cambridge, Mass., 1939); Minutes of the Meetings of the Justices, Church Wardens, and Vestrymen of the City of New York, 1694–1747, New York Public Library; Hamilton Andrews Hill, *History of the Old South Church (Third Church), Boston, 1669–1884,* 2 vols. (Boston, 1890), I, 417.

11. Distributions of taxable wealth in Boston, New York, and Philadelphia and of personal wealth in Boston and Philadelphia, based on these inventories and the lists, are summarized in *The Urban Crucible,* appendix, tables 3–7.

I have discussed the problems in using these sources, and ways of compensating for built-in distortions, in "Urban Wealth and Poverty in Pre-Revolutionary America," *Journal of Interdisciplinary History,* 6 (1976), 547–555, 566–574. For probate records and their use see also Gloria L. Main, "Probate Records as a Source for Early American History," *WMQ,* 32 (1975), 89–99; Main, "The Correction of Biases in Colonial American Probate Records," *Historical Methods Newsletter,* 8 (1974), 10–28; and Daniel Scott Smith, "Underregistration and Bias in Probate Records: An Analysis of Data from Eighteenth-Century Hingham, Massachusetts," *WMQ,* 32 (1975), 100–110.

12. Quoted in David J. Rothman, *The Discovery of the Asylum: Social Order and Disorder in the New Republic* (Boston, 1971), p. 4.

13. Estimates for poor relief in the three cities throughout the period are based on the sources cited in *The Urban Crucible,* appendix, table 10.

14. Quoted in Bernard Bailyn, *The New England Merchants in the Seventeenth Century* (Cambridge, Mass., 1955), p. 193.

15. Samuel Estabrook, *A Sermon Shewing that the Peace and Quietness Of a People Is a main part of the Work of Civil Rulers . . .* (New London, Conn., 1718), p. 18, quoted in Richard L. Bushmann, *From Puritan to Yankee: Character and the Social Order in Connecticut, 1690–1765* (Cambridge, Mass., 1967), p. 5.

16. Quoted in Darrett B. Rutman, *Winthrop's Boston: Portrait of a Puritan Town, 1630–1649* (Chapel Hill, N.C., 1965), p. 162.

17. Milton M. Klein, "Democracy and Politics in Colonial New York," *New York History,* 40 (1959), 237.

18. Jon C. Teaford, *The Municipal Revolution in America: Origins of Modern Urban Government, 1650–1825* (Chicago, 1975), p. 16.

19. Randolph to William Blathwayt, July 20, 1689, in Robert N. Toppan and Alfred T. S. Goodrich, eds., *Edward Randolph; Including His Letters and Official Papers 1676–1703,* 7 vols. (Boston, 1898–1909), VI, 289–290.

20. Randolph to Blathwayt, July 20, 1689, ibid., 289–292. Thomas Hutchinson, a later chief justice of the colony, remembered Dudley in his history of Massachusetts as the most despised man in Boston at the time. *History of the Colony of Massachusets-Bay . . . ,* I (London, 1760), 391–392. For Dudley's fate at the hands of the Boston crowd see also Everett Kimball, *The Public Life of Joseph Dudley: A Study of the Colonial Policy of the Stuarts in New England, 1660–1715* (New York, 1911), pp. 52–53.

21. Quoted in T. H. Breen, *The Character of the Good Ruler: Puritan Political Ideas in New England, 1630–1730* (New Haven, 1970), pp. 171–172.

22. Ibid., p. 173.

23. Willard, *The Character of a Good Ruler* (Boston, 1694), quoted ibid., p. 176.

24. Gershom Bulkeley, "Will and Doom" (1692), quoted ibid., p. 177.

25. Christopher Hill, *The World Turned Upside Down: Radical Ideas during the English Revolution* (New York, 1972), p. 11.

26. Ibid.

27. Charles M. Andrews, ed., *Narratives of the Insurrections, 1675–1690* (New York, 1915), pp. 175–176.

28. "Abstract of Colonel Nicholas Bayard's Journal," *NYCD,* III, 601; Address of the Militia of New York to William and Mary, ibid., 584.

29. Quoted in David S. Lovejoy, *The Glorious Revolution in America* (New York, 1972), pp. 282–284.

30. In 1698, in a tract written for the anti-Leislerians, it was claimed that the Leislerians "did force pillage, rob and steal" £13,959 of property in the city during Leisler's administration. *A Letter from a Gentleman of the City of New York* (New York, 1698), reprinted in Andrews, *Narratives of the Insurrections,* pp. 360–372.

31. Stephanus Van Cortlandt to Francis Nicholson, Aug. 5, 1689, *NYCD,* III, 610.

32. Lovejoy, *Glorious Revolution,* pp. 298–300; *A Letter from a Gentleman . . . ,* in Andrews, *Narratives of the Insurrections,* p. 364.

33. Julius Goebel, Jr., and T. Raymond Naughton, *Law Enforcement in Colonial New York: A Study in Criminal Procedure, 1664–1776* (New York, 1944), p. 83.

34. Quoted in Gary B. Nash, *Quakers and Politics: Pennsylvania, 1681–1726* (Princeton, 1968), p. 122.

35. Quoted in Ethyn W. Kirby, *George Keith, 1636–1716* (New York, 1942), p. 56.

36. Robert Turner to Penn, June 15, 1692, quoted in Nash, *Quakers and Politics,* p. 154.

37. Penn to the Board of Trade, April 22, 1700, and Penn to Charlewood Lawton, Aug. 18, 1701, Penn Letter Book (1699–1703), HSP, quoted ibid., p. 162.

38. Quoted ibid., pp. 174–175.

2. The Port Towns in an Era of War

1. In general, statistics for tonnage and for per capita imports throughout the period are drawn from *Historical Statistics of the United States, Colonial Times to 1970,* 2 vols. (Washington, D.C., 1975), II, 1168, 1176–78, 1180–81. For corrections, sources for individual years, and graphic summaries see *The Urban Crucible,* appendix, figs. 2 and 3.

2. Bernard Bailyn and Lotte Bailyn, *Massachusetts Shipping, 1697–1714: A Statistical Study* (Cambridge, Mass., 1959), pp. 102–105.

3. Ibid., pp. 63–64.

4. Herbert L. Osgood, *The American Colonies in the Eighteenth Century,* 4 vols. (New York, 1924), I, 434, 442.

5. Quoted in Arthur H. Buffinton, "External Relations (1689–1740)," in Albert Bushnell Hart, ed., *Commonwealth History of Massachusetts: Colony, Province and State,* 4 vols. (New York, 1927–30), II, 76.

6. Jeremiah Dummer, *A Letter to a Noble Lord . . .* (Boston, 1712).

7. Cotton Mather, *The Bostonian Ebenezer* (Boston, 1698).

8. Curtis P. Nettels, *The Money Supply of the American Colonies before 1720* (Madison, Wis., 1934), p. 255.

9. Tables of silver prices in Massachusetts currency are generally derived from the data in Andrew McF. Davis, *Currency and Banking in the Province of Massachusetts Bay,* 2 vols, (New York, 1901), I, 368–370. See Roger W. Weiss, "The Colonial Monetary Standard of Massachusetts," *Economic History Review,* 27 (1974), 586–587, for a slightly refined table and *The Urban Crucible,* appendix, table 12, for my own refinements, based on values given in Boston inventories.

10. Quoted in Nettels, *Money Supply,* p. 258n.

11. Mather, *Marah Spoken To* (Boston, 1718), p. 1.

12. Published anonymously in 1719 and 1720, both pamphlets were probably written by John Colman, a Boston merchant.

13. Bellomont to Lords of the Treasury, Dec. 14, 1698, *NYCD,* IV, 438.

14. Kenneth Scott, "The Church Wardens and the Poor in New York City, 1693–1747," *New York Genealogical and Biographical Record,* 99 (1968), 157–164; Raymond A. Mohl, "Poverty in Early America, a Reappraisal: The Case of Eighteenth-Century New York City," *New York History,* 50 (1969), 5–28.

15. The tax list of 1709 and the poor-relief accounts are reprinted in Peter J. Parker, "Rich and Poor in Philadelphia, 1709," *PMHB,* 99 (1975), 3–19.

16. Charles Tilly, "Food Supply and Public Order in Modern Europe," in Tilly, ed., *The Formation of National States in Western Europe* (Princeton, N.J., 1975), p. 428.

17. *Diary of Samuel Sewall, MHS Coll.,* 5th ser., VI (Boston, 1879), 281.

18. Quoted in Perry Miller, *The New England Mind: From Colony to Province* (Cambridge, Mass., 1953), p. 330.

19. *A Dialogue* . . . (Boston, 1714), *CSM Pub.* 10 *(Transactions, 1904–06),* 344–348.

20. "My Son, fear thou the Lord . . . ," ibid., pp. 348–352.

21. *An Addition to the Present Melancholy Circumstances of the Province* . . . (Boston, 1719), in Andrew McF. Davis, ed., *Colonial Currency Reprints,* 4 vols. (Boston, 1910–11), I, 389.

22. *An Addition to the Present Melancholy Circumstances* . . . , ibid., pp. 358–359.

23. Quoted in Stephen Foster, *Their Solitary Way: The Puritan Social Ethic in the First Century of Settlement in New England* (New Haven, 1971), pp. 132–134.

24. *A Letter to an Eminent Clergy-Man* . . . (Boston, 1720), in Davis, *Currency Reprints,* II, 233–234.

25. Quoted in Miller, *New England Mind,* p. 322.

26. Quoted ibid., p. 315.

27. Carl Bridenbaugh, "The Press and Book in Eighteenth-Century Philadelphia," *PMHB,* 65 (1941), 5.

28. G. B. Warden, *Boston, 1689–1776* (Boston, 1970), p. 93.

29. Ibid., p. 67.

30. John Bridger to William Popple, July 9, 1719, *Documentary History of the State of Maine,* ed. James P. Baxter, *Collections of the Maine Historical Society,* 2d ser., X (Portland, 1907), 127.

31. Jerome R. Reich, *Leisler's Rebellion: A Study of Democracy in New York, 1664–1720* (Chicago, 1953), p. 156.

32. Norris to Penn, Dec. 2, 1709, Norris Letter Book, 1709–1716, p. 112, HSP.

33. Logan to Penn, Nov. 22, 1704, *Pennsylvania Archives,* 2d ser., VII (Harrisburg, 1890), 16.

34. Isaac Norris to Penn, Oct. 11, 1704, Norris Letter Book, 1704–1706, p. 2.

35. Logan to Penn, Feb. 3, 1708/09, in Edward Armstrong, ed., *The Correspondence of William Penn and James Logan* . . . , 2 vols. (Philadelphia, 1879–80), II, 313.

36. Logan to Penn, Nov. 22, 1704, *Pennsylvania Archives,* 2d ser., VII, 16.

37. Governor John Evans to Board of Trade; Sept. 29, 1707, *CSP Colonial, 1706–1708,* no. 1126.

3. Urban Change in an Era of Peace

1. F. J. F. Schantz, Frank R. Diffenderffer, et al., *Pennsylvania—The German Influence in Its Settlement and Development,* pt. 7, *Proceedings of the Pennsylvania-German Society,* 10 (1900), 32–37; Wayland F. Dunaway, *The Scotch-Irish of Colonial Pennsylvania* (Chapel Hill, N.C., 1944), pp. 28–42; R. J. Dickson, *Ulster*

Emigration to Colonial America, 1718–1775) (London, 1966); James G. Lydon, "Philadelphia's Commercial Expansion, 1720–1739," *PMHB*, 91 (1967), 407–408.

2. John Duffy, *Epidemics in Colonial America* (Baton Rouge, 1953), pp. 50–54, 33, 36; John B. Blake, *Public Health in the Town of Boston, 1630–1822* (Cambridge, Mass., 1959), pp. 47–51, 247–250.

3. Logan to William Penn, Sept. 8, 1713, *Pennsylvania Archives,* 2d ser., VII, 39.

4. For ship arrivals and number of passengers see Gary B. Nash, "Slaves and Slaveowners in Colonial Philadelphia," *WMQ,* 30 (1973), 227n–228n. For arrivals in 1749, *Poor Richard's Almanack for 1750 . . .* (Philadelphia, 1749).

5. Sharon V. Salinger, "Colonial Labor in Transition: The Decline of Indentured Servitude in Late Eighteenth-Century Philadelphia," *Labor History,* 22 (1981), 165–191.

6. Quoted in Almon W. Lauber, *Indian Slavery in Colonial Times within the Present Limits of the United States* (New York, 1913), p. 292.

7. Slightly varying statistics on slave imports from 1701 to 1764 are presented in *Historical Statistics of the United States, Colonial Times to 1970,* 2 vols. (Washington, D.C., 1975), II, 1173, and James G. Lydon, "New York and the Slave Trade, 1700–1774," *WMQ,* 35 (1978), 382.

8. Kenneth Scott, "The Slave Insurrection in New York in 1712," *New-York Historical Society Quarterly,* 45 (1961), 43–74.

9. Ferenc M. Szasz, "The New York Slave Revolt of 1741: A Re-Examination," *New York History,* 48 (1967), 215–230.

10. Quoted in Davis, *Currency and Banking,* I, 443.

11. *New-England Courant,* Feb. 22, 1724/25.

12. *A Discourse Concerning the Currencies . . .* (Boston, 1740), in Davis, *Currency Reprints,* III, 328.

13. See *The Urban Crucible,* appendix, table 13.

14. Carl Bridenbaugh, *The Colonial Craftsman* (Chicago, 1961), p. 145.

15. Annual intentions to marry are tabulated in Lemuel Shattuck, *Report to the Commissioners of the City Council Appointed to Obtain the Census of Boston for the Year 1845* (Boston, 1846), pp. 71–72.

16. Infant baptisms, recorded in newspapers beginning in 1732, are summarized in ibid., pp. 71–72.

17. Francis Rawle, *Some Remedies Proposed for the Restoring the Sunk Credit of the Province of Pennsylvania* ([Philadelphia], 1721), pp. 6–7.

18. Logan to John Andrews, Aug. 14, 1722, quoted in Richard A. Lester, *Monetary Experiments: Early American and Recent Scandinavian* (Princeton, 1939), p. 66; Governor William Keith to the Lords of Trade, Dec. 18, 1722, *CSP Colonial, 1722–23,* p. 190.

19. William Keith, *A Collection of Papers . . .* [London, 1740], quoted in Lester, *Monetary Experiments,* p. 70.

20. Harrold E. Gillingham, "Cesar Ghiselin, Philadelphia's First Gold and Silversmith, 1693–1735," *PMHB,* 47 (1933), 244–259.

21. Quoted in Lester, *Monetary Experiments,* p. 117.

22. *The Account Stated* [New York, 1734]; *New-York Weekly Journal,* April 8, 1734.

23. Quoted from the preamble of the law authorizing the paper money issue by Lester, *Monetary Experiments,* p. 118.

24. Carl Bridenbaugh, *Cities in the Wilderness: The First Century of Urban Life in America, 1625–1742* (1938; reprint, New York, 1964), p. 393; Foster, *Solitary Way,* p. 147.

25. Rothman, *Discovery of the Asylum,* p. 5.

26. "The Diary of John Comer," *Collections of the Rhode Island Historical Society,* VIII (n.p., 1893), 78.

27. Benjamin Colman to Samuel Holden, May 8, 1737, Colman Papers, II, MHS.

28. The letters were published as part of Governor Belcher's proclamation condemning the rioters in the *Boston Weekly News-Letter,* April 21, 1737.

29. *Boston Weekly News-Letter,* April 21, 1737.

30. Colman to Holden, May 8, 1737, Colman Papers, II.

31. Belcher to Richard Waldron, July 12, 1733, Dec. 3, 1733. *MHS Coll.,* 6th ser., VI (Boston, 1893), 324, 438.

32. E. P. Thompson, "Patrician Society, Plebeian Culture," *Journal of Social History,* 7 (1974), 403.

33. "Address in Opposition to Issuing More Paper Money," in "Letter-Book of Samuel Sewall," *MHS Coll.,* 6th ser., II (Boston, 1888), 235–289.

34. *The Melancholy State of this Province . . .* (Boston, 1736), in Davis, *Currency Reprints,* III, 142.

35. Quoted in Patricia U. Bonomi, *A Factious People: Politics and Society in Colonial New York* (New York, 1971), p. 113.

36. Stanley N. Katz, ed., *A Brief Narrative of the Case and Trial of John Peter Zenger, Printer of the New-York Weekly Journal, by James Alexander* (Cambridge, Mass., 1963), p. 20.

37. Ibid., p. 34.

38. Timothy Wheelwright [pseud.], *Two Letters on Election of Aldermen* [New York, 1734].

39. Ibid.; *New-York Weekly Journal,* March 18, May 20, July 8, 1734.

40. *A Word in Season . . .* [New York, 1736].

41. William Smith, *The History of the Late Province of New-York, From its Discovery to the Appointment of Governor Colden, in 1762,* in *NYHS Coll., 1829* (New York, 1830), pp. 34–35.

42. *Letters and Papers of Cadwallader Colden,* in *NYHS Coll., 1917* (New York, 1918), p. 179.

43. *New-York Weekly Journal,* March 18, 1733/34; May 20, July 8, July 15, 1734; March 3, 1735; May 30, 1737.

44. Smith, *History of New-York,* p. 41.

45. [Lewis Morris], *Some Observations on the Charge Given by the Hon. James DeLancey . . . to the Grand Jury . . .* (New York, 1733).

46. "History of Governor William Cosby's Administration," *Colden Papers,* IX, 298, in *NYHS Coll., 1935* (New York, 1936).

47. *New-York Gazette,* March 11, 1733/34, quoted in Patricia U. Bonomi, "The Middle Colonies: Embryo of the New Political Order," in Alden Vaughan and George Billias, eds., *Perspectives on Early American History: Essays in Honor of Richard B. Morris* (New York, 1973), p. 87.

48. Norris Letter Book, 1716–1730, pp. 369, 381, 395, 399.

49. *Pa. Votes,* II, 1459–1460.

50. Logan, *The Charge Delivered from the Bench to the Grand Jury* (Philadelphia, 1723).

51. Ibid.

52. Lloyd, *A Vindication of the Legislative Power* . . . (Philadelphia, 1725).

53. *A Dialogue Between Mr. Robert Rich and Roger Plowman* [Philadelphia, 1725].

54. [Logan], *A Dialogue Shewing What's therein to be found* (Philadelphia, 1725).

55. The fullest statement of the ordinary Pennsylvanian's complaints against an insensitive proprietary elite is William Keith's forty-five-page pamphlet, *The Observator's Trip to America, in a Dialogue between the Observator and his Countryman Roger* ([Philadelphia], 1726).

56. [Logan], *A Dialogue Shewing What's therein to be found.*

57. Patrick Gordon to John Penn, Oct. 18 and Oct. 22, 1726; Logan to John Penn, Oct. 17, 1726, Penn Papers, Official Correspondence, I, 239, 247, 237, HSP; Norris to Jonathan Scarth, Oct. 21, 1726, Norris Letter Book, 1716–1730, pp. 474–475.

58. Logan to Thomas Penn, April 24, 1729; Patrick Gordon to Springett and John Penn, May 2, 1729, Penn Papers, Official Correspondence, II, 54, 57; *Minutes of the Provincial Council of Pennsylvania,* 16 vols. (Philadelphia and Harrisburg, 1852–53), III, 352–355, 360–361.

59. *American Weekly Mercury,* Dec. 21, 1733.

60. *Pennsylvania Gazette,* March 24, April 1, 1736; *American Weekly Mercury,* April 22, 1736; *Pennsylvania Gazette,* April 15 and 22, 1736; *American Weekly Mercury,* April 22, 1736; *Pennsylvania Gazette,* April 29, 1736.

61. *A Just Rebuke to a Dialogue betwixt Simon and Timothy* . . . (Philadelphia, 1726).

4. War, Religious Revival, and Politics

1. Mather, *Theopolis Americana* (Boston, 1710), quoted in David Levin, ed., *Bonifacius: An Essay upon the Good* (Cambridge, Mass., 1966), p. xvii.

2. William B. Weeden, *Economic and Social History of New England,* 2 vols. (1890; reprint, New York, 1963), II, 547n.

3. James G. Lydon, *Pirates, Privateers, and Profits* (Upper Saddle River, N.J., 1970), p. 210.

4. *BTR,* XIV, 98–99.

5. Thomas Hancock to Miss Thomas and Adrian Hope, May 24, 1745, quoted

in Joel A. Shufro, "The Impressment of Seamen and the Economic Decline of Boston, 1740 to 1760" (M.A. thesis, University of Chicago, 1968), p. 31.

6. W. T. Baxter, *The House of Hancock: Business in Boston, 1724–1775* (Cambridge, Mass., 1945), pp. 98–110.

7. Ibid., p. 78n.

8. Shufro, "Impressment," p. 29, citing J. Osborne to William Pepperall and Peter Warren, Feb. 5, 1745, Belknap Papers, MHS.

9. *BTR*, XV, 369.

10. *Boston Gazette*, Aug. 27, 1751.

11. *BTR*, XIV, 99–101.

12. Petition of a "Number of Inhabitants" to the town, Aug. 14, 1744, *BTR*, XIV, 57; and selectmen's petition to the House of Representatives, May 28, 1746, *BTR*, XIV, 99–101.

13. Nathaniel Appleton, *The Cry of Oppression* (Boston, 1748), pp. 34–37.

14. *Boston Evening Post*, Feb. 1, 1748.

15. Lydon, *Pirates, Privateers, and Profits*, p. 154.

16. *New-York Weekly Post-Boy*, June 20, 1748.

17. Randolph Shipley Klein, *Portrait of an Early American Family: The Shippens of Pennsylvania across Five Generations* (Philadelphia, 1975), p. 66; Carl Bridenbaugh, *Cities in Revolt: Urban Life in America, 1743–1776* (New York, 1955), p. 15.

18. William Douglass, *Summary, Historical and Political, of the . . . Present State of the British Colonies in North-America,* I (London, 1750), 540.

19. Murray G. Lawson, "The Boston Merchant Fleet of 1753," *American Neptune*, 9 (1949), 207–215.

20. *BTR*, XIV, 221, 238; Petition of the Town of Boston, Feb. 11, 1756, Massachusetts Archives, Boston, CXVII, 55–68.

21. Petition of the Town of Boston, April 1758, Massachusetts Archives, CXVII, 395–396.

22. Quoted in Duffy, *Epidemics in Colonial America*, p. 58.

23. *BTR*, XIV, 85.

24. "Persons Warned Out of Boston, 1745–1792," Records of the Boston Overseers of the Poor, MHS.

25. *Durable Riches* (Boston, 1695), and *Concio and Populum* (Boston, 1721), quoted in Foster, *Solitary Way*, pp. 135, 137.

26. *BTR*, XII, 104–105, 111, 114, 116, 156, 159–162, 165–168, 172; Bridenbaugh, *Cities in the Wilderness*, p. 393, and *Cities in Revolt*, p. 320; Foster, *Solitary Way*, pp. 147–148. The fullest account of the workhouse is in Stephen Edward Wiberley, Jr., "Four Cities: Public Poor Relief in Urban America, 1700–1775," (Ph.D. diss., Yale University, 1975), pp. 88–98.

27. *BTR*, XII, 159–160; quotes from the workhouse rules, *BTR*, XII, 234–241.

28. *The Society for Encouraging Industry . . . Articles of Incorporation . . . with a List of Subscribers* (Boston, 1748; reprint, 1754), p. 3.

29. *Report of the Committee for the Society for Encouraging Industry . . .* (Boston, 1752).

30. *Boston Weekly Post-Boy,* Feb. 12, 1752.

31. Charles Chauncy, *The Idle-Poor Secluded from the Bread of Charity* (Boston, 1752), p. 19.

32. Samuel Cooper, *A Sermon Preached in Boston, New England before the Society for Encouraging Industry and Employing the Poor* . . . (Boston, 1753), p. 23.

33. *Boston Gazette,* Aug. 14, 1753.

34. Chauncy, *A Sermon Preached* . . . , pp. 9–17; *Industry and Frugality Proposed* . . . (Boston, 1753), p. 10.

35. *Pennsylvania Gazette,* Sept. 12, 19, 26, 1754.

36. William Alexander to John Stevens, Aug. 23, 1750, Alexander Manuscripts, Box IX (Stevens), NYHS.

37. Franklin to Joseph Galloway, Feb. 17, 1758, *PBF.*

38. James DeLancey, *The Charge* . . . *To the Gentlemen of the Grand-Jury for the City and County of New-York* . . . (New York, 1733); and *The Charge* . . . *to the Gentlemen of the Grand-Jury* . . . (New York, 1734).

39. *Letters and Papers of Cadwallader Colden,* IV, 122, 161, in *NYHS Coll., 1920* (New York, 1921).

40. DeLancey, *The Charge* . . . *to the* . . . *Grand-Jury* . . . (1734), p. 7.

41. Colden to Gov. George Clinton, Dec. 27, 1748, *Letters and Papers of Cadwallader Colden,* IV, 185.

42. Paul S. Boyer, "Borrowed Rhetoric: The Massachusetts Excise Controversy of 1754," *WMQ,* 21 (1964), pp. 341–344.

43. Thomas Gordon, *The Craftsman: A Sermon* . . . (New York, 1753), pp. iii–xiii, xxv, xxvi.

44. *Pennsylvania Journal,* April 22, 1756.

45. "Philo-Reflector" in preface to Gordon, *The Craftsman,* pp. ii, v.

46. Quoted in Alan Heimert, *Religion and the American Mind from the Great Awakening to the Revolution* (Cambridge, Mass., 1966), p. 15.

47. William G. McLoughlin, *New England Dissent, 1630–1833: The Baptists and the Separation of Church and State* (Cambridge, Mass., 1971), p. 335.

48. Quoted in Bridenbaugh, *Cities in the Wilderness,* p. 424.

49. Perry Miller, *Jonathan Edwards,* (New York, 1949), p. 166.

50. Quoted ibid.

51. Timothy Cutler to Zachary Gray, Sept. 24, 1743, quoted in Eugene E. White, "The Decline of the Great Awakening in New England: 1741 to 1746," *New England Quarterly,* 24 (1951), pp. 37–38.

52. White, "Decline of the Great Awakening," p. 40.

53. *Boston Evening Post,* Aug. 2, 1742; Miller, *Jonathan Edwards,* p. 172.

54. *Boston Evening Post,* Feb. 8, 1742.

55. Miller, *Jonathan Edwards,* p. 173, quoted Chauncy, *Enthusiasm described and caution'd against* . . . (Boston, 1742), p. 15.

56. *Boston Evening Post,* Aug. 2, 1742.

57. Ibid.

58. Harry S. Stout, "Religion, Communications, and the Ideological Origins of the American Revolution," *WMQ,* 34 (1977), 527.

59. Robert Zemsky, *Merchants, Farmers, and River Gods: An Essay on Eighteenth-Century American Politics* (Boston, 1971), p. 119.

60. Quoted in John C. Miller, "Religion, Finance, and Democracy in Massachusetts," *New England Quarterly,* 6 (1933), 33.

61. Quoted ibid., p. 48.

62. [William Rand], *The Late Religious Commotions in New-England considered* . . . (Boston, 1743), p. 13.

63. Douglass, *A Post[s]cript* . . . , in Davis, *Currency Reprints,* IV, 78.

64. Alan Heimert and Perry Miller, eds., *The Great Awakening: Documents Illustrating the Crisis and Its Consequences* (Indianapolis and New York, 1967), p. lxi.

65. Jonathan Mayhew, *Seven Sermons* . . . *Preached at a Lecture* . . . *in August, 1748* (Boston, 1749), quoted in Heimert, *Religion and the American Mind,* p. 252.

66. Jonathan Edwards, *A Dissertation Concerning the Nature of True Virtue* . . . , in *The Works of Jonathan Edwards,* 10th ed. (London, 1865), quoted in Heimert, *Religion and the American Mind,* p. 252.

67. Gilbert Tennent, *A Solemn Warning to the Secure World from the God of Terrible Majesty* [Boston, 1735], pp. 56–57, 102, quoted in Heimert, *Religion and the American Mind,* pp. 306, 32.

68. Edwards, "Christian Charity: or, the Duty of Charity to the Poor, Explained and Enforced," in Edwards, *Works,* II, 164–165, quoted in Heimert, *Religion and the American Mind,* p. 250.

69. Heimert, *Religion and the American Mind,* p. 93.

70. *PBF,* II, 241n.

71. Quoted in John Lax and William Pencak, "The Knowles Riot and the Crisis of the 1740s in Massachusetts" *Perspectives in American History,* 10 (1976), 176.

72. *BTR,* XIV, 217.

73. Shirley to Josiah Willard, Nov. 19, 1747, in Charles H. Lincoln, ed., *Correspondence of William Shirley, Governor of Massachusetts and Military Commander in America, 1731–1760,* 2 vols. (New York, 1912), I, 406; Hutchinson, *History of Massachusets,* II, 431.

74. Quoted in Lax and Pencak, "Knowles Riot," pp. 196–200.

75. *An Address to the Inhabitants of the Province of Massachusetts-Bay* . . . (Boston, 1747), pp. 4–5.

76. *Boston Independent Advertiser,* Jan. 25, 1748.

77. Hutchinson, *History of Massachusets,* III, 8.

78. Vincent Centinel [pseud.], *Massachusetts in Agony: Or, Important Hints to the Inhabitants of the Province* . . . (Boston, 1750), pp. 3–5, 8, 12–13.

79. *New-York Weekly Mercury,* Dec. 24, 1753, Jan. 7, 14, 21, 1754.

80. William Allen to John Penn, March 27, 1741, Penn Papers, Official Correspondence, III, 143.

81. Richard Hockley to Thomas Penn, Nov. 1, 1742 and Nov. 18, 1742, Penn Papers, Official Correspondence, III, 241–243.

82. Richard Peters to Thomas Penn, Nov. 17, 1742, Peters Letter Book, 1737–1750, HSP.

83. *PBF*, III, 200–201.

5. The Seven Years' War and Its Aftermath

1. Stanley McCrory Pargellis, *Lord Loudoun in North America* (New Haven, 1933), p. 290n.

2. James DeLancey to William Pitt, March 17, 1758, *NYCD*, VII, 343.

3. Lydon, *Pirates, Privateers, and Profits*, pp. 157–159; Virginia D. Harrington, *The New York Merchant on the Eve of the Revolution* (New York, 1935), pp. 303–305.

4. Bridenbaugh, *Cities in Revolt*, pp. 63–64, 335, 338.

5. Thomas C. Barrow, *Trade and Empire: The British Customs Service in Colonial America, 1660–1775* (Cambridge, Mass., 1967), pp. 160–163; Nicholas B. Wainwright, "Governor William Denny in Pennsylvania," *PMHB*, 74 (1950), 457–472; Richard Pares, *War and Trade in the West Indies, 1739–1763* (London, 1963), pp. 446–468.

6. Paul L. Ford, ed., *The Journal of Hugh Gaine, Printer*, 2 vols. (New York, 1902), II, 8–9.

7. For New York mariners' pay see Jesse Lemisch and John K. Alexander, "The White Oaks, Jack Tar, and the Concept of the 'Inarticulate,'" *WMQ*, 29 (1972), 122, 124. For mariners' wages in Philadelphia see *The Urban Crucible*, appendix, table 2; *NYHS Coll., 1891* (New York, 1892), pp. 503–504, 513, 516.

8. Lydon, *Pirates, Privateers, and Profits*, p. 208.

9. Joel A. Shufro, "Boston in Massachusetts Politics, 1730–1760" (Ph.D. diss., University of Wisconsin, 1976), pp. 296–297, 330 for codfish exports. The reports of various craft leaders to the selectmen regarding the decline of their trades are in Massachusetts Archives, CXVII, 58–60, 67. The selectmen's petition to the legislature, based on these reports, is in *BTR*, XIV, 280–281.

10. *BTR*, XIV, 303.

11. Quoted in Weeden, *Economic and Social History*, II, 678.

12. Memorial of William Bollan to the King, April 11, 1764, quoted in John Gorham Palfrey, *History of New England*, 5 vols. (Boston, 1865–90), V, 143n.

13. Massachusetts Archives, XCIV, 161, 193, 333.

14. "Muster Rolls of the New York Provincial Troops," in *NYHS Coll., 1881* (New York, 1882), pp. 162–167, 170–175, 206–213, 292–309, 374–379; *Pennsylvania Archives*, 2d ser., II (Harrisburg, 1890), 484–485, 487–488, 491–494.

15. *Boston Post-Boy*, April 28, 1760.

16. Am 1809, Boston Public Library; *BTR*, XXIX, 89–100.

17. *Boston Post-Boy*, June 3, 1765, cited in Arthur M. Schlesinger, *Colonial Merchants and the American Revolution, 1763–1776* (1918; reprint, New York, 1968), p. 57; Bridenbaugh, *Cities in Revolt*, p. 281.

18. *The Late Regulations respecting the British Colonies* . . . (Philadelphia, 1765), quoted in Marc Egnal and Joseph A. Ernst, "An Economic Interpretation of the American Revolution," *WMQ*, 29 (1972), 17.

19. Watts to Scott, Pringle, Cheap and Co., Feb. 5, 1764, *Letterbook of John Watts: Merchant and Councillor of New York,* in *NYHS Coll., 1928* (New York, 1929), p. 228.

20. Quoted in Harrington, *New York Merchant,* p. 323.

21. Marc Egnal, "The Business Cycle in Colonial America" (paper presented at the annual meeting of the Organization of American Historians, April 18, 1975), pp. 5, 24.

22. Billy G. Smith, "The Material Lives of Laboring Philadelphians, 1750 to 1800," *WMQ,* 38 (1981), 163–202; William S. Sachs, "Agricultural Conditions in the Northern Colonies before the Revolution," *Journal of Economic History,* 13 (1953), 284–285.

23. Smith, "The Material Lives of Laboring Philadelphians," pp. 175, 178–179; *New-York Gazette,* Jan. 22, 1761, cited in Bridenbaugh, *Cities in Revolt,* p. 233.

24. *Pennsylvania Gazette,* Jan. 24 and 31, 1765; Gary B. Nash, "Poverty and Poor Relief in Pre-Revolutionary Philadelphia," *WMQ,* 33 (1976), 14.

25. James Freeman Notebook, June 29, 1764, MHS.

26. *Minutes of the Common Council of the City of New York, 1675–1776,* 8 vols. (New York, 1905), VI, 403–404.

27. Quoted in William H. Williams, "The 'Industrious Poor' and the Founding of the Pennsylvania Hospital," *PMHB,* 97 (1973), 436.

28. *Pa. Votes;* VII, 5506, 5535–5536.

29. *New-York Gazette,* Aug. 26, 1762.

30. L. H. Butterfield ed., *Diary and Autobiography of John Adams,* 4 vols. (Cambridge, Mass., 1961), I, 294.

31. E. P.Thompson, "Patrician Society, Plebeian Culture," *Journal of Social History,* 7 (1974), 384.

32. Norris Account Book, 1752–1761, pp. 12, 22–25, 35, HSP.

33. Alfred F. Young, "Pope's Day, Tar and Feathers, and 'Cornet Joyce, jun.': From Ritual to Rebellion in Boston, 1745–1775," pts. I and II (manuscript made available through the courtesy of the author). The next three paragraphs are based principally on this pioneering investigation of artisan culture in Boston during the late colonial years.

34. "Memoir of Isaiah Thomas," in Thomas, *The History of Printing in America,* 2 vols. (Albany, 1874), I, xxix.

35. *An Address to the Freeholders and Inhabitants of Massachusetts-Bay* (Boston, 1751), pp. 5–6. The pamphlet was taken almost verbatim from *Cato's Letters,* no. 69, first published in book form in London in 1724; but its virtue, Phileleutheros explained "is not altogether lost by crossing the Atlantic."

36. *New-York Gazette,* July 11, 1765, quoted in Bernard Friedman, "The Shaping of the Radical Consciousness in Provincial New York," *Journal of American History,* 56 (1970), 794.

37. *Pennsylvania Journal,* April 22, 1756. For a general account see Ralph L. Ketcham, "Benjamin Franklin and William Smith: New Light on an Old Philadelphia Quarrel," *PMHB,* 88 (1964), 142–163.

38. [David James Dove], *The Lottery* [Germantown, Pa., 1758], pp. 5–6.

39. "Dialogue between X, Y, and Z," *PBF,* VI, 295–306.

40. William Smith to Archbishop Secker, Nov. 27, 1759 in Horace Wemyss Smith, ed., *Life and Correspondence of the Rev. William Smith,* 2 vols. (Philadelphia, 1880), I, 220–227.

41. William Allen to———, quoted in Theodore Thayer, *Pennsylvania Politics and the Growth of Democracy, 1740–1776* (Harrisburg, 1953), p. 90; Richard Hockley to Thomas Penn, Aug. 22, 1755, quoted in James H. Hutson, "Benjamin Franklin and Pennsylvania Politics, 1751–1755: A Reappraisal," *PMHB,* 93 (1969), 309n.

42. Shirley to the Lords of Trade, Dec. 1, 1747, in Lincoln, *Correspondence of Shirley,* I, 418.

43. *Boston Gazette,* May 5, May 12, 1760.

44. Bernard Bailyn, ed., *Pamphlets of the American Revolution,* I (Cambridge, Mass., 1965), 411.

45. "An Impartial Account of the Conduct of the Corkass By a Late Member of that Society," *Boston Evening Post,* March 21, 1763.

46. Tom Thumb [Samuel Waterhouse], *Proposals for Printing, . . . by Subscription the History of Vice-Admiral Thomas Brazen . . .* ([Boston], 1760).

47. *Boston Gazette,* Dec. 28, 1761; [Oxenbridge Thacher], *Conciderations on the Election of Counsellors, Humbly Offered to the Electors* ([Boston], 1761).

48. *Boston Evening Post,* March 14, 1763.

49. Brooke Hindle, "The March of the Paxton Boys," *WMQ,* 3 (1946), 461–486.

50. Quoted in James H. Hutson, *Pennsylvania Politics, 1746–1770* (Princeton, 1972), p. 97.

51. *The Scribbler . . .* ([Philadelphia], 1764), *PBF,* XI, 387–390.

52. [Isaac Hunt], *A Letter From a Gentleman in Transilvania To his Friend in America . . .* (New York, 1764), p. 4.

53. [Isaac Hunt], *A Humble Attempt at Scurrility,* pp. 39–41; [Anon.], *A Conference Between the D . . . L and Doctor D . . . E* [Philadelphia, 1764]; [Anon.], *Exercises at Scurrility Hall . . .* (Philadelphia, 1764); *An Answer to the Plot* [Philadelphia, 1764]; [Hugh Williamson], *What is Sauce for a Goose is also Sauce for a Gander* (Philadelphia, 1764).

54. [Hunt] *Letter From a Gentleman in Transilvania,* p. 10; James Pemberton to John Fothergill, Oct. 11, 1764, Pemberton Papers, HSP.

55. *The Election Medley* (Philadelphia, 1764).

6. The Stamp Act

1. William Gordon, *The History of the Rise, Progress, and Establishment of the Independence of the United States of America . . . ,* 4 vols. (London, 1788), I, 178.

2. [Samuel Waterhouse], *Proposals for Printing by Subscription the History of Adjutant T. Trowel and J. Bluster* [Boston, 1764].

3. Henry A. Cushing, ed., *The Writings of Samuel Adams,* 4 vols. (New York, 1904–08), IV, 67. In his article on devaluation in the *Boston Evening Post,* Dec. 14, 1761, Hutchinson said the poor lived too well. He was quoted and refuted by Otis in *Boston Gazette,* Dec. 28, 1761.

4. Bernard to the Board of Trade, Aug. 31, 1765, in William Cobbett, ed., *The Parliamentary History of England,* XVI (London, 1813), 129–131; Bernard to Halifax, Aug. 31, 1765, Francis Bernard Papers, IV, 158–160, Houghton Library, Harvard University.

5. James Gordon to William Martin, Sept. 10, 1765, *MHS Proc.,* 2d ser., XIII (1899–1900), 393; Henry Lloyd to William Butler, Aug. 29, 1765, quoted in Dirk Hoerder, *Crowd Action in Revolutionary Massachusetts, 1765–1780* (New York, 1977), p. 109.

6. *BTR,* XVI, 152.

7. Douglass Adair and John A. Schutz, eds., *Peter Oliver's Origin & Progress of the American Revolution: A Tory View* (Stanford, Calif. 1967), p. 54; Hutchinson to Thomas Pownall, March 8, 1766, Massachusetts Archives, XXVI, 207–214.

8. Quoted in Edmund S. Morgan and Helen M. Morgan, *The Stamp Act Crisis: Prologue to Revolution* (1953; reprint, New York, 1963), p. 181.

9. Quoted in F. L. Engelman, "Cadwallader Colden and the New York Stamp Act Riots," *WMQ,* 10 (1953), 560–565.

10. Robert R. Livingston to Gen. Robert Monckton, Nov. 8, 1765, *MHS Coll.,* 4th ser., X, (Boston, 1871), 559–561; Montressor Journal, in *NYHS Coll., 1881* (New York, 1882), p. 336.

11. Montressor Journal, p. 336; Engelman, "New York Stamp Act Riots," pp. 560–561, 571–572.

12. Livingston to Monckton, Nov. 8, 1765, *MHS Coll.,* 4th scr., X, 559–562.

13. General Thomas Gage to Secretary of State Henry Seymour Conway, Nov. 4, 1765, in Clarence E. Carter, ed., *The Correspondence of General Thomas Gage,* 2 vols (New Haven, 1931–1933), I, 71.

14. Roger J. Champagne, *Alexander McDougall and the American Revolution in New York* (Schenectady, N.Y., 1975), p. 14.

15. Quoted in Morgan and Morgan, *Stamp Act Crisis,* p. 209.

16. *New-York Gazette,* April 4, 1765, quoted in Friedman, "Radical Consciousness," pp. 789–790.

17. *New-York Gazette,* June 6, 1765, quoted ibid., p. 790.

18. *New-York Gazette,* Sept. 26, 1765; Friedman, "Radical Consciousness," p. 792.

19. [Samuel Wharton] to Franklin, Oct. 13, 1765, *PBF,* XII, 315–316; Benjamin H. Newcomb, "The Stamp Act and Pennsylvania Politics," *WMQ,* 23 (1966), 265.

20. Hughes to Franklin, Oct. 12, 1765, *PBF,* XII, 301; Deborah Franklin to Franklin, Nov. 3, 1765, ibid., p. 353.

21. Joseph Galloway to Franklin, Sept. 20, 1765, *PBF,* XII, 270; William Bradford to New York Sons of Liberty, Feb. 15, 1766, quoted in Francis Von A. Cabeen, "The Society of the Sons of Saint Tammany of Philadelphia," *PMHB,* 25 (1901), 439.

22. Hughes to the Stamp Commissioners, Oct. 12, 1765, in *Pennsylvania Journal,* Sept. 4, 1766, Supplement.

23. Quoted in Arthur L. Jensen, *The Maritime Commerce of Colonial Philadelphia* (Madison, Wis., 1963), p. 161.

24. Douglass, *A Letter to [a] Merchant in London* . . . (Boston, 1741), in Davis, *Currency Reprints,* IV, 76.

25. Adair and Schutz, *Peter Oliver's Origins & Progress,* p. 65.

26. Gage to Conway, Sept. 23, 1765, in Carter, *Correspondence of Gage,* I, 67.

27. Gage to Conway, Dec. 21, 1765, ibid., 78–79.

28. Gage to Conway, Nov. 8, 1765, ibid., 72–73.

29. Gage to Conway, Sept. 23, 1765, ibid., 67.

7. The Onset of Revolution

1. *Pennsylvania Gazette,* Jan. 9, 1772.

2. Richard B. Sheridan, "The British Credit Crisis of 1772 and the American Colonies," *Journal of Economic History,* 20 (1960) 161.

3. *Pa. Votes,* VII, 5830.

4. Nina Tiffany Moore, ed., *Letters of James Murray, Loyalist* (Boston, 1901), p. 132.

5. "On the Price of Corn, and Management of the Poor," *London Chronicle,* Nov. 29, 1766, *PBF,* XIII, 512–516.

6. *Pa. Votes,* VII, 6148–6149, 6097–99. Wiberley, "Four Cities," pp. 188–197, gives details on the dispute. The overseers' complaints are recorded in their minutes for Jan. 22, 1770, City Archives, Phiadelphia.

7. Philip Padelford, ed., *Colonial Panorama 1775: Dr. Robert Honyman's Journal for March and April* (San Marino, Calif., 1939), p. 18.

8. Almshouse Managers' Minutes, Nov. 3, 1775, City Archives, Philadelphia.

9. "On the . . . Management of the Poor," *PBF,* XIII, 515.

10. Minutes of the Overseers of the Poor, June 15, 1769, City Archives, Philadelphia.

11. *New-York Gazette,* Nov. 13, 1769.

12. *New-York Gazette,* Aug. 13, 1767; "List of New York Coachowners, 1770," Du Simitière Papers, HSP.

13. Treasurer's Accounts, Records of the Contributions to the Relief . . . of the Poor, I, 12, City Archives, Philadelphia.

14. Hutchinson to Richard Jackson, Oct. 20, 1767, quoted in Bernard Bailyn, *The Ordeal of Thomas Hutchinson* (Cambridge, Mass. 1974), p. 97.

15. John McCleary to Samuel Abbot, Feb. 12, March 6 and 13, 1771, Papers of Samuel Abbot, Box 14, folder 18, Baker Library, Harvard University.

16. *To the Inhabitants of Pennsylvania in General, and Particularly Those of the City and Neighbourhood of Philadelphia* (Philadelphia, 1779).

17. William G. McLoughlin, "The American Revolution as a Religioius Revival: 'The Millennium in One Country,'" *New England Quarterly,* 40 (1967), 102; Adam Smith, *The Wealth of Nations,* ed. E. Cannan (New York, 1937), p. 674.

18. H. James Henderson, "The Structure of Politics in the Continental Congress," in Stephen G. Kurtz and James H. Hutson, eds., *Essays on the American Revolution* (Chapel Hill, N.C., 1973), p. 183.

19. J. G. A. Pocock, *The Machiavellian Moment: Florentine Political Thought and the Atlantic Republic Tradition* (Princeton, 1975), p. 472.

20. Robert J. Taylor, ed., *The Papers of John Adams*, I (Cambridge, Mass., 1977), pp. 106–107n.

21. Cushing, *Writings of Samuel Adams*, IV, 67.

22. Quoted in Hoerder, *Crowd Action*, p. 155.

23. Ibid., p. 156.

24. Quoted in Hiller B. Zobel, *The Boston Massacre* (New York, 1970), p. 75.

25. John C. Miller, *Sam Adams: Pioneer in Propaganda* (1936: reprint, Stanford, Calif., 1960), pp. 195–196.

26. Pauline Maier, "Reason and Revolution: The Radicalism of Dr. Thomas Young," *American Quarterly,* 28 (1976), 245–246.

27. Quoted in Miller, *Sam Adams,* pp. 206–207.

28. Hutchinson to Lord Dartmouth, Dec. 2, 1773, quoted in Hoerder, *Crowd Action,* p. 258.

29. Miller, *Sam Adams,* p. 302.

30. Ibid., p. 110.

31. Quoted ibid., p. 207.

32. *Proposals, for Erecting and Encouraging a new Manufactory* [New York, 1770].

33. Nicholas Varga, "Election Procedures and Practices in Colonial New York," *New York History,* 41 (1960), 267, citing *New-York Journal,* April 12, 1770.

34. Quoted in Bernard Friedman, "The New York Assembly Elections of 1768 and 1769: The Disruption of Family Politics," *New York History,* 46 (1965), 17–18.

35. Quoted in Carl Lotus Becker, *The History of Political Parties in the Province of New York, 1760–1775* (1909; reprint, Madison, Wis., 1960), p. 111n.

36. Gouverneur Morris to John Penn, May 20, 1774, reprinted in Michael Kammen, *Colonial New York* (New York, 1975), p. 344.

37. Quoted in Becker, *Political Parties,* p. 116n.

38 Thomas Young to John Lamb, Nov. 19, 1774, quoted in Roger J. Champagne, *Alexander McDougall and the American Revolution in New York* (Syracuse, N.Y., 1975), p. 74; Becker, *Political Parties,* p. 117n., quoting John Adams.

39. "The Respectful Address of the Merchanicks in Union . . .", quoted in Edward Countryman, "Consolidating Power in Revolutionary America: The Case of New York, 1775–1783," *Journal of Interdisiplinary History,* 6, (1976), 659.

40. *Pennsylvania Chronicle,* March 27, 1767. For further complaints about the inequitable use of tax funds see ibid., Sept. 18, and Oct. 2, 1769.

41. *The the Free and Patriotic Inhabitants of the City of Phila. and Province of Pennsylvania* (Philadelphia, 1770).

42. *Pennsylvania Chronicle,* July 5, 1770.

43. *Pennsylvania Gazette,* Sept. 27, 1770.

44. Quoted in Charles S. Olton, *Artisans for Independence: Philadelphia Mechanics and the American Revolution* (Syracuse, N.Y., 1975), p. 53.

45. Ibid., pp. 54–55.

46. *A Trademan's Address to his Countrymen* (Philadelphia, 1772).

47. *Pennsylvania Gazette,* Sept. 22, 1773, quoted in Olton, *Artisans for Independence,* p. 56.

48. *Pennsylvania Packet,* April 30, 1776.

Index

Adams, John, 163, 223
Adams, Nathaniel, family (Boston), 8
Adams, Samuel, Jr., 188, 210; populistic politics of, 140, 174, 194, 224, 225, 228, 229, 231, 232; and "Christian Sparta," 176, 245; and Boston Caucus, 186
Africa: trade with, 6, 42, 47
Albany Congress (1754), 148
Albany (N.Y.), 40
Alexander, James, 88, 109
Alison, Francis, 180
Allen, James (Boston), 174
Allen, James (Philadelphia), 198
Allen, William, 180, 194
Andros, Sir Edmund, 21–24, 28, 48
Anglican church (Church of England), 197, 202, 218, 232; animosity toward, 21, 125, 126–127; and merchant elite, 48, 171, 182; and King's College, 123, 125, 126–127; Presbyterians vs., 126, 181, 182, 196–197, 239, 244, 245; vs. Quakers, 126, 169, 170; and immigrants, 145, 181
Appleton, Nathaniel, 107, 108, 207, 230
Apprenticeship, 2, 7, 35; poverty and, 67, 115; slavery replaces, 69. See also Indentured servants; Labor; Slavery
Apthorp, Charles, 103
Artisans: intergenerational continuity of, 5, 8; social status of, 8, 35, 163–166, 220; merchant elite vs., 13, 27–28, 29–31, 81, 87, 124, 173, 233, 240–241, 243; as officeholders, 14, 17, 27, 63, 90, 230, 231, 233, 240, 241; economic controls on, 18, 28, 47, 50, 163; appeal to and mobilization of vote of, 49, 53, 56, 88–

90, 93–96, 143, 169, 173–175, 233, 239; and slave competition, 68, 69, 164, 206; Franklin's Junto of, 76, 170, 182; and war prosperity, 151–153, 241; and Stamp Act, 185, 186–188, 191, 192, 193, 194–196, 198–199; internal stratification of, 209, 233, 234–235, 238–239, 244; and Mechanics Committee(s), 230, 237, 238, 239, 240–241, 242; and secret ballot, 235 236, 238. See also Labor; Political life and power; Wages; Wealth
Avery, Capt. John, 41
Avery, John (of "Loyal Nine"), 186
Awakeners. See Great Awakening

Bayard, Nicholas, 41, 56–57
Belcher, Andrew, 13, 46, 48
Belcher, Gov. Jonathan, 81, 83, 134; and inflation, 86, 133, 140
Bellomont, Earl of (Richard Coote), 41, 42, 55, 56
Bernard, Gov. Francis, 171, 172, 173
Bettering House (Philadelphia), 202, 207, 210–212, 213, 214, 217
Beverly (Mass.), 115
Birth rate, 74, 120
Blacks. See Slavery
Blackwell, Gov. John, 29, 30
Boardinghouses, 120
Bollan, William, 174
Boston Caucus, 53–54, 64, 123, 171, 173–174, 175, 186–187, 198, 225, 227
Boston economic conditions, 93, 111–112, 122, 145, 186; population, 1, 9, 33, 53, 56, 66, 68, 71, 73, 78, 110, 114, 146, 201; shipping, 1, 33–34, 36,

Roberdeau, Daniel, 217
Rowe, John, 230
Rush, Benjamin, 207, 224, 244, 245

Salaries. *See* Wages
Salem (Mass.), 3, 66, 104, 117
Sauer, Christopher, Jr., 181
Schuyler, Philip, 239
Schuyler family, 54
Scots, Scots-Irish. *See* Immigrants
Scott, John Morin, 192
Scull, Nicholas, 76
Sears, Isaac, 192, 193, 238, 244
Self-interest, and public good. *See* Political life and power
Seven Years' War (1755–1762), 115, 147–148, 224; impact of, 149, 155, 158–159, 163, 166, 176, 192, 193, 198, 200, 203, 204, 206, 208, 213, 247
Sewall, Samuel, 13
Shipbuilding, 147; slump in, 34, 50, 74, 77, 79, 113–114, 152, 202; wartime, 33–35, 101, 109, 154. *See also* Boston economic conditions; New York City economic conditions; Philadelphia economic conditions
Shippen, Edward, 111
Shipping. *See* Boston economic conditions; New York City economic conditions; Philadelphia economic conditions
Shirley, Gov. William, 133, 139, 153, 171; economic policy of, 71, 134, 140–141; and Louisbourg expedition, 104, 105
Shute, Gov. Samuel, 52, 53
Sibbald, Capt. John, 110
Silver Bank, 133–134
Simpson, Samuel, 221
Slavery, 6–7, 66, 75, 219; and slaves in social structure, 2, 6–7, 135, 198, 220, 231; and slave trade, 6–7, 42, 68–70; of Indians, 6, 68, 69; and slaves as wealth, 10, 42, 67, 68, 69; and abolitionism, 68, 132, 137, 206, 239; and import duties, 68, 70, 177; as competitive labor, 68, 69, 164, 206; and slave revolts, 69, 70; decline of, 69–70, 77, 206; of women, 69, 120; and slaves in West Indies, 100, 108
Sloughter, Gov. Henry, 25, 28
Smallpox, 43, 66, 113–114, 118, 160
Smith, Adam, 221, 222

Smith, John (of "Loyal Nine"), 186
Smith, William (New York), 88, 125
Smith, William (Philadelphia), 169, 170, 180
Smith, William, Jr., 192
Smuggling. *See* Trade
Social structure, 3–4, 122, 246–247; position of slaves, 2, 6–7, 135, 198, 220, 231; and mobility, 4–6, 8–9, 14, 30–32, 39, 221, 222, 239; artisans in, 8, 35, 163–166, 220; and wealth, 9–13, 38, 141, 165–166, 223; merchants and shopkeepers in, 9, 27, 89, 92, 188, 223; professionals in, 9; widows in, 10, 38, 39; and politics, 17, 18–19, 21–24, 27–31, 38–39, 46–49, 51–56, 62, 84, 168–170, 182–183, 198–199, 224–247; and officeholding, 19, 27, 63, 86, 90, 174–175, 230–231, 233, 241; antagonisms within, 22–29, 83–85, 140–141, 142–143, 146, 166, 171, 175–176, 186–199, 210, 213, 221, 229, 233, 234, 238, 241–242, 246–247; and clergy's view of mob, 23, 48, 51, 85, 116, 121, 135–136, 137; mariners in, 38–39; and laboring class "idleness," 93, 116, 121, 229; and religious revival, 128–132, 135–137, 166; categories redefined, 162–163; Evangelicals in, 220–221
Society for Encouraging Industry and the Employment of the Poor (Boston), 118
Society for the Encouragement of Arts, Agriculture, and Economy (New York), 160
Society for the Relief of Poor and Distressed Masters of Ships (Philadelphia), 208
Society of Friends. *See* Quakers
Solemn League and Covenant, 229–230, 232
Sons of Liberty: Boston, 188, 195, 209, 227; New York, 192, 234, 237; Philadelphia, 194–195
South Carolina, 68, 85
South Sea Bubble, 100
Spain, 1, 146; English war with, 101–104, 109, 110, 126
Spinning and weaving, 116, 118–121, 214, 216; and linen manufactories, 118–121, 143, 160, 161, 210, 211, 214, 216–217, 218, 232